Marketing Literature

Also by Claire Squires

PHILIP PULLMAN, MASTER STORYTELLER: A Guide to the Worlds of *His Dark Materials*

PHILIP PULLMAN'S *HIS DARK MATERIALS*: A Reader's Guide

ZADIE SMITH'S *WHITE TEETH*: A Reader's Guide

Marketing Literature

The Making of Contemporary Writing in Britain

Claire Squires

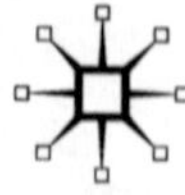

First published 2007 by
PALGRAVE MACMILLAN
Houndmills, Basingstoke, Hampshire RG21 6XS and
175 Fifth Avenue, New York, N.Y. 10010
Companies and representatives throughout the world

PALGRAVE MACMILLAN is the global academic imprint of the Palgrave Macmillan division of St. Martin's Press, LLC and of Palgrave Macmillan Ltd. Macmillan® is a registered trademark in the United States, United Kingdom and other countries. Palgrave is a registered trademark in the European Union and other countries.

ISBN-13: 978–1–4039–9773–9 hardback
ISBN-10: 1–4039–9773–X hardback

This book is printed on paper suitable for recycling and made from fully managed and sustained forest sources. Logging, pulping and manufacturing processes are expected to conform to the environmental regulations of the country of origin.

A catalogue record for this book is available from the British Library.

Library of Congress Cataloging-in-Publication Data
Squires, Claire.
Marketing literature: the making of contemporary writing in Britain/
Claire Squires.
p. cm.
Includes bibliographical references (p.) and index.
ISBN 1–4039–9773–X (alk. paper)
1. Literature publishing—Great Britain. 2. Fiction—Publishing—Great Britain. 3. Books—Great Britain—Marketing. 4. English fiction—20th century—History and criticism. I. Title.
Z326.S67 2007
070.50941—dc22 2007016438

10 9 8 7 6 5 4 3
16 15 14 13 12 11 10 09 08

Printed and bound in Great Britain by
Antony Rowe Ltd, Chippenham and Eastbourne

Contents

Preface

Over the course of the 1990s and 2000s, the same period addressed in this book, I have had the good fortune to pursue my fascination with literary fiction and its publishing while located at several universities and publishing companies. My interests were initially nurtured at the Universities of York and East Anglia, both of which placed strong emphasis on the study of contemporary writing. Later, professional experience working as a publisher at Hodder Headline informed my understanding of the literary fiction market, and I learned much by working with Carole Welch and the Sceptre imprint, and with energetic and enthusiastic colleagues. The specific shape of this project began to manifest itself in the late 1990s and early 2000s as a DPhil thesis at the University of Oxford. During this period I was supervised by Professor Hermione Lee, whose inspiring and articulate interest meant I always left tutorials with a desire to extend my knowledge of my subject, and which has made an invaluable contribution to its development. I was also fortunate to have two very rigorous and engaged examiners for my thesis, Dr Peter McDonald and Professor Juliet Gardiner, who made suggestions which have substantially aided its transition to book form. Later, Professor David Finkelstein provided me with insightful commentary which assisted that transition further. Since 2002, I have worked as a lecturer at the Oxford International Centre for Publishing Studies at Oxford Brookes University, which has provided me with a stimulating location both in which to extend my knowledge and understanding of contemporary publishing markets, and in which to discover the great benefits of supportive colleagues. The strong ethos of professional commitment, communication and enjoyment fostered within the Centre has provided me, and my work, with a perfect home, and I'm proud of my association with its staff and students.

In revising my original work for publication, I wish to make particular acknowledgement to the School of Arts & Humanities at Oxford Brookes, which has facilitated its completion through the funding of a period of research leave. I also benefited from an award from the AHRC Research Leave Scheme in 2006 (RL/113023). The British Academy and AHRB funded the postgraduate study that initiated this project, and I was given financial support in order to attend numerous conferences and seminars by the English Faculty, the Graduate Committee and Wolfson College (all at the University of Oxford), Oxford Brookes University and the British Academy. The opportunities they provided me with to attend conferences, seminars and colloquia in the UK and further afield have enabled the development of this book, both through the preparation of early drafts, and in discovering an invaluable international network of research colleagues.

Earlier versions of this work have been published in a variety of guises. Some of the material in Chapters 1 and 2 previously appeared as 'Novelistic Production and the Publishing Industry' in *A Companion to the British and Irish Novel 1945–2000*, edited by Brian Shaffer. A brief version of the *Bridget Jones's Diary* case study appears in the chapter 'The Global Market 1970–2000' in *A Companion to the History of the Book*, edited by Simon Eliot and Jonathan Rose. I previously wrote about *Trainspotting* in the *Edinburgh Review* (101), in the article '*Trainspotting* and Publishing, or Converting the Smack into Hard Cash'. The *Edinburgh Review* (103) also published my article 'A Guide to Literary Prizes'. A version of my work on crossover writing for children and adults appears in the chapter 'Literary Prizes, Literary Categories and Children's Literature in the 1990s–2000s' in *Pre- and Post-Publication Itineraries of the Contemporary Novel in English*, edited by Vanessa Guignery and François Gallix.

Many people have discussed ideas, shared information and showed interest in my work, and thus they have helped my thinking to take shape. I interviewed a number of publishers, literary agents, literary journalists and other participants in the literary marketplace in constructing this study: Gillon Aitken; Clare Alexander; Eric Anderson; John Carey; Kirsty Fowkes; David Godwin; Martyn Goff; Jamie Hodder-Williams; Philip Gwyn Jones; Pat Kavanagh; Mark Le Fanu; Robert McCrum; Bud McLintock; Andrew Miller; Geoff Mulligan; Alexandra Pringle; Robin Robertson; Peter Straus; and Erica Wagner. Many others have spoken to me informally. Richard Knight of Nielsen Bookscan provided me with market data. Chris Fowler, the Publishing Subject Librarian at Oxford Brookes University, has facilitated my quest for resources, and the librarians at the Bodleian have also aided my research. I would also like to acknowledge the publishers of this book, Palgrave Macmillan, in particular Paula Kennedy and Christabel Scaife. I hope that the experience of working with a lecturer in Publishing has not been too self-reflexive a process. Thanks also go to Jo North for her editorial help. For their invaluable assistance with the cover, I thank Laura Davison, Chrissy Leung and The QI Bookshop.

Finally, I'd like to thank friends and family who have provided me in turn with intellectual camaraderie and welcome distraction. Particularly, I'd like to thank Kirstie Blair, Caroline Campbell, Laura Davison, Chloë Evans, Rosie Holland, Aboliçao Oxford Capoeira, Jane Potter, Eleanor Purser, Julia Reid, Dan Scroop, DeNel Rehberg Sedo, and Christine, Michael, Julie and Dorothy Squires. Finally, a big thank you to the wonderful Blea Tarn Team, for whom I house-sat during the closing stages of writing this book. The fumes of generator diesel will always come to mind when re-reading these final pages!

Introduction

A writer in a small room typing on a laptop; a publisher in an office looking through a pile of scripts; a marketing department discussing cover designs; a bookseller in a shop stacking a pile of books; a supermarket shopper adding a bestselling novel to the weekly grocery trolley; a journalist on television debating one of the week's new publications; a prize judge in a dinner jacket announcing a decision; an author talking to an audience at a festival; a commuter in a packed train immersed in a novel; a circle of readers drinking wine and discussing books; a sandy paperback lying next to suntan cream and towel. All these images are part of the contemporary literary marketplace. Between them seems to run some sort of narrative, a network linking people, objects and activities. But how should these images be defined? Does it matter which image comes first, or what the order of the narrative is? What conflicts and alliances does the juxtaposition of images create?

This book, *Marketing Literature: The Making of Contemporary Writing in Britain*, is an examination of these images and the processes that link them. It is an investigation into the conditions of and contexts for the publishing of contemporary writing in Britain. It considers the changing social, economic and cultural environment of British publishing at the end of the twentieth and beginning of the twenty-first centuries, examining the book trade in a period of notable change. These changes include the processes of conglomeration and globalisation of publishing companies; the demise of the Net Book Agreement (NBA) and retail price maintenance; developments in retail practice; rapidly rising production figures; the emergence of new and competing leisure industries and information technologies; and a perceived switch of publishing power from editorial to sales and marketing. This is also a period in which, despite earlier prognostications of the death of the book and the continuing rise of other leisure industries and technological developments, the publishing industry and its products have been strong commercial and cultural forces. Leading literary writers such as Martin Amis, Irvine Welsh and Zadie Smith have commandeered pages of feature coverage as well as gossip column inches, and phenomenally successful books such as J. K. Rowling's *Harry Potter* series (1997–2007) and Dan Brown's *The Da Vinci Code* (2003) have sold millions of copies of their works, dominated the bestseller lists and made their authors rich.[1] Literary prizes – notably the (Man) Booker, but also a legion of others including the Whitbread (latterly Costa) Awards and the Orange Prize – have promoted writing and also contributed to mid-term canon formation. Technological advances have offered opportunities as well as challenges: book sales on the internet; spin-off merchandising; desk-top publishing (DTP); and print on demand (POD) production.

The focus of this book is on the marketing of literature, and specifically on the impact marketing has on literature's production and reception. Publishers have utilised the techniques and strategies of book marketing since the inception of print culture, but the contemporary period has seen a striking intensification of marketing activity and the increasing commodification of the literary marketplace. *Marketing Literature* explores these activities.

Definitions

Marketing Literature: The Making of Contemporary Writing in Britain extends a range of terms which are crucial in the definition of its parameters, and, moreover, are central to its argument. The first, and most important of these in terms of the development of the book's thesis, is *marketing*. There is a vast body of marketing theory and practice, although rather less in specific relation to the publishing industry. This is examined in more detail in Chapter 2: 'Literature and Marketing'. The definition that this book proposes of marketing, however, is a catholic one, and also one that goes beyond the definitions that might be found in a marketing textbook. That definition includes the acts of a publisher's marketing and press departments: for example, the production of point of sale (POS) materials, advertising, reading events and publicity campaigns. It also includes the decisions publishers make in terms of the presentation of books to the marketplace, in terms of formats, cover designs and blurbs, and imprint. All these are activities that a generic book marketing plan might involve, and in the heightened age of marketing of the 1990s and 2000s, might be thought necessary to a book's successful entry into the marketplace. The definition of marketing offered here, however, goes beyond these activities to encompass the multiplicity of ways in which books are presented and represented in the marketplace: via their reception in the media; their gaining of literary awards; and their placement on bestseller lists, to give only a few examples. Marketing is conceived *as a form of representation and interpretation,* situated in the spaces between the author and the reader – but which authors and readers also take part in – and surrounding the production, dissemination and reception of texts. In *Marketing Literature,* marketing is the summation of *multiple agencies* operating within the marketplace, by which contemporary writing is represented and interpreted, and in which contemporary writing is actively constructed. Marketing, as Chapters 2 and 3 develop in more detail, is in a very real sense, *the making of contemporary writing.*

This definition of marketing develops from the academic discipline of the history of the book and the sociology of literature. It is one that is firmly based in material culture, and which analyses literature via the institutions and processes that produce and consume it. As such, it draws on a rich academic field. Chapter 2 explores this field, and draws analogies between that field and the field of marketing theory and practice. The essential role played by *communications,* both with regards to the book as a means of communication, and as a method of conveying marketing messages to potential target markets, is central to this argument. Therefore, Chapter 2 explores in some detail the potential for a *theory of book marketing* drawing on diverse academic fields and methodologies.

In addition, this study takes as a key element in the construction of its definitions the language, organisational structures and operational tendencies of the publishing industry itself. The publishing industry, over its centuries of existence, has developed its own methods for discussing and defining its products and its activities, through its day-to-day operations, its trade press and through a variety of other source materials ranging from memoirs to consultancy reports. The publishing industry is frequently typified as a garrulous one, built – in the twentieth century at least – upon the basis of the business lunch, personal relationships and communication networks. The communicative nature of the industry has spawned its own form of metacommentary, which this study takes up both as an object of study in its own right, and as a tool in understanding the industry. This has an impact on the sources and methodology of the study. A thorough understanding of the publishing industry is to be derived at least in part from the industry's own well-established discourses of self-explanation.

A key area in which publishing's self-definitions are conscripted to this study, is in terms of the definition of *literature* and particularly of *literary fiction*, which *Marketing Literature* takes as its primary focus. A simple definition of the 'literary' might say that 'literary' writing (including literary fiction, poetry and non-fiction) is writing of a certain (high) standard. 'Literary' is then an assurance of quality, a guarantee that what is to be approached here is 'good' writing. The standards for judging the writing, and the values underlying the process of judgement, should be open to interrogation. In the course of *Marketing Literature* the impact of ideological subtexts on the marketplace, in terms of the construction of value, is investigated. Another notion of the 'literary' might be ventured via formalist poetics. Gérard Genette's problematisation of the attempt to establish 'literariness' in *Fiction and Diction* (1991), however, sees such a venture caught between the impulses of form and content, the 'constitutivist' and 'conditionalist' interpretations.[2] Genette's call to plurality needs, for the purposes of this book, to include a definition that can be applied to the structures of the publishing industry as well as its products.[3] Forging a reconciliation between formalism and the mechanisms of the industry is too large a project to embark on in the Introduction, and it is perhaps in the sociological structuralism of Pierre Bourdieu, which is considered in Chapter 2, that such a reconciliation can begin to occur.

To a publisher, literary fiction is described in two ways, one more formal, and one more contextual, and both of which may initially seem to defy definition. The first way is by a process of negation, as Steven Connor summarises in his brief but informative overview of 'Economics, Publishing and Readership' in *The English Novel in History 1950–1995* (1996).[4] Connor writes that, 'Literary fiction is usually defined by negation – it is *not* formula fiction or genre fiction, *not* mass-market or bestselling fiction – and, by subtraction, it is what is left once most of the conditions that obtain in contemporary publishing are removed.'[5] The first half of Connor's statement certainly holds with regard to publishers' definitions, although the chronology of definition causes a problem with regards to the process of 'subtraction'. It assumes an a priori genre division, whereby 'literary' fiction is only defined after more obvious genres have been categorised. This definition is therefore more of a formal than a contextual definition. 'Literary' fiction, Connor suggests, is the fiction published by a company that cannot be described in more formally, or formulaically, generic terms: it is not crime or science fiction, romance or fantasy. Any subject, or plot line, could potentially pertain to a literary novel. It could include elements of more closely defined genre fiction (in the 1990s, for example, there was a vogue for literary thrillers), but formal undefinability is its prevailing characteristic.[6] Because of the formal undefinability of literary fiction – a non-generic genre – genre becomes a dynamic and mutable property of its marketing, in which fashions shift and shape literary taste, and novels (and indeed works of non-fiction) which are situated at the borders of literary and other genres offer some of the most revealing sites of negotiation to the analyst. The blurring of genre boundaries, particularly when undertaken for promotional purposes, is considered in Chapter 3 and several of the case studies in Part II. Genre, including the genre of literary fiction, is a marketing concept in publishing: a definition not for its own sake but one which has commercial implications. This is certainly where *Marketing Literature* departs from the second part of Connor's definition. 'The conditions that obtain in contemporary publishing' refers more to the definitions of 'commentators [who...] maintain a Leavisite sense of the fundamental antagonism between the fiction market and the literary novel'.[7] In such a definition, the literary novel is *not* involved with the conditions of the market, in fact is set apart from – or above – it by its very nature. The definition that this book adheres to is that the literary novel exists – as it has since its inception as a literary form – under market conditions just as other, 'genre', fiction does. This is a central argument of the book, as it is of print culture more generally.

The second, contextual, definition of literary fiction to be derived from the structures and processes of publishers may at first appear to be meaninglessly circular, and yet it is perhaps one of the most significant methods of industry categorisation. Literary fiction is that published by literary imprints such as Hamish Hamilton, Jonathan Cape, Picador, Sceptre and Viking. What is important about the definition is the dialogue between the imprint and the individual novel or novelist, where each mutually defines the other, thus altering definitions as the years go by. The example of the imprint Picador, developed through the case studies of *American Psycho* (1991) and *Bridget Jones's Diary* (1996), illustrates this.[8] Imprint, however, is not the only (nor, to the reading public, the most visible) means of structural and contextual segmentation. Other industry and book-trade related factors that play a part in constituting the 'literary' are book prizes, material considerations (such as cover designs and book formats), media coverage, bookshop design and bestseller lists. All these factors play important roles in the contingent and shifting definition of the literary, and are examined in detail in this book.

The marketing of the books examined as case studies in Part II displays in empirical detail how such factors contribute to definitions of literariness, and the introductory section to the publishing histories explains in more detail the rationale behind the choice of titles. All, in some way or another, could be described as literary, and most – though not all – are fiction. All are also examples of *contemporary writing*, a third term from the title of this book in need of definition.

The publishing histories included in Part II range in publication date from 1991 to 2004. Part I of *Marketing Literature* gives a longer historical overview, in order to depict the historical and contextual backgrounds to the case studies. In terms of literary study and periodisation, a variety of different dates have been offered by literary historians to differentiate the contemporary period from the modern, the post-war, and even the postmodern. Rationales are provided in terms of perceived shifts in literary form and content as well as politics, economics and sociology. Randall Stevenson's Volume 12 of *The Oxford Literary History*, quizzically entitled *The Last of England?* (2004), for example, surveys the period from 1960–2000. James F. English, following the critical promptings of theorists including David Harvey and Anthony Giddens, and the political positioning of the country through the Thatcher government of 1979 onwards, posits a period break of the late 1970s in his Introduction to *A Concise Companion to Contemporary British Fiction* (2006).[9] Both of these recent studies tease at the edges of their periodisation, and literature's interactions with society, politics and economics. While paying attention to these factors, this study once again adheres to the periodisation of *publishing* history which, although interconnected with literary, political and economic history, has its own specific chronology. Chapter 1 explores this specific history in detail. The prevailing argument made is that, because of the shifting market conditions of the 1970s onwards, the last two decades of the twentieth century underwent an intensification in the marketing activity surrounding literary fiction. This intensification came about through a variety of factors including the increased financing available to publishing, conglomeration and globalisation and competition at all levels. This intensification has had the effect of increasing the visibility and impact of marketing activity on literature. The altering retail landscape has also had a strong impact on books and their marketplace reception. Thus, the period covered by *Marketing Literature*, following the historical and contextual overview offered in Chapter 1, is the 1990s and 2000s. This means that the material studied in this book is from the very recent past, which both requires and makes possible particular methodological processes.

Material conditions and methodologies of knowledge

The broad economic and business contexts of the publishing industry in the last decades of the twentieth century, as Chapter 1 explores, stress the centrality of marketing to the publishing process. It is these acts of marketing upon which this book concentrates, and the approach that it takes towards the literary novel is firmly based in market conditions. The book is located within an interactive network of forces, with a form that mutates according to the myriad demands, pressures and desires that are placed upon it. *Marketing Literature* begins from the premise that the study of literature benefits greatly from investigations into the conditions of its production and reception, and thus it falls into the academic field of the history of the book.

The very title 'history of the book', however, indicates a temporal positioning with regards to its subject matter that is at variance with *Marketing Literature*. In Thomas R. Adams and Nicolas Barker's 'A New Model for the Study of the Book' (1986), an essay at the heart of the theoretical debate concerning the discipline, the authors comment that 'posterity [will] come [...] to study our own time'.[10] The comment, though made specifically in the context of the material deterioration and conservation of books, is revealing. Its assumption is that only in the future can the present be studied, insisting on a temporal distance between the historian and his or her period of study. This distance is not available to *Marketing Literature*, and in some ways it is not desirable. The perceived need for 'posterity' has inflected the history of the book so as to skew study away from the contemporary period.[11] Of course, by a process of accumulation there are likely to be fewer existing studies of the 1990s than of the 1890s. Nonetheless, there is a disappointingly low number of studies of the material conditions of contemporary writing. Moreover, the work undertaken in the contemporary period is largely directed towards particular sectors of the market. Contemporary literary fiction is much less commonly dealt with than 'genre' or mass-market fiction in its industrial context. The paucity of academic study of the period means there is much room for original research to be undertaken.

Inevitably, studying the contemporary period means that there will be a lack of hindsight, and this book makes no claims that the works discussed as case studies here will be discussed in ten years' time, let alone in one hundred. The dust has not settled, canons are still in formation, and the marketing of each novel – which includes the agencies of canonisation and books such as this one – is an ongoing process.[12] A lengthy time lapse, though, would alter the project of this book, necessitating lengthier, archaeological reconstructions of the contexts and placing a different emphasis on the case study texts. The choice of books for the case studies is made not with an eye to the future, but to the present and very recent past. Although each of the novels may still be read decades or even hundreds of years in the future, the appeal that they will make will not be the same as the influence they currently exert. Hence, *Marketing Literature* is an exploration of an industry and its products in transition. Recording this period of transition means that the focus is inevitably that of the period itself. Thus, the renaming, and reorienting, of 'the history of the book' as the study of 'material cultures', or 'literary sociology', or the 'institutions of literature', also apply to *Marketing Literature* in the repositioning of the discipline, and the interrogation of its tenets. Adams and Barker's anxiety about what evidence will remain for posterity to study demonstrates, ironically, the advantage of *not* waiting for posterity.

In writing about contemporary literary fiction in the context of its industry now, *Marketing Literature* also contests a cultural divide in the choices of genre and period made by the history of the book, which tends to operate in one of two ways. The first is a means of proliferating research topics on literature already fully accepted into the canon, an argument based on the premise that if a text, or author, is thought to be important, the conditions of their production must be too. As such, there are studies of the material culture of Shakespeare, Charles Dickens and James Joyce, to name but a few whose publishing histories provide particularly unusual or interesting examples. The second is a means of incorporating certain texts and their contexts into academic study, which might otherwise be rejected by the more value-laden mores of traditional English Literature departments. The attention given to romance fiction in a variety of recent scholarly publications is one example.[13] Hence, mass-market and genre fiction become legitimate topics of study: if a cultural artefact reaches a large audience it must be of importance, even if some might find it distasteful or simply 'badly' written. Very good studies have been produced to either of these remits, and the two sides share a validating belief in the study of the network of forces acting on the transmission of the book. Yet the two sides of the history of the book suffer, often unwillingly, from the legacy of English Studies in its tendency both to social discrimination between elite and mass audiences, and to textual discrimination via the imposition of literary hierarchies.[14] By working in a period in which the contested processes of canonisation are only just beginning, the aim here is to work towards narrowing the cultural divide that is all too easily perpetuated by the history of the book. The study of the industry in transition, and the emphasis on the present and recent past, then, is part of the intellectual enterprise of *Marketing Literature*.

There is, nonetheless, a growing body of work focused on the material culture of the contemporary period of literary history which this book draws on. Much, though not all, of this has appeared since the turn of the millennium. John Sutherland's earlier *Fiction and the Fiction Industry* (1978) and *Bestsellers* (1981) were formative works in the study of the contemporary fiction industry, but concentrate largely on genre fiction.[15] His more recent *Reading the Decades: Fifty Years of the Nation's Bestselling Books* (2002), published to accompany a BBC series of the same year, is, as Sutherland himself states, not so much 'a research dissertation [...] as something more in the nature of an informed essay on what the British read, and why, over the last half-century'.[16] Clive Bloom's *Bestsellers: Popular Fiction Since 1900* (2002) also works best as a survey, though he does offer some valuable commentary on what constitutes a bestseller, which Part II looks at in more detail.[17] Connor's aforementioned 'Economics, Publishing and Readership' provides an articulate analysis of the historical and theoretical background to the period. Paul Delany's *Literature, Money and the Market* (2002) has a chapter on what he terms the 'postmodern literary system' of the 1980s and 1990s, and some useful conceptions of the literary marketplace in his Introduction.[18] The updated edition of John Feather's *A History of British Publishing* (2006) usefully extends its reach to the 1990s and 2000s, while the eventual appearance of *The Cambridge History of the Book in Britain Volume Seven 1914-2000* will provide a much-needed standard reference work for the period.[19] Recent volumes on post-war writing that have chapters on the publishing contexts include Stevenson's *The Last of England?*, Brian W. Shaffer's *A Companion to the British and Irish Novel 1945–2000* (2005) and English's *A Concise Companion to Contemporary British Fiction*.[20] John B. Thompson's *Books in the Digital Age* (2005) concentrates on academic and higher education publishing, rather than the fiction sector, but nonetheless offers insight into overall market conditions.[21]

There are also several studies which take a more particular perspective on the publishing industry and its associated agencies. These include *Writing: A Woman's Business: Women, Writing and the Marketplace* (1998), edited by Judy Simons and Kate Fullbrook, which offers some illuminating analysis of publishing, writers and readers, and through its range of essays demonstrates a strong interest in concepts of literary classification (serious/popular; literary/commercial).[22] More recently, Simone Murray's *Mixed Media: Feminist Presses and Publishing Politics* (2004) surveys in detail the feminist press movement.[23] Examinations of the publishing industry from a post-colonial angle, such as S. I. A. Kotei's 'The Book Today in Africa' (1981) and Philip G. Altbach's 'Literary Colonialism: Books in the Third World' (1975) began the exploration of the impact of the global structures of publishing, while Graham Huggan's *The Postcolonial Exotic: Marketing the Margins* (2001) puts these structures under stringent theoretical scrutiny.[24] Richard Todd's *Consuming Fictions: The Booker Prize and Fiction in Britain Today* (1996), a history and analysis of the prize, affords some fruitful contextual analysis of the contemporary literary novel, while on the same topic James F. English's *The Economy of Prestige: Prizes, Awards, and the Circulation of Cultural Value* (2005) also puts prize culture, including book awards, under the microscope.[25] Joe Moran's *Star Authors: Literary Celebrity in America* (2000), though concentrating for the main on the US, nonetheless provides an informed study of literary celebrity with some revealing UK examples.[26] Eva Hemmungs Wirtén's *No Trespassing: Authorship, Intellectual Property Rights, and the Boundaries of Globalization* (2004) also concentrates on the author, but from the perspective of the laws of copyright.[27] Laura J. Miller's *Reluctant Capitalists* (2006) is a fascinating account of the history of bookselling in the US, but there is no comparable volume on the particular conditions of the retail trade in the UK.[28] The various authors contributing to Stephen Brown's edited volume *Consuming Books: The Marketing and Consumption of Literature* (2006) examine a variety of publishing case studies, though they do not provide an overview of the contemporary marketplace.[29] Eric de Bellaigue's *British Book Publishing as a Business Since the 1960s* (2004) surveys the economic underpinning of the industry in the late twentieth century.[30]

There is an expanding corpus of publishing memoirs, biographies and house histories which touch on this period, including, recently, Joseph McAleer's *Passion's Fortune: The Story of Mills & Boon* (1999), Jeremy Lewis's biography of Allen Lane, the founder of Penguin Books (2005), and Elizabeth James's *Macmillan: A Publishing Tradition* (2002).[31] However, although Penguin is still very much alive as an imprint (having celebrated its 70th anniversary in 2005), Lane died in 1970 and Lewis's focus is on Penguin under its founder's reign. McAleer's history, while surveying the company's activity until as close to the present as possible, nevertheless concentrates on the pre-1972 period. James's *Macmillan* looks at the first 130 years of the company, from 1843 to the 1970s. Recent publishing memoirs, including *Stet* by Diana Athill (2000) and *Publisher* by Tom Maschler (2005), who were, respectively, editors at André Deutsch and Jonathan Cape, offer an individual's insight into the world of publishing and editing, although they both concentrate on decades prior to those upon which this book concentrates.[32]

Much, therefore, still remains to be done in this area, and as James notes in her Introduction to *Macmillan*, 'the writing and publishing of books is still going on [...] the History of the Book is not yet complete'.[33] The temporal positioning of *Marketing Literature* is, then, very close to its subject matter. As well as building on academic and historical accounts already available, *Marketing Literature* draws extensively on the wealth of sources produced by the trade itself and those closely related to it. These sources range from the trade press and the general media, to best-seller lists, publishers' and booksellers' marketing material, and reports produced by industry analysts. Before even considering the information that these sources divulge, it is taken as axiomatic that they are produced for a variety of different purposes, audiences and intents. Intended and incidental audiences, the conditions of the source's production, the varying degrees of truth, polemic and (mis-) information are all factors that must be borne in mind when using such material. Moreover, the use of such sources here is dual: for not only do they provide information about the marketing processes of the industry, but they also act as interpretive tools themselves, commenting upon publishing history as it happens and subsequent to its passage.

For the purposes of this book, primary research in the form of interviews with people working within the industry (including editors, literary agents, sales and marketing teams, journalists, prize administrators and authors) has been conducted. The problematic nature of personal testimony extends to these accounts, in their susceptibility to false memory, self-promotion and partiality. Nonetheless, these interviews, like the other sources used here, have a double purpose: both to convey information (some of which would be unavailable in any other form), and as interpretations of that information. They are, in other words, both the voice of the industry and a commentary upon it. This last point is crucial: the publishing industry is far from naïve but provides multiple, instantaneous and continuing interpretations of its own activities, which inform its continuing activity.

The contemporaneity of this project also has a bearing upon the sources. It is not possible for every statement that is made in the sources to be verified, and consequently interpretations are sometimes made on hints, rumours and assumptions that might, when posterity dawns – when and if, for example, publishers' material becomes more widely available in archives – be found to have been incorrect. However, as long as interpretations are made with an awareness of the potential for untruths and misleading information, working very close to the period of study allows for a greater understanding of the ephemeral sources that have nonetheless a vital impact on contemporary perceptions and representations. A factually incorrect interpretation in a newspaper, for example, nevertheless creates its own form of truth – or myth.

To have lived through a period is of course not the only means to understanding it, but the near-sightedness of the vision allows a representation in a way that is both particular and avoids the causal determinism of hindsight. In this respect, *Marketing Literature* takes its cue from the historiography of the present undertaken by those including Timothy Garton Ash, who, in his *History of the Present: Essays, Sketches and Despatches from Europe in the 1990s* (2000), rejects what Henri Bergson called the '"illusions of retrospective determinism"' for the immediacy of what people actually experienced and believed 'at the time'.[34] Included in this near-sighted vision is my own personal experience of working in the publishing industry, first in the press office and editorial department at Hodder Headline, then as a freelance, and latterly as an educator of future publishers at the Oxford International Centre for Publishing Studies at Oxford Brookes University.[35] This personal experience has been central both in framing the topic of this book, and in gathering information for it.

Importantly, though, a note on what this book is not. It is not the aim to provide a statistical analysis of the publishing industry (although quantitative data underpins much of its thinking). Numerous market analysts, including *The Bookseller*, Book Marketing Limited and Nielsen Bookscan, are much better equipped to perform this function. The primary focus is on, as the definitions suggest, marketing as a form of representation and interpretation. Marketing's function as a business practice feeds into its representational agencies, but to encompass this fully would require a very different sort of study to this one. Although concerned with all the agencies operating within the literary marketplace, including readers, *Marketing Literature* is also not a study of readership, although it addresses a variety of different ways in which patterns of reading influence the production and consumption of books. Contemporary aspects of the marketplace such as reading groups and meet-the-author events are mentioned, but more with regard to their place in the promotional circuit than their depiction of reading habits.

Narrative and structure

When the contemporary publishing industry is mentioned by the media and cultural pundits – and yoked with a discussion of the state of the novel – the debate frequently tends towards a polarisation of viewpoint. The negative opinions cite what they see as falling standards of production, the globalising monopolies of a handful of companies, and a perceived impoverishment of an industry that forgoes diversity and quality in the pursuit of profit. The more positive accounts see a renewed vigour in the marketplace, particularly in the arena of literary fiction, and refer to the numerous new book retailing outlets, with their emphasis on accessibility and consumer choice, and the central place and impact of books in the media. The tendency towards hyperbole is not restricted to the literary pages of newspapers and industry analyses: Carmen Callil and Colm Tóibín, in their introduction to *The Modern Library: The Two Hundred Best Novels in English since 1950* (1999), note that the period their volume covers 'has been [...] as sublime and exciting as any other for the novel', a comment that follows a litany of positive developments in the industry.[36] Negative accounts from chroniclers including André Schiffrin's *The Business of Books: How International Conglomerates Took Over Publishing and the Way We Read* (2000) constitute, as Simone Murray appositely termed it in her paper 'From Literature to Content: Media Multinationals, Publishing Practice and the Digitisation of the Book' (2002), a 'lament school'.[37] This 'school' may well draw on a tradition of cultural pessimism, but it is also a specific response to the economic and cultural circumstances of the period. D. J. Taylor, in *A Vain Conceit: British Fiction in the 1980s* (1989), opined that 'The publishing industry, like the Labour Party or the Church of England, exists forever in a state of crisis.'[38] The economic background of conglomeration and globalisation has been central in the creation of current market conditions, as the next chapter indicates, and positive or negative accounts are in response to these trends, concomitant industry developments, and opinions on the value of the contemporary publishing industry's output. Whether the commentator is a polemicist, enthusiast or apologist, there is a tendency to begin any account from a position that irrevocably colours it one way or another. When Steven Connor states that, 'It is possible to tell a very depressing story about the publishing and circulation of fiction from the 1970s onwards', he indicates the narratability – and inherent possibility for bias, exaggeration and personal colouring – of the process of describing the publishing industry.[39] These dichotomous accounts indicate that there is a need for a less polemic and more qualified analysis. Narrating any version of events is, of course, to make an interpretation, but it is the intention of this book to try to present as balanced a view as possible, one that allows an understanding of the industry to develop in the ensuing chapters in an unprejudiced manner. *Marketing Literature,* nonetheless, proceeds on the understanding that the material conditions of production are of vital importance in the consideration of literature. This study is thus emphatically contextual and as such, the place of literary criticism is secondary. Where, however, literary criticism begins to develop is in the intersections of text and context, in the places where the 'inside' of a book functions in conjunction, or conflict, with its 'outside'. Genre – the literary taxonomies that develop through marketing – is the key element in this dialogue of text and context as the discussion of genre in Chapter 3 emphasises.

Marketing Literature, then, provides an overview of the social, economic and cultural contexts for the production of contemporary writing in Britain, and analyses the specific conditions of the publishing industry at the turn of the twentieth and twenty-first centuries. It establishes a framework for understanding the marketing of contemporary writing which has both a theoretical underpinning and is based on industry practice. It investigates the impact of the contemporary publishing environment on genre, format and packaging, literary prizes, authorship and promotion, and reading. *Marketing Literature* concentrates on literary fiction and the processes of its commodification, but also extends into a consideration of genre fiction and children's writing. It develops a range of models of marketing success through the close examination of the publishing histories of a series of high-profile books, and demonstrates the central importance of the theory and practice of book marketing to constructions of literature and literary value.

In order to fulfil this brief, *Marketing Literature* divides into two parts. Part I has three chapters, the first of which, 'Publishing Contexts and Market Conditions', establishes the social, cultural and economic contexts for publishing in the period. It examines the conditions of British publishing, including the impact of conglomeration and globalisation, changing retail practice, new leisure and information technologies, the intensification of marketing activity and the commercialisation of the marketplace. Alongside an understanding of the circulation of literary fiction, it develops definitions of a publishing market sector which has undergone radical and significant change in recent years in both cultural and economic status. The second chapter, 'Literature and Marketing', considers more specifically the marketing of literature. It traces the development of the frequently heated debate about the relationship of literature to marketing in the decades preceding the 1990s and 2000s, and explores its contemporary manifestations. The chapter also develops the theoretical basis of the book. While firmly situated within the discipline of book history and the sociology of literature, and part of an emerging field of publishing studies, *Marketing Literature* also forges its own theoretical background via the linkage of marketing theory and practice to publishing history. This is accomplished through the focus on marketing as a form of representation and interpretation. In so doing, it seeks to extend our frameworks for understanding the institutional and economic contexts of literary discourse. Chapter 3, 'Genre in the Marketplace', considers the place of genre in the marketplace. It examines how publishers, booksellers and other intermediary agencies involved in the marketing of literature create cultural meanings through genre negotiations following the theoretical promptings of Chapter 2. The chapter discusses paratextual issues of packaging and formats, bookshop taxonomies, and the role of publishers' imprints and literary prizes in constructing and reshaping notions of literary value and taste.

Through the publishing histories of a series of high-profile books, Part II then interrogates a number of different ways of thinking about the relationship between marketing and literature. The case studies are split into three loosely themed chapters. Chapter 4, 'Icons and Phenomenons', discusses two of the highest-profile titles of the period: Louis de Bernières' *Captain Corelli's Mandolin* (1994) and Martin Amis's *The Information* (1995).[40] As well as being valuable case studies in their own right, they also indicate a wider sense of the contemporary market and attitudes towards it. The second sequence of books in Chapter 5 are 'Marketing Stories'. These reveal a variety of different models of marketing, including the instant global success, the slowly acquired cult status, the impact of winning prizes on a developing career, and the manipulation of the author figure. The books examined are Irvine Welsh's *Trainspotting* (1993), Pat Barker's *The Ghost Road* (1995) and Arundhati Roy's *The God of Small Things* (1997).[41] The final sequence of books in Chapter 6 are 'Crossovers': Bret Easton Ellis's *American Psycho* (1991), Helen Fielding's *Bridget Jones's Diary* (1996), J. K. Rowling's *Harry Potter* series (1997–2007), Philip Pullman's *His Dark Materials* trilogy (1995–2000), Mark Haddon's *The Curious Incident of the Dog in the*

Night-Time (2003) and David Mitchell's *Cloud Atlas* (2004).[42] These case studies consider the placement of novels in terms of imprint and packaging, and the impact this has on the construction of genre, value and textual interpretation.

In conclusion, *Marketing Literature* considers, through a summary of the book and a final case study of Zadie Smith's *White Teeth* (2000), the extent to which literature as a category might, occasionally and paradoxically, resist all forms of categorisation, and hint towards a form of writing beyond marketing.[43] The central argument of *Marketing Literature*, however, is that of its subtitle. Marketing is effectively the making of contemporary writing. In a very real sense, as the following chapters reveal, material conditions and acts of marketing profoundly determine the production, reception and interpretation of literature.

Part I

Marketing Literature: Contexts and Theory

1
Publishing Contexts and Market Conditions

The twentieth century was a time of great reorganisation in the British publishing industry. During this period, the production of literature would be affected by great upheaval in terms of ownership, operation and competition. In the course of the century, the ideology and culture of publishing would also come to be re-evaluated. Although some book historians have argued that the last two hundred years of British publishing have shown at least as much continuity as they have change in terms of rising production figures, merchandising, the mass-market paperback, the knowledge economy, and the exploitation of intellectual property, there have nonetheless been profound shifts.[1] This chapter details these shifts, and relates them to the specific market conditions of contemporary literary publishing.

In his memoir *Kindred Spirits: Adrift in Literary London* (1995), the publisher Jeremy Lewis, who worked for Chatto & Windus, depicted the upheaval in his industry by describing the changing office spaces in which he worked:

> the last ten years I spent with a small but well-regarded firm, which has since been absorbed into an American conglomerate and transplanted to a modern office block, all open-plan and winking VDUs, but was, when I went there in the late 1970s, the epitome of an old-fashioned literary publisher [...]
>
> the floors were covered with blue lino, the telephones were Bakelite and the furniture Utility [...] and the place was staffed by loyal, long-serving spinsters in cardigans and sandals, and – for much of the firm's history at least – amiable and highly civilised men with large private incomes [...][2]

Through his description of office spaces and their inhabitants, Lewis hints at some of the major changes in recent publishing history: the consolidation of small, often family-run companies into global multimedia conglomerates; the resulting new operational paradigms and in particular the ascendancy of marketing over the editorially led tradition; and the cultural transition from an industry populated by 'amiable and highly civilised men with large private incomes' to a highly commercialised, market-focused workforce which has overseen the intensification of marketing activity. These changes, alongside key developments including the impact of new technologies and competing leisure activities, alterations in the book retail environment, the interaction of publishing and society and, centrally to the argument of this book as a whole, the growth of literary celebrity and the commodification of contemporary writing, are addressed here.

Conglomeration and competition

The greatest transition in twentieth-century publishing has been in its changing patterns of ownership. At the beginning of the century, the British publishing industry was largely run by mid-sized, family-owned businesses, including such houses as Chatto & Windus (established 1876), Hodder & Stoughton (established 1868), The Bodley Head (established 1887), and one of the oldest family companies, John Murray (established 1768). By the end of the Second World War, this pattern remained largely the same, though with the addition of several key new companies, including Mills & Boon (1908), Victor Gollancz (1927) and Penguin (1935). By the end of the 1990s, however, this pattern had been completely overturned, with all market sectors being dominated by a very small number of multinational, multimedia companies. Mergers and acquisitions in the publishing industry before the Second World War were not unheard of – Stanley Unwin bought the flagging George Allen to form George Allen & Unwin in 1914, for example, and the nineteenth-century companies of Methuen, and Chapman and Hall, came together in 1938 – but they proliferated from the late 1960s onwards. The 1990s and 2000s continued this trend, with significant mergers and acquisitions including Bertelsmann's takeover of Random House in 1998 and Hachette's purchase of Hodder Headline in 2004. As Andrew Milner comments in *Literature, Culture and Society* (1996), 'The most significant shift under post-war late capitalism has [...] been that from national publishing empires to international media conglomerates.'[3]

The deregulation of the financial markets in the US and UK in the 1970s and 1980s was crucial in the intensification of publishing conglomeration. As Giles Clark explains in *Inside Book Publishing* (2001), deregulation 'led to increased availability of long- and short-term equity and debt financing allowing large publishers or their parents to take over medium-sized publishers, and small publishers to expand or start-up'.[4] This process of conglomeration has been analysed in numerous economic histories of the publishing industry, including in the occasional supplements produced by Bookseller Publications, *Who Owns Whom in British Book Publishing* (1990, 1998, 2002) which chart in textual and visual format the frenetic consolidation of publishing companies in this period.[5] The most comprehensive chronicler of recent economic publishing history is Eric de Bellaigue who, in a series of *Logos* and *Bookseller* articles that were revised and published in book format, examined *British Book Publishing as a Business Since the 1960s*.[6] In setting out the financial and business reasons behind this concentration, de Bellaigue comments on the perceived need for market share, economies of scale, concentration, cross-media synergy and focus, all of which factors have contributed in varying degrees to the types of groups into which publishing groups have been incorporated. He also notes that by the 1980s general publishing (as opposed to the academic, educational or Science, Technical and Medical (STM)), was dominated by seven publishers: HarperCollins, Hodder Headline, Macmillan, Penguin, Random House, Reed Consumer Books and Transworld.[7] Subsequent mergers have meant the further reduction of the number of these groups, as the trade section of Reed was sold to Random House, and Bertelsmann, the group owning Transworld, bought Random House. By 2001, five companies (Bertelsmann, Pearson, HarperCollins, Hodder Headline and Hachette) had just over 50 per cent of market share in the UK.[8] Hodder Headline, to take one example, had been formed as a group in 1993 when the 1986 start-up company Headline merged with the nineteenth-century Hodder & Stoughton. It was then bought by newsagent and book retailer WH Smith in 1999, and acquired John Murray in 2002. This last event occasioned much hand-wringing in the trade press and the media more generally, as the sale of John Murray, once the publisher of Lord Byron, Charles Darwin and Jane Austen, came to represent the succumbing of publishing history and family tradition to big business. A cartoon accompanying a *Bookseller* editorial on the sale visualised it as a modern multi-storey office block voraciously leaning over a small building (Hodder Headline's Euston Road premises and John Murray's famous offices in London's Albemarle Street).[9] When WH Smith divested itself of Hodder Headline in 2004, the purchase by Hachette (already Orion's owner) of the publisher concentrated the market yet further. This was compounded in 2006, when Hachette purchased the Time Warner Book Group.

A near oligopolistic control has thus came to exist in publishing in this period, and despite the very creditable performance of independents such as Faber and Faber and Bloomsbury (the latter having the advantage of rights to the *Harry Potter* series), the field of general publishing has increasingly become dominated by a small number of giant corporations rather than populated by small and mid-sized companies, as with earlier twentieth-century ownership patterns. Given the enduring importance of books in society, it follows that significant cultural and political power has therefore been invested in the hands of the same small group of conglomerates, and there has been much anxiety expressed about the changing patterns of ownership. The seeming prevention of Harper-Collins' publication of Chris Patten's book on Hong Kong, *East and West: The Last Governor General of Hong Kong on Power, Freedom and the Future* (1998), is frequently cited as an example of conglomerate intervention in editorial decisions.[10] Rupert Murdoch (head of News Corporation, HarperCollins' owner) infamously suppressed the book, as it was deemed detrimental to his business interests in China and the Far East.[11] The book was eventually published by Macmillan, however, and Patten's beleaguered editor moved to Penguin following the book's suppression.

This was a rare example of censorship dictated by political and business interests. Less overt forms of control exerted by conglomerate publishing are described by André Schiffrin in *The Business of Books*, which is provocatively subtitled *How International Conglomerates Took Over Publishing and Changed the Way We Read*. Schiffrin discusses how 'market censorship' – governed by profitability rather than politics – is as effective as ideological controls in curtailing the range of publishing activity.[12] The political and cultural autonomy of a nation's publishing industry is inevitably under duress when controlled by a small number of large agents, a recurrent theme in analyses of the late twentieth- and early twenty-first-century trade. The precise impact of this on fiction publishing is hard to discern, however, although some suggestions are made later in this chapter.

Giles Clark's analysis of the impact of the deregulation of the financial markets emphasises, however, that money has also been made available to small companies to be established or expand, and new technologies, including desk-top publishing software, print on demand and internet publishing, have cut down on costs and on the need for traditional production skills for new entrants into the market.[13] Thus, although market share has been highly concentrated in the period covered by this study, there has also been a rise of small operators, and an improvement in the technological and business practices available to them. The seemingly contradictory outlook for smaller companies in a market dominated by a small handful of multimedia conglomerates suggests the complexity of contemporary publishing markets, and a marketplace that can be – as the Introduction stated – depicted both negatively and positively. On the one hand, there is the reality of market control by an oligopolistic group. On the other, there are the very real possibilities for small and start-up businesses operating in new ways.

Publishers who are outside the small group of market leaders encounter particular problems in the supply chain in terms of unequal access to the market and hence difficulties in attracting customers to their products. The preferential discounts offered by large publishers to major retailers, and the high discounts demanded of small publishers by retailers, have meant that some independents have taken the decision to sell to larger companies (such as Fourth Estate's sale to HarperCollins in 2000) in order to access their negotiating power and distribution channels. De Bellaigue notes that in the UK there is no law prohibiting 'discriminatory discounts', by which publishers can favour particular retailers, thus resulting in publisher/retailer negotiations of a 'peculiarly tangled character'. Such tangles typically might include, in addition to the market-wide activity of consumer advertising, co-promotional payments for bookshop space. Commonly known in the trade as 'bungs', these payments to retailers from publishers secure front-of-bookshop or window display space for their products.[14]

The impact of the changing retail environment is examined in the next section of this chapter. Before moving on to this, there are some further implications of the processes of conglomeration on the literary marketplace. The first of these is structural. In the transformation from mid-sized family-run businesses to large multinationals, many once independent publishers have become incorporated into conglomerates. Publishers are thus both vertically integrated (publishing in both hard- and paperback) and include previously independent houses as imprints. Random House, for example, now includes a host of previously independent houses as imprints, including Jonathan Cape, Chatto & Windus, The Bodley Head, Hutchinson and the merged Harvill Secker (from Secker & Warburg and The Harvill Press). For observers of the contemporary British publishing scene, this offers a kind of living archaeology, in which the imprints contained within every large publishing company reveal a palimpsest history resulting from the conglomeration of the publishing industry, most particularly in the period from the 1960s onwards. The way in which these imprints are retained, along with their colophons can, Simone Murray has suggested in 'From Literature to Content', be likened to the display of hunting lodge trophies.[15] The collection of previously independent publishers as imprints displays – if nothing else – a conglomerate publisher with a strong acquisitive appetite. Imprints are also used within the publishing trade, however, to signal list identity and to demarcate genre divisions: Jonathan Cape and Harvill Secker as literary imprints, for example, and Hutchinson as a mass-market one. This role of imprints in marketing and categorisation is looked at more thoroughly in Chapter 3.

A further impact of the conglomeration of publishers is in the broader business groupings in which book publishers have found themselves. De Bellaigue charts the succession of different types of corporate owners of publishers: from a tendency in the 1960s and early 1970s to combine communications groups and publishers; to the purchase of UK publishers by US publishing groups; and later in the 1970s, the purchase of US by UK groups; and to a global marketplace from the late 1980s onwards with German, French, Australian and Canadian companies in addition to US and UK companies.[16] Publishers now tend to be subsumed into multimedia conglomerates: companies with interests in newspapers and magazines, film, television and radio, and new communications technologies. News Corporation, for example, besides HarperCollins, has newspaper, magazine, satellite and terrestrial television and film production and distribution interests. Viacom, owner of Simon & Schuster, has cable and broadcast television, film and television production, music, video, themes parks and cinemas. Publishers, therefore, have come to operate with other cultural and media industries for whom 'content' and intellectual property rights are central to their business. The possibilities for re-use of content have thus been intensified, with the idea that cross-media synergies within conglomerate groups would maximise profits for corporate owners. Books can be turned into films (and vice versa), merchandise is produced alongside television shows and spin-off books, and electronic games give print- or audio-based characters a repurposed form of life. Rowling's *Harry Potter* character and stories are a prime example of this. All this has meant, as Clark has put it in *Inside Book Publishing*, that the book trade has become 'part of the larger media leisure industry' as a result of changing patterns of ownership and the synergy between books and other leisure products and their producers.[17] Moreover, the possibilities of content repurposing have opened new revenue channels, in which the author, as content creator, can play a vital role. The consolidation of multimedia conglomerates has therefore occurred alongside the diversification of rights sales, content re-use, and the remodelling of the author as a content creator. The ascendancy of the literary agent, however, as the primary business manager of an author's rights, has militated against total control by the multinational multimedia groups. Literary agents frequently deem it fitting, in order to maximise profit and effective production and marketing, to break up rights sales. Contrary to global multimedia companies obtaining the rights to exploit all possible uses, literary agents have separated out rights, continuing to sell licences to different publishers in a number of territories, and to give film options and rights to companies who have no links to the original book publisher.[18]

The rise of literary agents as rights managers has increased competitiveness, as well as indicating the developing culture of marketing in British publishing. Another factor contributing to increasing competitiveness has been the rising level of book title production. The history of post-Second World War British publishing has been one of rapidly increasing production levels which accelerated yet more in the 1990s. Many of the mid-century shifts have to do with broader historical factors: the immediate post-war industry was extremely depressed; the book trade had been hit hard by the war. Before the Second World War, much of Britain's paper was imported, and the domestic paper-making industry was heavily reliant on imported raw materials. In 1940, paper rationing was introduced, and the trade negotiated the Book Production War Economy Agreement as a paper-saving measure. New title production in the war halved, falling from a total of 14 904 new books in 1939 to a wartime low of 6705 in 1943.[19] Post-war publishing, like many other aspects of life in Britain, entered a time of austerity, with paper rationing in place until 1949. The editor Diana Athill evokes in her memoir of the period 'those book-hungry days' of 'the post-war book famine'.[20] From the depressed point of 6747 new titles in 1945, production levels rose to 35 608 by 1975.[21] By 1985, there were 52 994 titles, and by 1996 title production had for the first time surpassed the 100 000 mark.[22] From 1975 to 2000, UK title output had almost tripled, and the first years of the new century saw the onward march of this trend, with the additional factor of print on demand titles pushing figures towards 200 000.[23] Simon Eliot, although arguing in 2003 that the entire period from 1770 onwards has been one of 'huge increases in the scale of production', nonetheless accepts that the figures over 200 years are 'as nothing when compared with the output of texts in the last thirty years'.[24]

Without doubt, the rapid rise in production has forced a more competitive market, with hundreds of thousands of new titles every year jostling for places on bookshop shelves and in the bestseller lists. Inherent in this is that the shelf life of books is short – worryingly so to many. The reversal of the traditional book economy of long-termism and the backlist towards a short-term, mass-market logic has been profound. In Schiffrin's indictment of the US industry in *The Business of Books*, for example, he remarks that 'Calvin Trillin once described the shelf life of a book as somewhere between that of milk and yogurt, and we joked that an expiration date ought to be stamped on every book cover. Now the stores do that for us, returning the books faster and faster.'[25] Indeed, the issue of returns, where in the majority of cases retailers can send back to the publisher or wholesaler unsold copies, is one of the greatest challenges to the British industry, persuading the UK Publishers' Association and the Department of Trade and Industry to commission a management consultancy report on the issue in 1998.[26] In addition to the financial and logistical issues of supply-chain management, short-termism encourages novelty, and the late twentieth century has seen a growing pressure on novelists to produce works of fiction with greater regularity, to counteract short shelf lives and the threat of returns, contributing in a major way towards the commodification of books, including those in the literary field.

One further implication of conglomeration has arguably had the most profound effect on the marketing of literary fiction, and that is the increased money made available to large publishers. As Clark makes clear, increased equity accelerated mergers and acquisitions, but also made money available to conglomerate publishers to spend on advances and marketing. The late twentieth century saw rapid rises in advance levels for the select few, a parallel rise in marketing spends, and a consequent intensification of marketing and promotional activity surrounding certain books and market sectors. This concentration of resources on lead titles has also had the effect of increasing competition. This competition can be internal as well as external – Transworld and Random House (both Bertelsmann companies), for example, compete for publishing projects, but there can even be internalised competition between imprints, between editors commissioning for the same imprint, and between individual titles on an imprint for a proportion of marketing spend. All this has meant an increasingly stratified market in which, despite rapidly increasing title production, resources and sales are heavily concentrated. Literary celebrity and highly visible books are two consequences of great importance to the marketplace, and to the argument of this book.

The book retail environment

Much of the recent history of conglomeration of publishing companies, as the previous section details, would suggest that it has been the primary driver of change in the production and reception of literature. Indeed, its effects have been profound on business practice, and particularly on the intensification of marketing activity. However, changes in the book retail environment have, arguably, had at least as strong an impact on the ways in which literature has been produced, marketed and received, and the strength of particular retailers and retailer types has altered the complexion of the literary marketplace.

The demise of the Net Book Agreement (NBA) in 1995 was seen by many in both symbolic and actual terms as symptomatic of the new retail market of the late twentieth century. The NBA, which came into being at the dawn of the twentieth century, was an industry retail price maintenance agreement, whereby retailers were bound to sell books at the minimum price set by the publisher. This agreement, which worked not on a legislative basis but on the sanction of refusing further discounted supply if the terms were broken, underpinned publishing and book retail practice for the majority of the twentieth century. It was unsuccessfully challenged in court in 1962, in a case in which the phrase 'books are different' (from the mass of consumer products) figured large in the argument in favour of the retention of price protection.[27] By the 1990s, retail price maintenance was once again seriously challenged, and after major publishers and retailers (notably Hodder Headline, Dillons and WH Smith) broke the terms of the agreement by offering books at discounted prices, the NBA was finally abandoned in 1995.

The post-NBA retail environment has seen the habitual discounting of lead titles, particularly in hardback editions, a range of books in 3 for 2 price offers, and book retail venues competing heavily in order to offer the cheapest prices. Such energetic discounting practices have seen many books discounted at dramatic rates, with the retail price of some market-leading books falling below half their recommended retail price.[28] The wild discounting practices that ensued after the end of the NBA suggest that by the end of the twentieth century and the beginning of the twenty-first, the market had not yet found its equilibrium between protectionism and competition. The heavy discounting by retailers of highly desirable consumer items such as the *Harry Potter* books has been questioned by some observers of the market. Whether it is effective business practice to offer the highest discounts on the most desirable items is questionable, but others might argue that it extends the reading market.[29]

In order to be able to offer such low price points, retailers with the requisite power in the marketplace demand increasing trade discounts from publishers. Publishers in their turn attempt the negotiation of authors' contracts based on the principle of royalties based on net receipts (i.e. the monies received from sales of the book) rather than on cover price. Small and independent bookshops find it impossible to compete, as they do not have the power to negotiate such strong deals with publishers, and in the case of very heavily discounted books are offered less discount from the publisher than some retailers – particularly supermarkets – were offering direct to consumers. Such practice has been satirised in a Posy Simmonds cartoon depicting the employees of an independent bookshop fastidiously calculating that it is cheaper to send someone out to buy a supermarket trolley full of books to sell on in their own shop than to order them from their normal wholesaler.[30] Similarly, small and independent publishers find it difficult to afford the discount that retailers habitually demand, and so their books are difficult to source via the shelves of Waterstone's or WH Smith. This is the 'discriminatory' or preferential discounting to which de Bellaigue refers, and means that the retail environment privileges larger publishers and retailers who can negotiate such deals, and leads to the practice of co-promotion, or 'bungs', within bookstores.

Commentators on the publishing industry have had much to say about this practice. The literary agent Giles Gordon roundly condemned it in an article in the *Bookseller*, 'Proper Publishing Goes Bung' (2002), bemoaning a decline in literary standards and decrying in provocative terms the nature of co-promotional practice, saying that 'the conglomerates not only offer the bookselling chains better terms to stock their books rather than those of their rivals, but also give bookshops baksheesh to put their titles in the window, at the front of the shop and in great heaps around the place.'[31] The consequence of this, states Gordon in no uncertain terms, is that 'crap is being promoted [...] at the expense of quality'.[32] For Gordon, this perceived bribery is symptomatic of the 'rise and rise of sales and marketing "teams" at the expense of editors'.[33]

In the weeks following Gordon's polemic, the *Bookseller* assessed co-promotional activity in more measured terms in Danuta Kean's article 'Bungs – Are They Fair Trade?' (2002).[34] Kean's account refuted the 'basic misconception' that 'prime instore retail space is granted to the highest bidder', suggesting instead that the contribution towards marketing costs happens only after the selection of books has taken place, and that numerous more literary titles, including Zadie Smith's *White Teeth* (2000) and Margaret Atwood's *The Blind Assassin* (2000), benefited substantially from inclusion in bookshop co-promotions.[35] For those publishers that enter into co-promotions, they have access to 'effective targeted marketing' via bookshop displays, the chain bookshops' 'extensive market research and consumer profiles', and hence, it could be argued, they are an indication of the increasingly sophisticated and professional publishing industry.[36]

Nonetheless, the typical prices quoted by Kean in 2002 for co-promotional activities give a fair indication of the difficulties that these might present to a small, independent publisher. She cites £5–6000 for a WH Smith promotion, £8–10 000 for Waterstone's, and the standard expectation of an additional 7 per cent discount to retailers for books in special promotions.[37] Working on the rough estimate that large publishers spend at least 5 per cent of their turnover on marketing and publicity, and with approximately a quarter of this amount spent on sales promotions, Kean calculated that Hodder Headline and Penguin would spend around £1.28 and £1.43 million respectively, whereas the then independent Harvill would have about £30 000 in their total budget.[38] The high co-promotional prices thus undoubtedly exclude smaller publishers from the very activities that generate substantial additional sales. According to Kean's analysis, the superior access that large groups have to co-promotions is symptomatic of consolidation: 'money talks, from the advances on offer at acquisition through above-the-line marketing spend to retail promotions'.[39] Once more, increased competition serves to stratify the market, to sustain the power of the oligopoly, and to make the sales and marketing practices of the few effectively restrict access to the market for the rest.

Kean mentions that one – though not the only – means by which retailers make the decision about which books to include in their promotions is past sales data.[40] This can have both an advantageous and a disadvantageous impact on access to the market, as it allows for books either to be picked up in later months that were not promoted heavily initially, or means that the books chosen for promotions are either already selling well or are from authors who have a strong sales record.

Precise sales data came about in the publishing industry with the advent of Electronic Point of Sale (EPOS) in the early 1990s, which enabled booksellers, through the scanning of bar codes, to monitor sales and stock closely. It also allowed publishers to have instant access to both their own and their competitors' sales information, and hence strong indications of themes, trends and seasonality in the market. The use of EPOS figures has been, like co-promotions, contentious, as a *Bookseller* article in 2000 indicated. Joel Rickett surveyed industry opinion: some publishers and literary agents maintained that EPOS has encouraged short-termism, whereby 'publishers and booksellers are losing confidence in authors when their early works fail to set the charts alight'. Others stated that sales figures are 'never allowed to obstruct [our] fiction acquisitions', and that they rely instead on the foresight of the editor and the effectiveness of marketing and publicity departments. One commentator in Rickett's article argued that over-reliance on EPOS is 'catch-up publishing. The role of the editor is to be ahead of the beat, whereas the role of BookTrack [the chief provider of sales data in 2000] is to be behind the beat.'[41] Inserted into this analysis about the use of new technologies in contemporary business practice, then, is again a debate about the place of the editor and the acquisitions process, the same issue Giles Gordon brought up with regard to co-promotional activity. Richard Knight, the managing director of BookTrack (which later become Nielsen Bookscan), staked his own claim in Rickett's article for what his company could do for books and their authors. It can be easier for new writers to get noticed:

> 'If you could get an early Pat Barker into the top 5000 chart, it may be easier and quicker for her to get established than when no one was sharing data and she had to come right to the top before anyone noticed her.' He recalls that *Longitude*, which was initially picked up only by Waterstone's, quickly spread across the retail landscape because other chains noticed it in the bestseller lists.[42]

Knight's view of how the publishing industry can function with more information about sales demonstrates how popularity can be rewarded more quickly by increased publisher support. Rather than an author having to undergo a seven-book apprenticeship, he or she may be recognised much earlier. Knight points out, moreover, that sales figures are not neutral, and are themselves used in marketing.[43] Books advertise on their own front covers that they are 'Number One Bestsellers' before they are even released. This is the type of promotional activity explained by the management consultant Winslow Farrell, in *How Hits Happen: Forecasting Unpredictability in a Chaotic Marketplace* (1998), dependent upon a world of 'increasing returns', where 'success accrues to the successful; market share begets market share'. However, as well as promotional activity and the use of sales data, central to this model of behaviour is 'word of mouth', however it is instituted and sustained: 'higher visibility [leads...] to more word of mouth. And so success accrue[s] in this reinforcing cycle.'[44] The impact of 'word of mouth', and the ways in which it functions in the marketing of literature, is explored in Chapter 2.

In addition to developments in retail activities and technologies during the course of the contemporary period, there has also been a marked change in the physical environment of bookshops, their patterns of ownership, and a diversification of sales outlets. The book retail environment, like the patterns of publishing ownership, has changed dramatically in the last decades of the twentieth century. Bookselling chains – with nationwide branches of Waterstone's, Dillons, Hammicks, Ottakar's, Books Etc and Borders, as well as WH Smith – came to dominate the landscape, with many independents losing their market share and even their livelihood. By 1999, these seven chains had 42 per cent of retail share of consumer books.[45] Mergers in the period meant that the Dillons brand ceased to exist after takeover by Waterstone's. The US chain Borders acquired Books Etc (although the brand still operates separately), and, in 2006, after referral to the UK Competition Commission, Waterstone's acquired Ottakar's, causing much debate in the trade and general media about the potential adverse effect of 'Wottaker's' (as the merger was dubbed) vast market share, estimated at almost a quarter of the retail market.[46] As with publishing groups, this has meant that market share is dominated by a very small number of very large players, leading to anxieties both about control of the market and homogenisation.

The diversification of sales outlets in the period, however, has meant that the consolidation of high street chain booksellers is not the only pattern of book retail. The decades from the 1980s onwards have also seen the growth of alternative venues for bookselling, principally with supermarkets and the internet. All major supermarkets, including Tesco, Asda and Sainsbury's, stock books, and by 2004 were estimated by the *Books and the Consumer* survey to have a 9 per cent volume share of books sold (high discounting in supermarkets, and their concentration on paperback sales, has meant that value in the same year was put at the lower figure of 5.6 per cent).[47] Although books have frequently been sold through non-conventional or dedicated bookselling venues in the past – Penguin Books achieved mass-market success through its sales in Woolworths, for example – the volume of sales through supermarkets in the contemporary period has been unprecedented.[48] Supermarket sales, alongside sales through other non-conventional outlets such as garden centres and toy stores, have had the impact of extending the reach of the publishing industry beyond the bookshop into the mass-market, and towards the 45 per cent of people who rarely, if ever, buy books, and the 25 per cent of the adult population that read very little, if at all.[49] Writing about the changing attitudes towards bookselling at the beginning of this period, the commentator Michael Lane commented in *Books and Publishers: Commerce Against Culture in Postwar Britain* (1980) that 'modern' publishers:

> believe that the sectors of the population they want to convert do not go into bookshops at all, so they have made some efforts to market their books where this public does go. The ideological shift entailed in this secularisation of the book is at least as important as the structural and institutional changes that have occurred.[50]

Lane's concept of the 'secularisation' of the book and its trade suggests a shift away from the sanctity of the book as a cultural artefact and towards a concept of it as a commodity. Although this argument might deny the historically mercantile nature of the book trade, and particularly of the form of the novel throughout its history, the late twentieth century undoubtedly witnessed a proliferation of the possibilities of non-bookshop sales, and an increase in their volume. That the economy of supermarket sales tends towards short-termism and concentration, with retailers stocking a very select number of titles for limited periods, means that this 'secularisation' has also resulted in, through homogenisation, a limiting of the diversity of the books on offer through this sales channel. The same report that brought to attention the vast numbers of people alienated by books and book buying also noted that many potential book buyers commented that they might buy more books in supermarkets if the environment were more conducive to doing so, and the available range was improved.[51] Critics of the mass-market would certainly argue that these forms of mass retailing bring distinct disadvantages to the book market, despite their potentially democratising aspects. The limited stock range in particular is a cause of concern.

The development of e-commerce, on the other hand, has worked towards increased diversity in the marketplace. Amazon.com set up its UK site, Amazon.co.uk, at the end of 1998, joining Blackwell's online, and followed in 1999 by Alphabetstreet, Countrybookstore.co.uk, Bol.com, WHSmith online, Waterstone's relaunched site and Ottakar's.[52] As with high street bookshops, UK-based online retailers have gone through a process of consolidation and change, with Amazon remaining an extremely dominant market leader throughout, taking up to 85 per cent of the online bookselling market in some accounts.[53] By 2000, internet sales of books had levelled at 5 per cent (lower than through supermarkets), but by 2004 it was put at 8 per cent, with the figure of 10 per cent being mooted by the following year.[54] Amazon's stock levels, and its capacity to offer a virtual shop front to print on demand titles, means that it can offer to the customer a vast range of titles of which even the largest of high street retailers could not dream. This has created an enormous backlist market and, contrary to the trend towards concentration, radically enabled the 'long tail' and the niche market, in Chris Anderson's formulation.[55] Amazon also offers customers the opportunity to grade and make comments on purchases through its Customer Comments facility, which can create lively discussion and online communities. Because of its capacity to collect consumer data, Amazon has developed sophisticated recommendation facilities based on individual consumer profiles, allowing direct marketing unparalleled in book retailing.[56] Perhaps the greatest legacy thus far of the e-commerce boom for book sales, therefore, has been not so much in terms of the erosion of traditional markets but through the way in which traditional retailers, and publishers, have been pushed to rethink positively their patterns of distribution, price promotion, trade practice and the buying environments created for consumers.[57]

Technological developments in the latter half of the twentieth century have also given rise to e-books and the alternative modes of delivery that they offer. Yet, despite prognostications of the death of the physical book in the 1980s and early 1990s, and much excitement about the possibilities of the e-book, electronic delivery of novels has yet to make any major impact on the market. Various writers, including the US horror writer Stephen King, have experimented with e-books and electronic delivery of their writing, but during the period covered by *Marketing Literature*, print books still dominate trade publishing (developments in academic, reference and STM publishing are a different matter, as Thompson's *Books in the Digital Age* details).[58]

Despite all these technological and retailing developments, this period has, as the previous sections on the power of the chains demonstrated, seen the continuing presence of the high street bookshop. The changing retail environment was not simply a matter of the growing dominance of the chains, though, but also of the development of the bookshop experience and the appearance of the American-style superstore in the UK. Miller's history of twentieth-century book retailing, *Reluctant Capitalists*, recounts in detail the history and impact of the book superstore in the US in the 1990s, with its leading proponents Barnes & Noble and Borders.[59] The superstore is a book retailing concept that Fiona Stewart investigated in *Superstores – Super News?* (1999), at the point at which the established US phenomenon began to take hold in the UK. As Stewart defined it, a 'superstore' is 'a huge store [...] with a lot of square footage'.[60] Yet it is not simply the size and quantity of stock that defines these shops, but also what Leon Kreitzman, writing in 1999 about 'the new retailing culture' in the *Bookseller*, termed 'the bookshop as social club'.[61] Hosting author and discussion events, with musical entertainment, late opening hours, serving food and drink, and holding a range of other stock including newspapers, magazines, stationery, toys, CDs and DVDs, such superstores are a composite of bookshop, library and café/bar, seeking, as Miller puts it, to serve the 'entertained consumer' in a 'multifunction' environment.[62] In 1999, Waterstone's opened a flagship store on Piccadilly in London. Its stock levels and square footage defeated all previous claims to be the UK's largest bookshop, and its spacious, multi-storeyed siting in a converted department store, refurbished with a bar, café, restaurant and events rooms, made it an outstanding example of the British incorporation of the US trend of the superstore, and a world away from the traditional image of the small, independent bookshop. So although a very competitive atmosphere in terms of shop floor size and market share was created – Borders' entry into the already well-populated university cities of Oxford and Cambridge, also announced in 1999, signalled the company's challenge to the supremacy of the existing UK chains – the added value of what superstores could offer as social settings to increase their customer footfall became just as relevant to the altering retail environment.[63]

Authorship and the commodification of fiction

The late twentieth-century arrival of conglomerate finance and the changing book retail environment, then, has intensified the culture of marketing in publishing. This culture, however, had been developing substantially throughout the course of the twentieth century, as each new generation of publishers caused consternation to the previous one by their market-based activities. Chapter 2 examines this changing publishing culture in more detail. It is apparent that shifting publishing practice and philosophy have affected the production and reception of the novel in the twentieth century. Increasing competition and advance levels have meant that publishers make greater financial outlay, which demands to be quickly recouped. Marketing activity has intensified, and the shift in publishing culture identified by Giles Gordon in his protestation against bungs – that from an editorially focused to a marketing-led publishing culture – extended.

The rise of literary agents is linked to this cultural shift, though it is also intrinsically part of the growing professionalisation and business-based practice of publishing of the nineteenth and twentieth centuries. The first British literary agents appeared in the mid-nineteenth century, and developed alongside professional organisations: the Publishers' Association, the Booksellers' Association and the Society of Authors, which were all established late in the nineteenth century.[64] The rise of the literary agent's power has grown alongside the diversification of rights sales in a global, multimedia leisure and information industry, with the agent effectively acting as the author's business manager. However, with a increasing stress on the central business of sales and marketing within publishing companies, particularly the conglomerate companies, literary agents have also extended their role of business and financial management to incorporate editorial functions, and to provide continuity in a period when editors frequently change company allegiance. There has been a concomitant move of editors of prestigious literary imprints into agenting, with examples including Georgia Garrett and Peter Straus (both exiles from Picador), David Godwin (from Jonathan Cape) and Clare Alexander (from Macmillan), suggesting, perhaps, that these figures have moved into agenting in order to continue to have a key, and consistent, editorial role in their authors' careers. Yet there are also examples of other editors who have moved from conglomerate companies to run smaller independents, including Stephen Page and Philip Gwyn Jones from HarperCollins to Faber and Faber and Portobello respectively, and Andrew Franklin from Penguin to Profile. There are also examples of editors, such as Alexandra Pringle (previously of Penguin), who turned to an agenting career but then switched back to Bloomsbury, and editors such as Carole Welch at Sceptre who have remained consistently with their companies for over a decade. Perhaps what all this suggests is that anecdotal evidence does hint at trends, but these cannot be fully established without a thorough sociological investigation of the career patterns of editors in the 1990s and 2000s, which has not yet been done. Nonetheless, the power of literary agents in the marketplace cannot be denied, as both their growth in number and profile demonstrates. Michael Legat calculates in *An Author's Guide to Literary Agents* (1995), using the *Writers' and Artists' Yearbook* as his statistical base, the rise in agencies from 39 in 1946, to over 80 in 1975, and 138 in 1995.[65] Of the individuals in the *Observer*'s subjective but nonetheless timely list of 50 'top players in the world of books', five were literary agents.[66] As literary agents operate primarily within the field of trade publishing, it is to be assumed that the impact of their growth and profile has been on the commodification of contemporary writing, through the increasing advance levels elicited from publishing companies, and the resulting marketing activity discussed earlier in this chapter. As the *Observer* commented on its choice of 50 in 2006, 'some readers will be dismayed to see it's the noisy marketplace not the editorial armchair that exercises most power in 2006'.[67]

In terms of patterns of authorship, evidence would suggest, however, that the increase in production, promotion and financial reward has not benefited every writer equally. In 2000, the Society of Authors published the results of a survey in which responding writers were asked to give their 'approximate total gross income arising directly from their freelance writing in the previous year'. The average overall figure was £16 600, with 75 per cent earning under £20 000 (under, in other words, the national average wage), and 46 per cent under £5 000. Despite a few high earners (5 per cent earning over £75 000), the overwhelming response to the survey suggested that as a profession in 2000 writing was badly remunerated, even poverty-stricken: as the survey succinctly phrased it, 'half earning less than an employee on the national minimum wage'. The survey closes with the pessimistic aphorism, 'Authorship is clearly much more than a job, but it too frequently pays less than a living wage.'[68] The 1998 update of Cyril Connolly's original 'Questionnaire: the Cost of Letters' (1946), *The Cost of Letters: A Survey of Literary Living Standards*, paints a picture of the economics of authorship as gloomy as that of its predecessor.[69] In the 1998 version, the novelist Jonathan Coe, offering advice to 'young people who wish to earn their living by writing', suggests that they 'Pay no attention to fairytales about new authors' multi-million pound windfalls'. As Coe concludes, large advances are as much a media phenomenon as a publishing one, and that the 'multi-million pound windfall [...] happens occasionally, and for some reason is the only kind of literary story the newspapers are interested in reporting'.[70] Coe's comments are overly harsh on the media, which reports on much more than publishing advance levels. Nonetheless, the variable degree of attention paid to authors and their books in time and marketing results in the creation of a hierarchy of marketability. 'Journalistic capital', to use English's phrase, is conferred on a few 'valuable' authors, making them, and their books, highly visible in the marketplace, while the rest are condemned to what Karl Miller calls a 'painful soundlessness in the utterance of authors'.[71] A concentration on celebrity and marketability has resulted in a squeezing of the midlist. For the authors high in the hierarchy of marketability, the authorial role is expanded far beyond that of writer of the text. In a culture of increasing commodification of the novel, authors give readings in bookshops, attend events at literary festivals, appear in the media and embark on promotional tours that can last months. By 2000, for example, the novelist Andrew Miller, whose first novel *Ingenious Pain* was published in 1997, had already been 'on the road' promoting his novels for two years.[72] In '"What is an Author?": Contemporary Publishing Discourse and the Author Figure', Juliet Gardiner estimates that 'the promotable fiction author who spends, say, a year writing a novel, will now spend considerably *more* than a year promoting it in a round of press, radio and television interviews, bookshop readings, and other events on publication – a circuit that is replicated whenever and wherever across the globe the book is subsequently published.'[73] The 'phenomenon of literary celebrity', as Joe Moran terms it, is central to the promotion of contemporary literary fiction.[74] Literary prizes – and particularly the Booker Prize for Fiction (since 2002, the Man Booker) – increase this commodification and celebritisation, with their success in directing media attention to the book world. This, then, is the promotional circuit, and for those writers who have achieved this level of promotional activity, it is the creator of their literary celebrity. This is an aspect of the contemporary marketplace that has been scrutinised – and theorised – in some detail, and the case studies of Part II examine instances of it.[75]

For others, however, the concentration of resources on a handful of titles risks the 'painful soundlessness' to which Karl Miller refers. Publishing companies organise their activity into schedules built on relatively rigid 'grid' patterns. The grids, which are frequently but not exclusively influenced by the size of advance level, demonstrate the relative importance of titles, and are a way of systematically planning company activity. Only a handful of 'leads' and 'supersellers' are released each month, and it is these few books that receive most attention.[76] These categories are revealing in analysis of publishers' marketing, not least because they are pre-publication categories that are highly indicative of publishers' intentions for their products. The categories may be informed by publishers' readings of potential consumer reception, but they are put in place before the books reach the marketplace. In *Star Authors*, Moran discusses the decision-making of the 'sales representatives in marketing meetings', concluding that, 'Publishers [...] only make serious efforts to publicize a small percentage of their list, and the gap between the so-called "leads" and the "midlist" (the books with modest advances and modest sales) is becoming wider.'[77] Moran is principally concerned with the US market, but his statement holds true for the UK in the 1990s and 2000s as well. This period has seen an increasing concentration of finances on a handful of titles, entailing a squeezing of the 'midlist'. One archetypal 'midlist' author, Catherine Feeny, wrote about her experiences 'down at my end of the business' in a supplement to the *Independent* on World Book Day 2000, first of all mentioning the work she and her peers do to supplement their income, and then concentrating on the promotion of her books:

> Publicity can only be viewed as cumulative. Most cumulative of all, according to publishers, is word of mouth. They believe it to be so effective, especially with lesser-known writers, that there really is no point in wasting money on big launches or hard advertising.[78]

Feeny's satirical attack on the holy cow of the publishing industry – word of mouth – shows a certain weariness with the attitudes of publishers towards their midlist writers. Feeny and Moran's comments suggest that money does indeed follow money, and that full promotional attention will only be granted to a few selected titles, whilst the rest have to make do with publicity that can be gained for free, or that the author him- or herself can generate.

In *Star Authors*, Moran comments on the ubiquity of writers in the late twentieth century, noting that an excess of publicity can be the cause of anxiety amongst cultural commentators, who adversely compare the 'hype' of the promotional circuit to a system of judgement based on perceived literary value. In her essay on literary journalism, 'Living on Writing' (1998), Lorna Sage also discusses the place of the author in the late twentieth-century media environment. She notes the increasing prevalence of the 'feature' alongside the more traditional review, and analyses how this extends the role of both author and book:

> Zest, curiosity, voyeurism, vicarious *paper*-living enter into book reviewing, there's no real boundary around the books, and indeed book pages merge more and more into features, and there's a constant rearguard action being fought by literary editors to keep their space,

> and to find ways of allowing books to look like books without losing their 'living' appeal.[79]

The result of all this attention to the 'living' appeal of the book is, according to Sage, a renewed emphasis on 'the life of the author', supplemented by the array of author-centred promotional events.[80] The argument Sage makes is more subtle than seeing the extension of the authorial role as simply concerned with literary gossip. Rather, it is a debate engaged with both the life and death of the author – the trope of celebrity and literary biography on the one hand, and the interrogation of the '*author-function*', in Foucault's terms, on the other. Thus, this is a period which has seen the 'rise and rise of literary biography', 'life-writing' and the memoir, as well as a fictional inscription of the debate '*inside* many contemporary novels'.[81] Writers respond to the contextual '*paper*-living', Sage argues, by an internalisation of the authorial voice. The author is resuscitated not only as author-promoter, then, but also in the act of writing itself, as the Conclusion considers.

All the activities and agencies detailed in this chapter, then, have worked towards the increasing commodification of fiction in the market-place, drawing on and contributing to the 'literary-value industry', as English and Frow have termed it, which has constructed and positioned contemporary writing.[82] The next chapter provides a further history and theory of these acts of literary marketing.

2
Literature and Marketing

Literature has long had a close yet difficult relationship to marketing. The publishing industry and other intermediary agencies involved in the transmission of reading matter work within a marketplace which, in addition to the demands of commerce, incorporates the values enshrined in cultural activity. This dual nature of the publishing industry is one that has led to the tension referred to by Lewis A. Coser, Charles Kadushin and Walter W. Powell in their oft-quoted dictum in *Books: The Culture and Commerce of Publishing* (1982), to the effect that, 'The industry remains perilously poised between the requirements and restraints of commerce and the responsibilities and obligations that it must bear as a prime guardian of the symbolic culture of the nation.'[1] Marketing, if taken broadly as the activity by which literature is brought to the commercial marketplace, is the catalyst for much of this tension, and in the specific form of publishers' and retailers' promotional activities, it is frequently taken both to symbolise and actualise the shifting relationship of art to business.

This chapter takes the relationship of literature and marketing as its central theme. It begins by tracing the development of the frequently heated debate about this relationship over the course of the twentieth century in the UK, and the influence of the changing market conditions described in the previous chapter upon the state of these relations. The chapter then goes on to expound the concept of marketing as a form of representation and interpretation, by linking marketing theory and practice to models of publishing and book history, and in turn extending our understanding of the institutional and economic contexts of literary discourse. The following chapter then explores how publishers, booksellers, the media and other agencies involved in the marketing of literature create cultural meanings through negotiations with genre in the marketplace. This chapter includes a discussion of how various aspects of marketing activity in its widest sense, including formats, packaging, imprints, branding, bookshop taxonomies and literary prizes, construct and reshape notions of literary value and taste; how, in other words, marketing can be said to be the making of contemporary writing.

The changing culture of publishing

In *Literature, Money and the Market,* Delany argues that the culture of marketing, in its transition from 'product differentiation' to 'market segmentation' and the cultural niche, is particularly appropriate to 'the market for reading matter', entailing 'a move from a vertical structure (a scale from highbrow literature to trash) towards a horizontal one by genres appealing to differentiated but formally equal groups of readers. Buyers [are] now [...] classified by their interests, gender, or life-styles, rather than their social rank.'[2] In his study, Delany traces this transition through the course of the late nineteenth and twentieth centuries. Publishing is, arguably, still struggling to accomplish the shift from a product-led to a market-led industry.[3] But in tracing this transition, Delany marks the transposition of a formulation of the market based on class or income categories ('social rank'), to one formulated by 'lifestyle choices'.

Yet the transition to this contemporary approach towards the market and the consumers of which it is composed follows a history of a more stratified, and stereotyped, attitude. Q. D. Leavis, for example, in her attempt to quantify cultural value in her sociological study *Fiction and the Reading Public* (1932), divided the readership of literary works into the categories of 'highbrow', 'middlebrow' and 'lowbrow'.[4] Q. D. Leavis saw this act of market division, which in her study largely falls along class lines, as being primarily established by the media, as 'each [of the categories' media representatives] has a following that forms a different level of public'.[5] The stratification of works into three categories, for Q. D. Leavis, has strong implications of value, as becomes apparent when she calls upon F. R. Leavis's *Mass Civilization and Minority Culture* (1930) to further her own argument. A ' "very small proportion of gold" ' is the valuation that coincides with the 'highbrow' and its 'very small minority audience'.[6]

Q. D. Leavis's formulation of the 'middlebrow' in particular is one that could potentially be applied to all of the 'literary' novels examined in *Marketing Literature*. However, the middlebrow is not a term used in contemporary publishing practice, and as the Introduction emphasised, this book attempts to analyse the industry through its own terms and structures rather than externally imposed ones. Book historical studies by Joan Shelley Rubin and Janice A. Radway have done much to recuperate the middlebrow from its negative connotations, the history of which Radway catalogues in *A Feeling for Books* (1997).[7] Radway, in seeing the editors of the Book-of-the-Month Club as explicitly distancing themselves from '"academic"' ways of reading, records an institution that positively positioned itself through the middlebrow.[8] This necessary, passionate and yet cautious act of recuperation justifies the term in historical context, and thus is appropriate as more than the 'serviceable [...] descriptive shorthand' that Rubin explores.[9] Following Delany's definitions of the shift in market in the course of the twentieth century, however, the terminology of the middlebrow – or indeed the high and lowbrow – becomes anachronistic in any description of the later decades. Within the academy, indeed, cultural studies has deconstructed the ideology of 'brows'; postmodernism has flattened hierarchies. John Seabrook comments in *Nobrow: The Culture of Marketing the Marketing of Culture* (2000) of the landscapes of contemporary culture that they are 'neither high nor low, and not in the middle [but rather...] outside the old taste hierarchy altogether'.[10] The mixed portfolios of contemporary, conglomerate publishers would indeed demonstrate that cultural output is not divided in this way by its producers, rendering redundant the hierarchical language of 'brows'. The implication, then, is that even if the term 'middlebrow' can be recuperated in its historical context, it is largely anachronistic to the culture of marketing and consumption of the late twentieth and early twenty-first centuries.

Opinions such as Q. D. Leavis's in the 1930s are indicative of the impact of the expansion of the reading public brought about by educational reforms of the late nineteenth century in Britain, which widened literary culture to a mass audience. In *The Intellectuals and the Masses* (1992), John Carey argues that one effect of this expansion of readership was a retrenchment by modernist writers in order 'to exclude these newly educated (or "semi-educated") readers, and so to preserve the intellectual's seclusion from the mass'.[11] This fear of the masses apparent in the modernists' reactions modulated in subsequent decades into a fear of the deleterious effects of mass readership on literature. Q. D. Leavis declared that 'novel-reading is now largely a drug habit', while the publisher Geoffrey Faber was vociferous in 1934 in his condemnation of the new reading public's impact on his industry:

> Literature now is in the hands of the mob; and the mob is stampeded. It moves in a mass, this way or that, and all its thinking is done for it. For those who will hit the taste of the masses the reward is very large. Hence an ever growing temptation to write for the herd, to publish for the herd, to buy for and sell to the herd [...] The whole nation reads to order. Books are, increasingly, written to order.[12]

Faber's polemic is couched in very unsympathetic terms, but his argument about the impact of market-focused publishing was widely shared. Richard Hoggart, whose analysis in *The Uses of Literacy* (1957) is much more sympathetic to the working classes, was nonetheless deeply concerned about what he called 'mass-publications'.[13] Effective distribution networks augmented this trend in books, newspapers and magazines:

> Popular reading is now highly centralized; a very large body of people choose between only a small number of publications. This is a very small and crowded country; today almost everyone can be supplied at almost the same time with the same object. The price paid for this in popular reading is that a small group of imaginatively narrow and lamed publications are able to impose a considerable uniformity.[14]

As publishing changed in both culture and shape in the course of the twentieth century, these debates about the expansion of the market, the desirability of market-based publishing and the marketing activity that surrounded it would intensify. The trial of *Lady Chatterley's Lover* (1928) famously exemplified the anxieties around the growth of the market. In 1959, a new Obscene Publications Act was passed in Britain. The first trial under the new law was that of Penguin's edition of D. H. Lawrence's novel in 1960. The book had originally been privately published, and already existed in an expurgated UK edition as well as in full-text imported copies. The much-discussed trial, which has achieved 'mythic status', as one historian of Penguin Books put it, and whose proceedings were edited and triumphantly published by Penguin in book form in 1961, hinged largely on the fact that the book was published in cheap paperback form.[15] The infamous address by the prosecution to the jury, premised as an upper-middle-class male reader, demonstrated clearly that the provocation caused by Penguin's publication was one of *access* to content as much as content alone. The prosecution asked, 'Is it a book you would have lying around in your own house? Is it a book that you would even wish your wife or your servants to read?'[16] In Steven Connor's analysis, the significance of this comment 'lies in its acknowledgement of the huge and troubling power of an immoderately enlarged readership for fiction, and the incipient collapse of the ideally homogenous culture of the past'.[17] The widening market of the twentieth century resulted, at least with some commentators of the time, in stereotyped attitudes towards the groups that formed that market, and also towards marketing activity, particularly if it was directed towards the mass-market. Moreover, within publishing itself, the tension aroused by the changing markets meant that each new generation of publishers caused consternation to the previous one by their market-based activities. In the 1930s, for example, Geoffrey Faber clearly felt himself to be a dying breed in the face of those who succumbed to 'publish for the herd'. Faber's commentary on these interwar years connects to other publishers' attitudes. The publishing industry that Fredric Warburg, the founder of Secker & Warburg, cherished, was based on the concept of the 'gentleman publisher', after which he entitled his memoirs *An Occupation for Gentlemen* (1959). Incensed by the advertising trends of Victor Gollancz, Warburg wrote about changes in marketing in the interwar period in colourful terms:

> The 'pony-and-trap' period of English publishing, virtually unchanged for fifty years or more, had been superseded by the 'automobile' epoch. Chief among the internal combustion engines was Victor Gollancz, with a very high horse-power. With the foundation of his firm in 1928, the revolution may be said to have begun. Then we saw the shape of things to come. Instead of the dignified advertisement list of twenty titles set out primly in a modest space, there was the double or triple column, with the title of one book screaming across it in letters three inches high. The forces of modernity had been loosed, the age of shouting, the period of the colossal and the sensation, had arrived. [...] Though Gollancz was the great innovator and the lettering of his advertisements the biggest and blackest of all, his competitors did not lag far behind. [They] beat the drum in an ever more shattering tattoo. Amid all this clatter, how could the quiet whisper of a Routledge advertisement, the gentle nudge of a Routledge promotion, be heard or felt by an over-stimulated public. If the merit of books was now to be measured by the height of the letters that advertised them, publishing, it could well be said, was no longer an occupation for gentlemen, but a real business, even perhaps a rat-race.[18]

In later years, Allen Lane, the founder of Penguin, and a much more democratic figure than either Faber or Warburg, nonetheless came to regret the direction his company, and publishing generally, was taking in the 1960s. As he explained in an interview in 1967, he believed that his conception of Penguin was being undermined:

> 'My idea when I started was to produce cheap books that were aesthetically pleasing.'
>
> He didn't approve of the way those bright young marketing people in London were jazzing up the covers. 'Quite vulgar, some of them, and quite misleading. [...]
>
> 'So much dignity was going out of my books. Some of the frightful young marketing whizz-kids just wouldn't realise a book is *not* a tin of beans.'[19]

Lane felt that the book's uniqueness as a product was under attack from a new wave of market-oriented publishers. His choice of a most prosaic comparison is done for comic effect, but nonetheless insists on the disparity between beans and books – on, in other words, the 'books are different' argument of the NBA. Yet as units manufactured for profit, sustaining the distance between one and the other was not always so easy or, in fact, desirable, as Lane's own shrewd distribution of Penguin through Woolworths demonstrated at the foundation of the company.

Some years previously in the 1960s, E. V. Rieu, the founding editor of Penguin Classics, encountered the new generation in the forceful shape of Tony Godwin, who wanted to redesign the series. Rieu wrote to Lane to express his anxieties: '"I find it hard to believe that you would allow a newcomer to the firm, without discussion with me, its editor, to mutilate a series that you and I had created in 1944 and have since made world famous".'[20] Rieu's language of mutilation suggests that the battles over the definition of publishing could indeed be bloody. Warburg, continuing his argument with the new breed of interwar publishers, turned his argument into one of class and commerce:

> A publisher, if he is not to be a wholly commercial operator, must put a lot of his own personality into his firm. It must reflect him directly or indirectly, and if it does it will have a recognizable character. [...] No doubt my view of a publishing house as having a personality can be regarded as highbrow. It will be said that a publisher is a tradesman who is not in business for his health; his job is to take a book that

> in his view has a sales potential and boost it to the skies, regardless of its merits or lack of them. This view I understand, respect, and profoundly disagree with.[21]

Warburg's cult of personality, and the ability of the publisher to make his mark on his company (the gendering of this statement is indicative of the period), would inevitably diminish in the transition from small and mid-sized companies to global conglomerates. Nonetheless, 'recognizable character' is something that publishers still attempt to retain through the preservation of imprints, as Chapter 3 explores.

Tony Godwin, the young publisher at Penguin whose ideas caused Lane and Rieu such anxiety, would take up the debate over the direction of the trade in a talk given to the Society of Young Publishers in 1967, after leaving Penguin. His talk was summarised in *The Bookseller*:

> 'The reason why publishing has been regarded as an occupation for gentlemen, [Godwin] suspected, had been because the upper class considered themselves – possibly they still did – as the custodians of culture [...] However, as a result of the education acts raising the school leaving age and the steady "democratization" of culture, the distinguished amateur in publishing was, he liked to think, being supplanted by the passionate professional.'[22]

Godwin's passionate advocacy of professionalism in publishing is an assault on the class-based cult of the 'distinguished amateur'. The establishment of feminist publishers such as Virago in the 1970s, with their policies of female workforces and revised editorial and gatekeeping policies, similarly worked to remove the gendered construction of the 'gentleman publisher', and more recent attempts to diversify the ethnic basis of the workforce have also sought to overturn homogeneity in publishing.[23] In the claim Godwin went on to make for professionalism, though, he quite specifically clung to the notion of the book's uniqueness and role in society, while calling for a holistic view of the publishing process.[24] The primacy of the editorial function was thus undermined, but only – in Godwin's vision – to the extent of ensuring that the commissioning process was integrated into, and supported by, the other publishing functions. The transition from editorial primacy to a holistic view of publishing has continued to provoke controversy, particularly in the emphasis this has placed on sales and marketing, and the corresponding shift in perspective from production to consumption. As Michael Lane identified in *Books and Publishers*, this has entailed both an economic and an ideological shift. In opposing 'traditional' and 'modern' models of publishing, he analyses the 'golden age myth of the editor as cultural entrepreneur' as incorporating 'the idea of intuitive and individual decisions', whereas the 'modernist' approach (his terminology is not to be confused with modernist artistic movements) is one of 'enlarging the book-buying public', requiring 'a more active approach to that audience'.[25] It is this sort of publisher, Lane goes on to argue, and as the previous chapter described, that has overseen the 'ideological shift' of the 'secularisation of the book', via the publisher's appeal to the population that does not normally go into bookshops. Writing in 1980, Michael Lane had yet to see the extent to which the modern publisher would go, with heavy selling through supermarkets, e-commerce and other non-traditional outlets. The book retail environment is one of the clearest indicators of the change in book trade philosophy: from the independent bookshop to the rise of the lifestyle bookstore. Looking back at the distinction Allen Lane made to refute modern marketing trends, it is ironic that the growth of supermarket sales of books in the 1990s would place books and beans in adjacent aisles, and in the same shopping trolley. The perceived difference of books is, as the previous chapter detailed, no longer sustained through the NBA. The demise of the NBA, as well as affecting business practice, had cultural implications for the concept of the book and its industry. The overhaul of the century-old practice in the 1990s both heralded and was symptomatic of a changing attitude in and towards publishing. The difference is still upheld in the UK taxation system (VAT – Value Added Tax – is not applied to books), and is the cause of recurrent debate about the tension between commerce and culture in the industry.[26] However, given that other products which are also untaxed or taxed at a lower rate include children's clothes, most food, and fuel, the 'difference' cannot be solely one of *cultural* value.

To claim that the development of new models of publishing practice has meant a steady progression towards a better, more consumer-oriented publishing industry would be controversial, however. The switch from an editorial emphasis to a sales and marketing one has continually caused concern, and arguably elevated the principle of commerce above that of culture. The rise of the conglomerates has brought in a greater fear of global control of communications media, as the case of Chris Patten's book in Chapter 1 indicated, and, arguably, a decline in politically engaged and radical publishing. The homogenisation of publishing – and of culture – may result. Moreover, if market-based publishing comes to mean an emphasis on sales figures and the bottom line at the expense of innovation, a meaningful future for literature and the novel is severely compromised. Some commentators on the book trade at the turn of the twentieth and twenty-first century already think that time has come. Schiffrin argues in *The Business of Books* that:

> Publishers have always prided themselves on their ability to balance the imperative of making money with that of issuing worthwhile books. In recent years [...] that equation has been altered. It is now increasingly the case that the owner's *only* interest is in making money and as much of it as possible [...] The standards of the entertainment industry are [...] apparent in the content of best-seller lists, an ever-narrower range of books based on lifestyle and celebrity with little intellectual or artistic merit.[27]

The vision Schiffrin has of the contemporary industry is a depressing one. Quantitative data and interpretive analysis are both much needed in order to assess whether this vision is in fact a reality. Yet, as Schiffrin himself remarks, this is a difficult thing to do: there is a paucity of information other than anecdotal to clarify the arguments for and against the deterioration of publishing practice under conglomerate rule and a sound methodological process for dealing with such data is unlikely to be established, given how mired such a process would be in the literary-value system.[28] Recent publishing history is undoubtedly an area that demands more attention from researchers in order to determine the current condition of the industry and its future effects on culture and society.

The aim of *Marketing Literature*, while contributing to the corpus of information on, and analysis of, recent publishing history, has a rather different aim than making pronouncements on the state of the industry. The aim is to analyse the effect of the marketing activity surrounding the production and reception of literature, the marketing activity that has intensified as a result of the processes of conglomeration detailed in the previous chapter. By 1999, then, the resultant clash of values of the literary marketplace were encapsulated by Catherine Lockerbie in a *Scotsman* article on World Book Day which drew on Allen Lane's earlier juxtaposition of books and beans:

> Yes, yes, books are uniquely transfiguring, soul-saturating artistic artefacts; they are also commodities to be bought and sold as surely as baked beans [...] Yes, yes, readers may clasp literary enlightenment

> in their trembling hands and feel the shift in their very synapses; they are also fools to be parted from their money.
>
> The two aspects of this strange business of the book trade dovetail neatly in World Book Day.[29]

Lockerbie summarises the paradox at the heart of publishing – 'this strange business of the book trade' – which struggles to combine, and justify, economic and cultural imperatives. Placing the demands of culture and commerce in direct opposition, however – as Coser et al.'s opening parry in *Books: The Culture and Commerce* might seem to do – is perhaps not the most fruitful way of analysing the contemporary literary marketplace. In their chapter on 'Literary Authorship and Celebrity Culture', English and Frow indicate the more subtle workings of the marketplace, saying that 'British fiction is, like any field or subfield of cultural activity, not simply the site of a grand struggle between art and money but a complex system in which different kinds of agents or players [...] conduct transactions involving distinct forms of capital [...], all of which are partially but none of which is perfectly fungible with the others.'[30] The seeming opposition between culture and commerce should, they argue, be deconstructed. In her ironic commentary on World Book Day, Lockerbie builds upon Allen Lane's assertion in order to paraphrase the heated debate between culture and commerce in the publishing industry, between the argument that books are different and that they are commodities like any other. But what her commentary also indicates is the inescapability of promotional activity in the 'strange business of the book trade', in which the social practices of reading are inextricably caught up with the economic imperatives of companies that produce reading matter. As English and Frow go on to comment, 'The intense celebrity culture of contemporary British culture, in short, is a symptom not of homogenization and simplification ("it's all about money now"), but rather of increasing complexity in the way that literary value is produced and circulated.'[31] In similar terms, Wernick's account of 'Authorship and the Supplement of Promotion' (1993), posits that there is now no space that is 'hors-promotion', or outside the promotional circuit and, as he goes on to explain:

> The well-founded suspicion [...] that behind every public act of communication someone is trying to sell us something, multiplies its effects by rebounding from the reader on to the writer: a cynicism which at once sows self-suspicion, and confronts the writer with a resistance to writing that writing itself must find a way to overcome.[32]

This vision of readerly and writerly cynicism in the face of the market is bleak, yet, as is clear, books continue to be produced and launched into the market at an ever-increasing rate. The Conclusion to this book gives space to the responses of writers to the marketing environment in which they find themselves. Rather than tackling this cynicism, and the anxieties of commentators such as Schiffrin, and instead responding to the call to investigate the 'increasing complexity in the way that literary value is produced and circulated', this chapter now turns to a consideration of its central argument: the idea of marketing as a form of representation and interpretation.

Towards a theory of book marketing

Marketing theory is a discourse that in itself commands an impressively large sector of publishing output, in terms of student textbooks and advice from business and management gurus. As well as informing the practice of marketing activity in a multiplicity of industries and organisations, this theory has also spawned its own academic meta commentary.[33] Publishers have drawn on this body of knowledge to inform their own activities, and have published a small handful of volumes that specifically distil marketing theory for publishers, and address particular issues of marketing in the book trade. Alison Baverstock's *How to Market Books* (2000) and Patrick Forsyth and Robin Birn's *Marketing in Publishing* (1997) take on the task of transmitting the vast body of marketing theory in practical book marketing terms.[34] Like many of the more general marketing textbooks, Forsyth and Birn begin with an exploration of definitions of marketing and the marketing mix:

> the Chartered Institute of Marketing has an official definition of marketing that reads: 'Marketing is the management process responsible for identifying, anticipating and satisfying customer requirement profitably.' Marketing guru Philip Kotler has defined it by saying: 'Marketing is the business function that identifies current unfulfilled needs and wants, defines and measures their magnitude, determines which target markets the organisation can best serve, and decides on appropriate products, services and programmes to serve these markets. Thus marketing serves as a link between a society's needs and its pattern of industrial response.' These certainly express something of the complexity involved; marketing is more than just the 'marketing department' – though management expert Peter Drucker was content to say simply 'Marketing is looking at the business

> through the customers' eyes', and indeed everything stems from exactly that.[35]

Forsyth and Birn's incorporation of these definitions emphasises the customer and target markets – in publishing terms, the potential reader. The Chartered Institute of Marketing's definition sneaks the notion of profit into its otherwise rather altruistic sounding statement by way of its final adverb: customer needs may be identified, anticipated and satisfied, but this three-pronged process is done for economic gain. Peter Drucker's simpler formulation belies what is actually a sophisticated statement, if the wealth of interpretive possibilities of seeing the book business from the perspective of readers is borne in mind. Philip Kotler's definition is perhaps the most productive of all for the broader definitions of marketing with which this book is concerned. The marketing processes that he defines as the 'link between a society's needs and its pattern of industrial response' makes it clear that marketing is not only advertising and publicity, or the level of promotional spend, but a reactive and proactive process, one that begins with an assessment of perceived desires and moves on to a production and promotion of products that try to fulfil them. 'Marketing', then, is what actually constructs the marketplace through its functional linkage of society and industry. The processes of marketing – those defined by Kotler as identification, definition, measurement, determination and decision – are all forms of representation, reaffirming the central assertion of this book, that marketing is itself a process of representation. Marketing in publishing is thus a vital, dynamic act, the creator of the literary marketplace.

Marketing is also frequently described as the process by which marketplace exchanges occur; the process by which goods, services and ideas are sold or provided to buyers or consumers in return for money, credit, donations, labour or goods.[36] The circularity from seller or provider to buyer or consumer and back again is reminiscent of some of the models that book historians use to understand the processes of print culture in both historical and contemporary contexts. Robert Darnton's 'What is the History of Books?' (1982) devised the communications circuit, in which the book's role as a communications device is foregrounded, mapping in its passage from author to publisher, printer, distributor and retailer to the reader, with the reader completing the circuit by 'influenc[ing] the author both before and after the act of composition'.[37] In so doing, Darnton constructs a commonsensical framework that links the various agents and intermediaries in the book trade, and which would also be readily identifiable to a present-day publisher as a version of the supply chain which eventually links the consumer back to the original supplier, the author. Darnton emphasises the need to comprehend and trace the transmission of the message that the book is communicating, and hence each of the groups or agencies that Darnton depicts works towards transmission within the communications circuit, propelling the book and the messages it contains on its journey.

The raggedness at the centre of the diagram that Darnton draws to describe his circuit, which has a vague mention of intellectual influences and publicity, economic and social conjuncture, and political and legal sanctions or, as he puts it later in the essay, 'other elements in society [...] which could vary endlessly' hints at a complexity that is belied by the commonsensical circuit.[38] Darnton does not attempt to provide a rigorously systematised integration of these 'other elements' into the communications circuit, firstly because it would overburden its coherence as a structure and thus work against Darnton's professed aim of counteracting book history's tendency to 'interdisciplinarity run riot', but secondly because they would make it increasingly difficult to sustain the model of transmission.[39] Ultimately, it is not possible to describe and integrate all these 'other elements', otherwise every history of the book would have to be prefaced with a history of the world.[40]

Darnton's desire to develop a coherent model for the study of the book is perhaps at variance with the competing forces of the agencies in the circuit and the 'other elements'. The emphasis on communication as the prime motivation for book production and reception is complicated by the 'other elements' – for example, the push for profit, the desire to create art for its own sake, or the wish for entertainment. These other motivations fit only with difficulty into the momentum of a circuit based on communication. Communication may be in the interest of profit, or art, or entertainment, but it is not the ultimate aim, and so is sometimes only a by-product of other motivations. The 'complexity' of the systems of valuation discussed by English and Frow does not fit into Darnton's model, which by streamlining its processes risks eliding all the competing and occasionally haphazard motivations at work in a book's history (even if it can cope very well with competing and haphazard *events*).

Thomas R. Adams and Nicolas Barker's 'A New Model for the Study of the Book' (1993) developed Darnton's communications circuit by questioning its person- (rather than book-) centred approach, which they believed 'ignores the sheer randomness, the speculative uncertainty of the book trade'.[41] Darnton's claim for 'conceptual coherence' is itself an imposition, not a found system within literary sociology.[42] A belief that 'books belong to circuits of communication that operate in consistent patterns, however complex they may be' is an archaeological one, as Darnton's terminology of 'unearthing those circuits' betrays.[43] Believing that the history of books is there to be understood if only enough archaeological activity is undertaken – and available remains found – obviates a more random history, where intentions go astray or are lost, where other motivations take control, and consequently where historians should not seek to find the truth but to make interpretations as well as they can, but always according to their own intentions, motivations, and historical and sociological situations.

Adams and Barker's development of Darnton's model begins with the position that using the person-centred emphasis on communication cannot account for 'the total significance of the book'.[44] The refinement to Darnton's circuit proposed by Adams and Barker seeks to remedy this by substituting Darnton's 'six groups of people' with 'five events in the life of a book – publishing, manufacturing, distribution, reception and survival'.[45] By focusing on the 'transmission' of the text, rather than the text's 'communication' of any specific message, and by the conversion of people into events, Adams and Barker's model proves itself more flexibly responsive to the variant modes of activity that affect the book.[46] The model also has the advantage of being less historically time-bound – the people of Darnton's circuit are by turns relevant or anachronistic depending on the period and location, whereas Adams and Barker's 'events' can be applied to more periods with less convolution. However, Adams and Barker's statement that the 'text [as] the reason for the cycle of the book' is, as with all overarching statements about the impetus behind books, questionable.[47] Adams and Barker do themselves refine the statement, seeing the motivation behind the first stage, 'publishing', as 'creation, communication, profit, preservation'.[48] The most important factors in 'manufacturing', though 'dependent on the decision to publish', are 'technology and economics'.[49] 'Distribution', the 'most obvious [force in the process,] is the desire to communicate, but the motive can take a variety of forms: to amuse, to instruct, to convince'.[50] Desire, configured in various ways and enacted by different agencies, is Adams and Barker's most fruitful description of the circuit. Regarding the 'nature of the movement and momentum that carries a book through its life cycle', they write that:

> The movement is initiated by the desires of the author and publisher when they launched the book on its way. The momentum is provided by the desire of others to possess the book. Again the most obvious

> of these desires is the wish to read the book, but to do so one must possess the object. Further, the desire to possess a book does not necessarily mean a desire to read it. Immediate reading is only one of the purposes for which people buy books. They may buy books to read later, an intention not always fulfilled, or for reference. But they may also buy a book because their position or function (or their view of that) demands it [...] Books may be bought just as furniture, to garnish a room; that too is use expressing status. Finally, there is the power conveyed by the book itself, an incalculable, inarticulate, but none the less potent factor in the mixture of motives that makes people want books. There is more to the possession of books than mere utility.[51]

Adams and Barker's construction of patterns of desire and fulfilment in the course of a book's life is an immensely suggestive articulation of the processes that it undergoes. Marketing, as the dynamic process by which desires for a book's transmission are both communicated and created, is consequently an important concept to deploy in the history of the book.

Adams and Barker end the explanation of their revised model with a note of caution about its use, particularly with regard to 'the external forces that exert influence on the circuit'.[52] As with Darnton, they shy away from providing a systematised account, claiming that another model may serve as well, as 'our scheme for the study of the book is [...] intended only as a point of departure.'[53] The step back from a full incorporation of the processes of marketing into their construction of desire and fulfilment suggests that their own caution about the provisional nature of their circuit is justified, as the 'external forces' need a much more comprehensive theorisation. An understanding of the 'external forces' which make each of the partners in a marketplace exchange willing to enter into that exchange is necessary, therefore, in the study of the marketing of literature. The construction and perception of 'value', as the element which makes the exchange of books a worthwhile activity in the eyes of both partners, is thus central to a theory of book marketing.

Turning to a rather different explanation of the marketplace, Pierre Bourdieu's concept of a 'field of cultural production' seeks to provide much more than a point of departure, particularly in his theorisation of external forces. His essay 'The Field of Cultural Production, or: The Economic World Reversed' (1983) provides a way of accounting for books' status as both cultural artefacts and economic products through theorisations of value.[54] Using varying concepts of value to describe cultural production was hardly an invention of Bourdieu's, though, as Q. D. Leavis's quantification of cultural value via the categories of 'brows' demonstrates. In her formulation, value is constructed in inverse proportion to audience size, not as an absolute but seen as created by an audience and established by the media. The negative assertions she makes about working-class reading habits and popular culture stem from this perception.[55] Given their very different critical provenance, Bourdieu's account of cultural production is surprisingly similar to Q. D. Leavis's. As the title of his essay suggests, cultural value, or 'cultural capital', to employ Bourdieu's terminology, is the 'reverse' of economic worth (or audience size), not necessarily because the 'herd' (Q. D. Leavis's term as well as Geoffrey Faber's) will choose works of low cultural value, but because the defining characteristic of a successful cultural work is 'disinterestedness'.[56] Disinterestedness is, broadly speaking, the fulfilment of values that have no bearing on economic or political profit. Bourdieu does not insist on a market division based on class lines, but the reverse of economic values in his system implies that a literary work that has a broad appeal is less 'autonomous[ly]' legitimate, in other words, of less merit in the cultural field.[57]

As Bourdieu explains, a unique recourse to either textual or contextual explanation is not sufficient to construct the field.[58] By rejecting either of these two methods of analysis – the one seeking to explain literature through examination of its internal, formal, aspects, and the other by reducing literature to a mechanistic theory of demand, production and consumption (implicitly a rejection of the Frankfurt School's Marxist theorisation of the culture industries) – Bourdieu builds instead upon his concept of the 'field'.[59] Describing the literary/cultural field is, for Bourdieu, a 'task [...] of constructing the space of positions and the space of the position-takings [...] in which they are expressed'.[60] The 'field' is hence a dynamic site, one in which the definition – or 'position' – of a literary work is forged through its relation to other literary works, as well as via the multiple agencies that are at work within the field. The field, then, encompasses not only the direct producers of the work in its materiality but, 'also the producers of the meaning and value of the work – critics, publishers, gallery directors and the whole set of agents whose combined efforts produce consumers capable of knowing and recognizing the work of art [...] In short, it is a question of understanding works of art as a manifestation of the field as a whole, in which all the powers of the field, and all the determinisms inherent in its structure and functioning, are concentrated.'[61] As a model, Bourdieu's 'field', through its dual emphasis on both 'material' and 'symbolic' production, offers a fluid mode of analysis. In short, it requires the commentator to investigate all the functionings of all the agents within a field if a work of art is to be understood, given that the work of art is 'a manifestation of the field as a whole'. The comprehensive project of 'reconstruct[ing] these spaces [within the field]' is then the investigative role of the literary sociologist.[62]

The persuasiveness of Bourdieu's model is that it can encompass discussions of the text itself (without resorting to Formalist or New Critical description), the writer (without an over-heavy reliance on biography), the audience (without resorting to sociological stratifications), the intermediate producers – the publishers, printers, and so on (without reducing them to a mechanistic role within a theory of social or economic relations) – and also the manifold agencies who create symbolic value, such as prize givers and critics (without forgetting their place in the field as a whole). Holding together such a variable set of producers, recipients and agencies can only be feasibly sustained through a structure of the magnitude of Bourdieu's field. The field incorporates both the position-takers and their acts of position-taking, and so, as Peter McDonald summarises in his exegesis of Bourdieu in *British Literary Culture and Publishing Practice 1880–1914* (1997), this 'structural sociology emphasizes the role of cultural intermediaries [...] and consumers. They are now not only functionaries in the circuit but symbolic brokers in the field.'[63]

The essential organisational principle used by Bourdieu is one of hierarchy, or rather domination and subordination, and the field is both a '*field of forces*' and a '*field of struggles*'.[64] The changes in position, and the active nature of position-taking within the field are the procedures through which literary history, genre transition and fashion can be described, as one type of novel becomes more popular, or critically acclaimed, than another, and new genres supplant the old. To appropriate Bourdieu's system, in this case to the field of late twentieth and early twenty-first century literary fiction publishing, then, it is necessary to ask who, in this particular field, can bestow 'literary or artistic prestige', on what terms, and how far such an award can ever be disinterested.[65] Who are the 'symbolic brokers', and how do they function? Who, or what, can both define the values of autonomous fulfilment but restrict them so completely that they have no impact on heteronomous success? Can a published text ever achieve total disinterestedness, thus allowing a calculation of cultural capital entirely disassociated from economic capital?

A publisher in this period would, arguably, base his or her decision to publish neither on bald economics nor on cultural value alone, but rather calculate the appropriateness of the text to the market that will receive it, which is, so to speak, playing the field. Depending on the publisher and the text, the decision might appear more or less cynical, more or less dependent on a dovetailing of product, market and audience. But although the value of each *book* may be calculated as a product, it is the text in combination with the context that tips the equation. That publishers themselves are frequently surprised by which of their products sell well and which do not is the most obvious indication that the value of a book as product is not easily calculable. Moreover, when a publisher makes an offer for a text, the financial and cultural calculation of value begins with the advance level, but the sum is revised throughout the course of the text's life, as sales are made, as the text progressively acquires readers and readings, and as the mechanisms of canon-making roll into place. Cultural value is consequently mutable, and shifts over time and under the aegis of different agencies. The transformation of text into book and product entails overlapping interpretations, incomplete translations, and a continual shifting of meaning from text to written and consumable object and back again.

Appropriating the 'field' as a structure through which contemporary publishing can be surveyed is not without its problems, however. The specific terminology of Bourdieu's example – 'bourgeois art' and 'art for art's sake' – derive from his reconstruction of the late nineteenth century in France.[66] The value-laden nature of this organisational principle too quickly suggests a delineation of the field into the markets for mass and elite audiences, as Q. D. Leavis's does. The value-judgements (of both literature and of society) thus entailed are neither the most fitting for the contemporary market, nor the most accurate in describing its products, producers or consumers. The focus of *Marketing Literature* is largely upon 'literary' fiction but, as the Introduction discussed, the distinction is a fluid one in publishing terms, and is certainly not intrinsically linked to audience size. Organising the contemporary literary field of the UK by the principles suggested by Bourdieu could lead to inappropriate and ultimately misrepresentative distortions. To say, as Bourdieu does, that, 'some box-office successes may be recognized, at least in some sectors of the field, as genuine art' is not really a sufficient explanation for how 'genuine art' can also be commercially successful.[67] The construction of value enacted by literary prizes is a prominent example of how, in the 1990s, cultural and economic capital combine. English, in his essay 'Winning the Culture Game: Prizes, Awards, and the Rules of Art' (2002), contemplates how Bourdieu's work might be applied to a study of artistic prizes in the latter half of the twentieth century through his consideration of the Booker and Turner Prizes (the latter for art rather than books). English introduces the concept of 'journalistic capital (visibility, celebrity, scandal)' as the mediating – and transforming – force between economic and cultural capital in the late twentieth century.[68] This is a world of marketing and promotion – in which value unravels in a most postmodern way, and meaning proliferates in a promotional circuit to *mise en abyme*. This is the world of which Wernick comments that there is 'no *hors-promotion*'. English contends that the 'rules no longer apply', and that the 'two discreet zones' of cultural and economic capital 'must be set aside' as a means of understanding the production of value.[69] Instead, English calls for the 'study of the concrete instruments of exchange and conversion whose rise is perhaps the most conspicuous feature of our recent cultural history': cultural prizes, corporate patronage and sponsorship, arts festivals and book clubs.[70] As English comments, 'these phenomena have generated a good deal of journalistic coverage and comment, but scholars have barely begun to study them in any detail, to construct their histories, gather ethnographic data from their participants, come to an understanding of their specific logics or rules and of the different ways they are being played and played with.'[71] English himself went on to answer his own call in *The Economy of Prestige* with specific reference to cultural awards. *Marketing Literature* does so with regard to the marketing of literature in Britain more generally, although literary prizes are an essential part of the field. For it is only by searching for the appropriate terminology and hence the specific structural paradigms for the contemporary period, that the dimensions of the field can be properly plotted. The next chapter, and all of the case studies in Part II, address this task specifically, in their empirical investigation of marketplace activity.

There is one caveat that must be made to the plotting of these coordinates, which is the impossibility of total reconstruction. Pressures of space and time are of course limiting factors when faced with the intimidating size of the field. There is also the irrecoverable or only partially recoverable nature of much of the material that would inform the process of reconstructing the field. Reconstruction can never be complete and, moreover – due to the nature of evidence discussed in the Introduction – will inevitably be partial. Nicolas Barker, in 'Intentionality and Reception Theory', an appendix to the volume in which he and Adams proposed their new model, discussed the nature of evidence in the history of the book in evolutionary terms: 'The process is one of Darwinian selection and survival: of all the different intentions involved, those of writer, editor or compositor, publisher, bookseller or reviewer, reader at first or second hand, or of those still further removed, only some survive to form that part of the general reception (and onward transmission) of the text.'[72] In a text's travel through time, intentional impulses will be scattered or obscured, thus forging the nature of its reception. Following the pattern of intentions lost or transformed, and receptions made, is the project of book history, with the history of the loss – through a history of constraint, censorship, arbitrariness – arguably as important as the history of the achievement. The history of the book, in its role in recuperating transmission, reception and the desires that motivate them, is itself, in other words, an intending intervention that, through its representations, influences the process and hence the field itself. It is thus part of that very 'journalistic capital' – or, to rephrase and subtly reorientate, 'scholarly capital' – that will occur in an analysis of contemporary literary fiction publishing.

As a process of representation, marketing is similarly subject to the vagaries of intention, communication and interpretation, as models of both reader response theory and marketing communications demonstrate. The study of reading and reception is notoriously difficult, although there have been very fine recent publications in this area.[73] Darnton, who comments in 'What is the History of Books?' that 'Reading remains the most difficult stage to study in the circuit that books follow', suggests supplementing the bibliographer's analytical tools, and the historian's archival scholarship, with more theoretical accounts of reader-response theorists.[74] In discussing how to render the historical practice of reading less 'mysterious', he describes how these theoretical accounts may be of use to the book historian by understanding 'literature as an activity', a 'construal of meaning within a system of communication'.[75] Darnton further elaborates in 'First Steps Toward a History of Reading' (1986) on the use a book historian may make of reader-response theory.[76] Even the more abstract theories, in their delineation of the relationship between author, text and reader, illuminate the relationship of book and reader, product and consumer. Certainly the interrogation of intentionality and the construction of the text as a communications device passing messages from author to reader, that awaits its more or less competent decoding, finds its parallel in Darnton's communications circuit, as well as in marketing communications. In order to make these theoretical postulations of use in reconstructing the contemporary literary marketplace, the historicisation of 'notions of fictitious audience, implicit readers, and interpretive communities' is imperative – and answers Michel Foucault's call for the study of contingent use, circulation and appropriation in 'What is an Author?' (1969).[77] Foucault's essay premises its answer on the historical contingency of copyright by which 'the author is the principle of thrift in the proliferation of meaning', a limiting agency on textual interpretation.[78] Foucault argues for this limiting agency of the 'author-function' to be weakened, though remaining aware that, 'It would be pure romanticism [. . .] to imagine a culture in which the fictive would operate in an absolutely free state, in which fiction would be put at the disposal of everyone and would develop without passing through something like a necessary or constraining figure.'[79] Nevertheless, the overthrowing of authorial intention for the more fluid 'constraining figure' opens the possibility of a very differently angled view of textual culture, based on the questions ' "What are the modes of existence of this discourse? Where has it been used, how can it circulate, and who can appropriate it for himself? What are the places in it where there is room for possible subjects? Who can assume these various subject-functions?" '[80] Foucault thus turns from biography and questions of authenticity to those of a quite different emphasis: the study of use, circulation and appropriation. Foucault's emphasis on historical contingency – the 'what', 'where' and 'who' of discourse use, circulation and appropriation – must be constantly recalled in order to be of use to the literary sociologist. As Darnton argues, a 'dual strategy' of 'textual analysis' and 'empirical research' is needed in order to 'develop a history as well as a theory of reader response'.[81]

How, then, could such a collaboration be actualised, and in what ways would this 'dual strategy' begin to develop answers to the 'what', 'where' and 'who' questions (as well as the 'when' and the 'why'), as Darnton suggests?[82] In their Introduction to *A History of Reading in the West* (1999), Guglielmo Cavallo and Roger Chartier call upon Stanley Fish as a collaborator in their 'dual strategy':

> A comprehensive history of reading and readers must thus consider the historicity of ways of using, comprehending and appropriating texts. It must consider the 'world of the text' as a world of objects, forms and rituals whose conventions and devices bear meaning but also constrain its construction. It must also consider that the 'world of the reader' is made up of what Fish calls the 'interpretive communities' to which individual readers belong. In its relation to writing, each of these communities displays a shared set of competencies, customs, codes and interests.[83]

Fish's notion of 'interpretive communities' is a remunerative concept for historians of the book, both for its theoretical implications and its empirical potential. In 'Interpreting the Variorum', Fish elucidates:

> Interpretive communities are made up of those who share interpretive strategies not for reading (in the conventional sense) but for writing texts, for constituting their properties and assigning their intentions. In other words, these strategies exist prior to the act of reading and therefore determine the shape of what is read rather than, as is usually assumed, the other way round.[84]

The process of 'writing texts' (which Fish also calls 'the business of making texts and of teaching others to make them by adding to their repertoire of strategies') as an act performed by the reader, is a theoretical account of how readers' reception of marketing activity effectively *makes* writing.[85] It is the 'interpretive strategies' that inform the reading and making of literary value, and 'interpretive communities' the groups who employ these strategies. That these strategies can be learnt (and, as Fish claims, taught) indicates that interpretive communities (and hence readers, meaning and making) are not fixed, but can change depending on how persuasive a given community and its teachers (or cultural guardians, or the media) are, and also on the competing strategies of rival communities. So, for example, a bestselling novel, to foreshadow the case study of *Bridget Jones's Diary* in Part II, might be thought of by one community as an extremely funny satire reflective of a social condition, and by another as retrograde, not at all amusing and an anachronistic stereotype, while a third community's strategies for the novel's interpretation might derive from its prior readings of another (much earlier) novel, Jane Austen's *Pride and Prejudice* (1813). That it becomes a bestselling novel at all is a result of interpretive strategies brought to bear on the book's consumption, or, in other words, a result of whether the interpretive communities who think the book worth buying are of sufficient size to place it in the bestseller lists.

The reader's 'making' of textual meaning also articulates the potential crossover of text and context. The encoding of the narrative's 'message' via a notion of narrative codes presupposes a reader's eventual decoding. The process of decoding is reliant upon context, even if that context could be purely isolated as the decoding process learnt from other texts – intertextuality, in other words. In actuality, though, decoding draws not merely on knowledge of linguistic and narrative codes but a broad contextual framework. Reading methods, then, are institutionalised by a conventionalising of codes. Certain establishments – the academy, schools, reading groups, peers and the critics, for example – have the power to enforce particular interpretations. Fish's notion of 'interpretive communities', although situating the text's mode of being more radically in the readers themselves, is similarly reliant on what might loosely be called collective feeling, or, more politically, group coercion. Interpretation thus needs a community to formulate and sustain it. The power and persuasiveness of each of the communities is what then produces the text's cultural meaning. The fierce debates over the canon are a paradigmatic example of this, with the choice of whether to include or exclude a book hence a definition of its cultural meaning.[86] That meaning is not fixed, however, as a 'resisting reader' – Judith Fetterly's term for a feminist reader's rejection of the imposition of codes in the academy – can refuse or alter canons and their meanings.[87] Other groups and institutions involved in the processes of defining books – textually and contextually – are faced with similar struggles. Literary prizes are one example. Recent ethnographic and cultural studies of reading groups also demonstrate these processes.[88] How do members of reading groups form their groups? How do they constitute their reading activity alongside other social practices? How do they choose the texts they read and discuss, and how are these choices affected by gender, age, ethnicity and publishers' marketing? How are the discussions of the texts conducted? Such developing bodies of knowledge take theoretical concepts of reader-response and analyse them in their sociological setting, offering a clear example of how the theories can be co-opted within a historicising analysis, in order to inform understandings of value and meaning-making. If interpretive strategies are taken to include everything from a group's literacy rate and language competence, to its ethnicity or gender, and to its awareness of specific rhetorical literary tropes, the concept of interpretive communities – particularly if the communities' strategies are understood to develop from textual, paratextual, intertextual and contextual agencies – is a richly suggestive one. Nonetheless, the process of reconstructing such communities risks stereotyping their reactions, and the reactions of the individuals within them. In Avi Shankar's investigation of the reading group phenomenon, for example, he explains his preconceptions of how group discussions would function, and how these preconceptions were undermined in the course of his investigations:

> Given the similarity of group members in terms of their life stage, life experiences, shared history and sociological backgrounds, I expected

> that they would form a Fishian interpretive community and produce similar understandings or at least moves towards a consensual, shared understanding or interpretation of the book in question during their discussions. This, however, seems rarely to be the case with the book groups I encountered and there often exists a sharp divide between the 'loved it' or 'hated it' camps, making for a lively or interesting meeting.[89]

It could be argued that this insistence on difference, on the 'lively' or 'interesting' debate arising at the meeting (noted also in Jenny Hartley's lengthier study of reading groups) could in fact be part of the interpretive communities' shared code: that books should promote conversation, even argument.[90] However, perhaps more generally what it suggests is that anyone seeking to reconstruct readers' receptions of texts and the marketing activity surrounding them should beware of stereotyping group reaction. This conclusion both accords with and extends Delany's sense of the late twentieth-century book market. In an environment in which 'market segmentation' is more relevant than 'product differentiation', social rank will not classify buyer behaviour. However, with Shankar's reading group members, it would seem that 'their interests, gender, [and] life-styles', although influencing their joint purchase or borrowing of the book under discussion, does not necessarily extend to their reading responses. So although marketing activity profoundly influences consumer decisions and readerly interpretations, it is – as an act of representation – still open to debate and argumentation. Marketing, like the texts with which it deals, is open to interpretation by communities and individuals within those communities.

The close alliance of communications theory to elements of reader-response theory is another similarity between discourses ripe for further research development, as is the similarity of the book historical circuit to the feedback loop incorporated into more complex communications models, through which, as Chris Fill phrases it in *Marketing Communications: Contexts, Contents and Strategies* (1999), 'an organisation enters into dialogue with its various audiences'.[91] The synchronies between theories, both in terms of their structures and the disruptions which challenge them, point towards an understanding of the marketing of literary fiction that is situated within the structures of the industry in its definitions, but is informed by a nexus of overlapping discourses. An illustration of this can be found in the role that the media plays in the marketing and communication of books. Alison Baverstock's pragmatic view of this role in *How to Market Books* is as an opportunity for '"Free"

Advertising', and for the publishers' publicity department 'to inform public opinion and re-orientate popular debate, or simply to spread information by word of mouth' as well as to 'achieve the real aim: larger sales'.[92] Yet the impact of the media on book sales is difficult to quantify, unlike the effect of a book winning a literary award, the immediacy of which can be seen translating into sales figures.[93] One of the primary means by which potential book consumers are informed of literary prize winners, however, is through media reports (the other is through strap-lines on the books themselves and through bookshop promotions and point of sale materials).[94] As such the publicity created by literary awards is incorporated into the general activity of 'free' advertising to which Baverstock refers. Nevertheless, literary editors including Erica Wagner, Literary Editor of *The Times*, profess themselves to be uncertain of the extent to which a review increases sales.[95] The advent of off-the-page selling, in which newspapers act as bookshops, ending reviews with details of how to buy through the papers' designated supplier would certainly provide some interesting statistical evidence of patterns of purchasing, as well as provoking debate about the media's collusion in the book's promotion by its direct benefit from sales. Robert McCrum, Literary Editor of the *Observer*, also expressed doubt about the effectiveness of good reviews on a book's sales, believing that, 'A book will only really sell on a large scale (as a bestseller) by word of mouth, a process that is like alchemy.'[96] In effect, what McCrum suggests is that reviews can give voice to the author and their book, but the voice alone is not enough to achieve widespread sales.

This alchemical process of 'word of mouth' is one frequently discussed with regards to the publishing industry, with *Captain Corelli's Mandolin*, one of the case studies of Part II, being seen as its most successful 1990s exponent. The language of magic and mystification, as the phenomenal success of the *Harry Potter* series self-reflexively demonstrates, hovers over word of mouth.[97] Some demystification in considering what this process might be is necessary, as the individual case studies in Part II point out. P. R. Smith states in *Marketing Communications* (1998) that 'Of all the elements of the communications mix, [word of mouth] is by far the most potent on a one-to-one basis.'[98] In interview, McCrum went on to suggest that word of mouth 'can be broken down into constituent parts, but essentially there is a process of transformation which is the only way a book can sell so many copies'.[99] Both Smith, and Chris Fill in his version of *Marketing Communications*, though, attempt to theorise word of mouth and suggest how the theory can be put into practice by marketers. Fill sees word of mouth as 'one of the most powerful marketing communication tools' which, 'if an organisation can develop a programme to harness and accelerate the use of [...] effectively, the more likely it will be that the marketing programme will be successful'.[100] Thus, both Fill and Smith build word of mouth into their models of communication, with Fill defining the process as:

> [the] motivations to discuss products and their associative experiences [which] vary between individuals and with the intensity of the motivation at any one particular moment. For organisations in particular it is important to target messages at those individuals who are predisposed to such discussion, as this may well propel word-of-mouth recommendations and the success of the communications campaign. The target, therefore, is not necessarily the target market, but those in the target market who are most likely to volunteer their positive opinions about the offerings or those who, potentially, have some influence over members.[101]

Such volunteers derive from the marketing groups of 'opinion leaders, formers and followers'.[102] Where the media and similar agencies fit into the model is as 'opinion formers', who, as Smith explains, 'are formal experts whose opinion has influence, e.g. journalists, analysts, critics, judges, members of a governing body. People seek their opinions and they provide advice.'[103] The cultural authority and the power of recommendation invested in these opinion formers is thus apparent, just as it is for the literary prize judge or media-based reading groups such as Channel 4's Richard & Judy, discussed in the *Cloud Atlas* case study in Part II.

To trace in full detail the quantitative impact on sales by the media would require a different kind of analysis than that engaged in here. Rather, *Marketing Literature* makes a more qualitative analysis of the impact of the media, one that has to do with the creation and construction of audiences for a book. Discussing '"free" advertising', Baverstock states that 'Features and reviews of books in the media are one of the most influential ways of shaping reading habits.'[104] Wagner, although uncertain about how far reviews influence buying habits, still sees part of her role to provide a guide to (good) books for the reader and in her analysis there is a clear link between influencing her readers and creating an audience for the book.[105] Wagner and her fellow literary journalists guide the readers of their own newspapers towards certain titles and, through extracts of their quotations on later editions of the books, may also assist decisions in a shop or library about which title to purchase or borrow. The reviewer then is a mediator, a 'filter', as Robert McCrum puts it, but also, in his or her role in communicating the book, part of the process of marketing communications, an opinion leader in word-of-mouth recommendation and hence influential in 'shaping reading habits' and, moreover, of constructing meanings that are then affirmed or contested by readers.[106] Literary editors' awareness of their audience – the influence of, to varying degrees, the reader of the newspaper, the newspaper's proprietors, the literary establishment, even the author of the book – place them at the centre of a nexus of desires, some conflicting and some mutually supportive. Indeed, Fill defines marketing communications as a reciprocal process in which:

> an organisation/brand [attempts] to create and sustain a dialogue with its various constituencies. Communication itself is the process by which individuals share meaning. Therefore for a dialogue to occur each participant needs to understand the meaning of the other's communication.[107]

Once more, this is a depiction of the feedback loop of communications theory, or the circularity of the communications circuit. The idea of dialogue also fits with Karl Miller's notion of sound and soundlessness in the reception of contemporary writing discussed in the previous chapter with regards to contemporary authorship. For the conflicting or supportive desires create the noise of the communications circuit, and the various interpretive communities whose reading habits are shaped are also the segmented consumers in the marketplace. The demographic basis for segmentation estimated by McCrum for his pages in the *Observer* (homeowning, probably living in the South, middle class ABC1, etc.) is appended to a wealth of other 'bases for segmentation', as Fill enumerates.[108] The journalist, writing the book review, then, is a very visible, frequently self-reflexive participant in the dialogue, and so the choices that he or she makes are highly indicative of the processes of marketing and the concomitant creation of reading communities.

In her article about the process of literary reviewing, Lorna Sage describes it as a performative process of '*writing reading*', where reviewers turn their own reading into further material to be read.[109] Following Darnton, the link from reader to writer is the one that sees 'the circuit run [...] full cycle'.[110] In terms of marketing theory, the group of readers that comprise the reviewing community and the larger literary-value industry are 'opinion formers' – readers in a position of privileged authority, with an advantaged capacity for communicating the book to other potential readers, and thus part of the representational processes of marketing, including sales. As Sage puts it, as a reviewer, 'You swap words for money, you reprocess reading into writing and commentary. You describe, paraphrase, quote, reperform, "place" and help sell (or not) the books you're reviewing.'[111] The traces left by reviewers – the reviews themselves – mean that the critical reception of books is one particular area of reading and reception that can be studied with relative ease.[112] Yet embedded in these specialised forms of reading and writing undertaken for the book review are a discourse, history and purpose of their own, not all of which stem from marketing processes. The volume of essays in which Sage's 'Living on Writing' appears, *Grub Street and the Ivory Tower: Literary Journalism and Literary Scholarship from Fielding to the Internet* (1998), appraises the continuum, differences, and sometimes tensions, between academic and journalistic literary criticism, thus indicating an alternative field in which the reviewing process occurs. Reviewing, as well as an act of reading, is an act of writing in itself: McCrum, for example, asserts that the review, as well as being 'a transmitter of information' is also 'a piece of work in its own right'.[113] As Boyd Tonkin, Literary Editor of the *Independent* discussed in an article about reviewing in *The Bookseller*, this is an aspect that means that, '"The interests of literary editors and publishers are incompatible and always will be."'[114] The issue of audience is vital to the review as 'a piece of work in its own right', and hence '*writing reading*' can itself extend beyond the media circuit to be published in book form: *Several Strangers: Writing from Three Decades* (1999) by Claire Tomalin, former Literary Editor of the *New Statesman* and *Sunday Times*, is one example from the 1990s.[115]

Aware of the other agencies at work in the marketplace, Forsyth and Birn explain in *Marketing in Publishing* the need for the active intervention of publishers' marketing in the communications circuit:

> the market is demanding, unpredictable, dynamic and fickle. Even the best titles cannot be left to sell themselves, and marketing is, necessarily, a vital part of the publishing business.[116]

Market unpredictability is not quite the same thing as the randomness identified by Adams and Barker, although Forsyth and Birn's insistence that it is the responsibility of publishers to guard against it through careful marketing is a suggestion of how intentionality may go astray in the circuit of communications. In *How Hits Happen*, Farrell rejects a notion of randomness for one of 'complexity' (yet another discourse – this time of quantum physics), and suggests how the dynamic and seemingly unpredictable marketplace can be managed and turned towards making 'hits happen'. His account of the development of a software program to model individual consumers and their interactions has been taken up with particular regard to publishing by John Mitchinson, then Group Marketing Director of Orion, in a *Bookseller* article in 1999, 'Bestseller Genes':

> Th[e] application of complexity theory to business delivers a model of commercial reality that is chaotic but not random; obscure but not meaningless. It puts the onus on us to make the meaningful connections. As Winslow Farrell puts it: 'making sense is the most powerful form of action'. By applying some of these concepts to the bestseller, I believe we can begin to free ourselves from the role of passive observers.[117]

Mitchinson's particular application of Farrell's ideas to publishing bestsellers and how marketing can both understand and then create them is an interesting business model, though an examination of its potential productivity is not the aim of this book. What is perhaps more relevant to this study, beyond the synergistic understanding of communication in the creation of bestsellers, is Farrell's call to '"making sense"', or as Farrell himself phrases it:

> we have seen how emergent behavior is often decentralized, adaptive, and emanates both from the agents in a system *and* their interactions. This type of emergence simply cannot be understood or represented by taking a large system apart and then putting it back together again [...] Therefore in our work we don't seek an equation that describes the market: *We try to enable the market to describe the equation.*[118]

Farrell's prompt to understanding the market through the 'agents in a system *and* their interactions' is fascinating in its similarities to Bourdieu's call to reconstruct the field of cultural production: not a breakdown of individual taxonomies but an exploration of relationships of power and communication. The explanation of Farrell's method – an attempt to '*enable the market to describe the equation*' – is clearly one with specific outputs in mind, that consist of a much more active intervention in the marketplace than an academic study would undertake. Nonetheless, the aim of *Marketing Literature* is to develop an understanding of the active processes of marketing and the relationships of which they consist, rather than to draw a static picture of the marketplace. As Mitchinson's summary of Farrell's work has it, 'although we cannot "manage" a complex system, we can train ourselves to recognise patterns and developing structures.'[119] Thus, through the fusion of marketing theory, constructions of literary value, book historical models and the empirical examples provided by case studies, this developing theory of book marketing is developed and applied in the case studies contained in Part II, and in the next chapter, which considers the construction of genre in the marketplace.

3
Genre in the Marketplace

Of the link between reading and writing in his communications circuit, Darnton put it that:

> The reader completes the circuit because he influences the author both before and after the act of composition. Authors are readers themselves. By reading and associating with other readers and writers, they form notions of genre and style and a general sense of the literary enterprise, which affects their texts.[1]

Genre, then, is a crucial component in the marketplace, as it is one of the primary means by which authors and readers communicate, and one of the methods by which both writing and reading can be studied in their publishing contexts. The philosopher Benedetto Croce, writing on aesthetics in 1902, refuted the theoretical separation of literature into genre categories, seeing the only use of such divisions as practical, indeed purely physical:

> The books in a library must be arranged in one way or another. This used generally to be done by a rough classification of subjects [...]; they are now generally arranged by sizes or by publishers. Who can deny the necessity and the utility of such arrangements? But what should we say if someone began seriously to seek out the literary laws of [...] those altogether arbitrary groupings whose sole object was their practical utility? Yet should any one attempt such an undertaking, he would be doing neither more nor less than those do who seek out the *aesthetic laws* which must in their belief control literary and artistic kinds.[2]

Reducing the only proper relevance of classification to that of practical utility, or to what David Duff, in his commentary in *Modern Genre Theory* (2000) on Croce's assertions terms 'purely pragmatic purposes such as arranging books on shelves', Croce might seem to deny the importance of genre as a strategy in constructing cultural value.[3] Yet the relevance of practical utility cannot be denied, nor in fact is it, by Croce. By the turn of the twentieth and twenty-first centuries, the necessity of finding arrangements for the 100 000+ books produced yearly by the UK industry is readily apparent. The prolific and diverse nature of the marketplace demands it; the sheer number of individual product lines calls out for some sort of taxonomy, and so the multiple agencies in the field of literary publishing provide them via a variety of processes. Marketing is central to this taxonomic enterprise, providing the practical organisational structures that deliver the taxonomies. This chapter investigates some of these organisational structures, but also considers the cultural meanings created by categories, and how the tenets of practical utility do, in contradiction to Croce, reach towards notions of generic form, if not '*aesthetic laws*'.

David Duff, providing a definition of 'genre consciousness' at the beginning of *Modern Genre Theory*, denotes both 'conscious' and 'unconscious' components. The conscious component he sees as 'manifest in the explicit use made of generic categories and terminology by writers, critics, booksellers, publishers, librarians and other cultural institutions'. This foregrounded use is the one found in material and contextual representations of texts, and is the more visible element of the publishing industry's taxonomic enterprise. The unconscious component is 'suggested by the attempts of many writers, readers and critics, especially in the modern era, to conceal or repress their dependence on genre'. Such resistance to genre 'dependence' might well develop from the value-laden divisions between 'genre' and 'literary' fiction. The extent to which this unconscious component is present in the period under consideration here – or, indeed, whether a more flirtatious and more conscious mingling by individual writers with genre taxonomies occurs – is reliant on the historical specificity conjured up by Duff in the final remark of his definition, to the effect that, 'The forms to which genre-consciousness takes, and the intensity with which it is experienced, are subject to both personal and historical variation.'[4]

In *Genres in Discourse* (1990), Tzvetan Todorov theorises changing patterns of genre, paying particular attention to the manner in which genre functions in relation to society. He notes that 'It is because genres exist as an institution that they function as "horizons of expectation" for readers and as "models of writing" for authors.'[5] Todorov's articulation of genre as an 'institution' is an understanding of texts in their material and contextual situations. Genre, then, is as much an agency in the publishing field as publishers, booksellers and the other symbolic brokers, though it also affects and is affected by them. Writers and readers are located within the communication circuits of book production and knowledge transmission both in accordance with and reaction against dominant genres. As Todorov continues in *Genres in Discourse*:

> On the one hand, authors write in function of (which does not mean in agreement with) the existing generic system, and they may bear witness to this just as well within the text as outside it, or even, in a way between the two – on the book cover; this evidence is obviously not the only way to prove the existence of models of writing. On the other hand, readers read in function of the generic system, with which they are familiar thanks to criticism, schools, the book distribution system, or simply by hearsay; however, they do not need to be conscious of this system.[6]

As such, genre becomes a central – in Todorov's view, perhaps the central – concern of literary study.[7] Genre is the system through which art interacts with society, by which 'a society chooses and codifies the acts that correspond most closely to its ideology; that is why the existence of certain genres in one society, their absence in another, are revelatory of that ideology and allow us to establish it more or less confidently.'[8] This ideological function of genre is addressed in some of the case studies of the next chapter, particularly in that of Bret Easton Ellis's *American Psycho*.

Fashion is an important part of the ideology of genre. Boyd Tonkin, contributing a subject essay on historical fiction to the *Good Fiction Guide* (2001), comments on its fluctuating fortunes:

> Thirty years or so ago, the historical novel had dropped below the horizon of respectable attention. The romantic gestures that thrilled Victorian readers had dwindled into the folderol of swashbucklers and bodice-rippers in pulp fiction, kitsch movies and television serials [...] history (for serious novelists) was a no-go area.
>
> Yet, by the century's end, historical fiction commanded a prestige and acclaim unknown since its heyday. As I write, *Captain Corelli's Mandolin* [...] by Louis de Bernières, a period romance whose methods and motifs Walter Scott himself could have grasped at a

> glance, has just sold its millionth copy. Around a quarter of the titles that have appeared on the Booker Prize shortlists since 1975 count as historical novels of one brand or other.[9]

Tonkin's essay indicates how snobbery and prejudices attach and are detached from genre, and also how genre hierarchies come into play. The impact of these attitudes might be found, for example, in the author Andrew Miller's decision to turn from the critically acclaimed path of his first two historical novels to a contemporary setting for his third, after he 'kept hearing [him]self described as a "historical novelist" '.[10] Apart from a dissatisfaction with being stereotyped, evident here is also a sense of the danger of being described as an author writing in a devalued genre, and this is thus an example of genre functioning as a model of writing for authors that draws upon the horizons of expectation of readers. A. S. Byatt also debates the fashion and durability of historical fiction in *On Histories and Stories: Selected Essays* (2000):

> I think it can be argued that the 'historical' novel has proved more durable, in my lifetime, than many urgent fictive confrontations of immediate contemporary reality. I think it is worth looking at the sudden flowering of the historical novel in Britain, the variety of its forms and subjects, the literary energy and real inventiveness that has gone into it. I want to ask, why has history become imaginable and important again? Why are these books *not* costume drama or nostalgia?[11]

Byatt's passionate advocacy of the historical novel responds to the criticisms made by commentators such as George Walden, which are referred to in the case study of *The Ghost Road* in Part II. The ripostes Byatt finds in *On Histories and Stories*, however, should be supplemented by an understanding of the contextual background of genre formulation, and the centrality of the marketplace Richard Todd refers to in *Consuming Fictions* with regards to the 'self-conscious commercial categorization' in the popularity of the Rushdie and Byatt historical models of writing, following the success of their novels *Midnight's Children* and *Possession*, confirming Booker's place in (re-)establishing the genre.[12]

Two comments about literary fashion and genre transition – one from a theoretician of genre; and one from a practical guide to authorship – illustrate both the mechanisms of genre change and its pitfalls. Ireneusz Opacki, in 'Royal Genres' (1963) writes:

> at the point of transition from one literary trend to another, there takes place a revaluation of the hierarchy of genres: a previously secondary genre, because it possesses features which are especially serviceable to the new trend, rises to the top. Its promotion was determined by its distinctive features in the earlier phase of development. Now, once it becomes a royal genre, it imparts these distinctive features, which brought about its promotion, to other genres.[13]

In *An Author's Guide to Publishing* (1998), Michael Legat refers to what he terms 'Bandwagon books':

> As soon as a certain style of book becomes a bestseller – usually something which is sufficiently different from the normal range of publications to become almost a new genre – half the authors in the world seem ready to leap onto the bandwagon, rushing to their word-processors to produce imitations [...] There are two reasons why books of this kind are not often successful: the first is that few of these imitators are talented enough to write books which are anywhere near as good as the originals; the second is that such fashions in writing can often change remarkably rapidly, and allowing for the normal delay in getting a publisher to accept your book and then publish it, the fashion may have disappeared.[14]

Legat's advice for the potential writer of the 'bandwagon' book is a cautionary tale in which the 'royal genre' first dictates reception and is then rebuffed by it, as the discussion of the Bridget Jones imitators in Part II demonstrates. It is with these mechanisms of change that the successes and failures of literary production occur, and its sometimes wilful stipulations draw on changing conventions of taste, style and popularity.

What ends up on which particular shelf, for how long and to what effect, are the questions that an examination of genre in the marketplace causes to be asked. This chapter, through an analysis of some of the paratextual and contextual representations of marketing, examines some of the key mechanisms and institutions of literary categorisation in the contemporary market. The study of publishing, the study of literary history, and the study of wider social contexts – a sociology of genres – all develop through such analysis. The remainder of the chapter considers the methods by which the publishing industry categorises its products, concentrating on books as material objects, branding, imprints, bookshop taxonomies and literary prizes.

Books

How books look – the appearance of the material product – is reliant to a large degree on the imprint on which they are published, and as such imprint and materiality are inextricably linked.[15] This investigation of industry categorisations begins with individual objects before moving towards a consideration of branding and imprints. This section of the chapter deals with the materiality of texts, the methods by which texts are rendered material, and the impact of such actions. This is the realm of the paratext, which Gérard Genette defines in *Paratexts: Thresholds of Interpretation* (1997) as:

> what enables a text to become a book and to be offered as such to its readers, and, more generally, to the public. More than a boundary or a sealed border, the paratext is, rather, a *threshold*, or – a word Borges used apropos of a preface – a 'vestibule' that offers the world at large the possibility of either stepping inside or turning back.[16]

Genette turns the physical borders of the book – its cover, its pages – into a more fluidly metaphorical site. He presents the paratext as an invitation, which may be accepted or rejected, and at which the potential reader either 'step[s] inside or turn[s] back'. This invitation is one of marketing's methods of appeal, by which texts are represented to the potential reader. Hence, in *Paratexts*, Genette furthers the textual and contextual distinction by dividing the paratext into factors relating to the physical book itself – the 'peritext' – and those external to it – the 'epitext' – such as sales presenters and point of sale materials.[17] This section concentrates on three of the most instantly visible – and hence most obviously marketable – peritextual areas: design; format; and the copy or 'blurb', both on the cover and in the preliminary pages inside the books. It is important to note, though, that these peritextual elements are intimately related to epitextual materials and representations, as marketing is an inextricable fusion of both.

In *An Author's Guide to Publishing* (1998), Michael Legat deals with the issue of cover design as frequently problematic in the relationship between authors and publishers, by offering reassurance to the authorial anxiety that '*The jacket design is a travesty of my book*'. He responds:

> The most frequent complaints about jackets concern fiction when the artwork does not follow your descriptions of the characters or the scene portrayed. Good jacket/cover artists understand that they

> should reflect the contents of the book with a fair degree of accuracy, but many feel that they have a licence to adapt in order to make what they consider a better picture, and this is why, for instance, your blue-eyed blonde heroine may turn up on the jacket looking like a Spanish señorita.[18]

Legat's jokey tone suggests that the author must, despite his or her misgivings, accede to the demands of the publisher and cover artist. The 'licence to adapt' is not just a concession to the greater aesthetic good ('a better picture'), however, but a marker of the distinction between the author's text, or manuscript, and the marketable book, or commodity. Legat's earlier discussion of cover design further explains why he thinks the author should give way to the authority of the publisher, 'jackets and covers [...] are a vital sales tool, and if the sales department in particular is satisfied with the general design, the author may have to bow to their belief that it is acceptable [...] publishers tend to put credence in their own expertise, and may simply tell you bluntly that your skill is in writing the book, and theirs in knowing best how to sell it.'[19]

This moment of authorial anxiety is symbolic of a stage when authors lose control of the publishing process, as the text is reinterpreted in its material form. As Juliet Gardiner expounds in 'Recuperating the Author', it is also highly suggestive for considerations of genre:

> There is no appurtenance more indicative of the text's journey from private to public space, more manifest both of the proprietorship of the text (since that is where his/her signature first and most boldly appears) – and at the very same time, his/her letting go of that meaning. It positions the author on the boundary of the text's meaning: she/he envisages the jacket as representing the interior of the book: its *content*, what has *been* written – as far as possible its unique nature – whereas the publisher insists that it is the book's *circulation* that must be represented – its destination – the market it is to find by analogy with books of the same genre, the futurity of its appeal.[20]

How, then, are such paratextual reinterpretations made, and what is their impact? To explore this question, *Marketing Literature* proposes a hyp[illegible]thetical mini-genre, the 'Crime Boys'. Four key novels in [illegible]othetical genre are Emlyn Rees's *The Book of Dead Authors* [illegible]artyn Bedford's *The Houdini Girl* (1999), Rupert Thomson's

The Book of Revelation (1999) and Toby Litt's *Corpsing* (2000).[21] These four novels, textually and paratextually, are situated at the borders of genres – between the crime/thriller and literary fiction. Their state of formal indefinability is both reflected in the books' physical forms, and asserted by the material and contextual negotiations that accrue to the texts through the processes of marketing. The paperback editions are used in exploring the peritextual reinterpretations that contribute to this mini-genre, as the choice and positioning of review extracts add a revealing layer to the peritext. (Some of the books appeared in earlier hardback editions.) This abbreviated form of analytical bibliography pays attention to Philip Gaskell's call in *A New Introduction to Bibliography* (1972) to the merits of functionality, though it provides a more impressionistic description than Gaskell might approve, primarily because of the focus here on the representative factors of image and text rather than their histories of transmission.[22]

The Book of Dead Authors, Emlyn Rees's first novel, was issued by its publisher as a Headline Review paperback in B format (198mm × 129mm). The front and back covers and spine of the paperback edition have a bright red background, and a single, iconic image repeated on all three. The image is of a male body, visible from the torso downwards, wearing knickers, suspenders, stockings and high heels. The body is seemingly hanging, dead, from an unseen rope. The image descends from the top left-hand corner of the front cover, from the same position though with a smaller version of the image from the back cover, and in a tiny version coming directly down from the top of the spine. Martyn Bedford's *The Houdini Girl* is his third novel, and was issued by Penguin in A format (178mm × 111mm) paperback. It features a double-cover effect, with the outer front cover illustrated with a deep red velvet stage curtain, sprinkled with stars. Typography takes up most of the first cover space, with cut-outs in the letters 'D' and 'R' of 'THE HOUDINI GIRL', through which can be seen part of the second cover: a made-up eye and brow through the 'D' and a lipglossed mouth through the 'R'. The second front cover is a photograph of a young woman spied through the letters of the outer front cover, lying on a bed. Rupert Thomson's *The Book of Revelation* is his sixth novel, published as a B format Bloomsbury paperback. The front cover consists of the image of a red light bulb, wired into a bare fitting, set against a white background. Toby Litt's *Corpsing* is his third book. Published by Penguin in A format, it features a bright red background to the front and back covers and spine. The front cover has an image of two bullets, one, marked 'LILY', crumpled and fallen over, the other, upright and intact, marked 'CONRAD'. The spine features images of the bottom of two bullets. The back uses a *trompe l'oeil* effect of a bullet entry through the book cover. Another noteworthy element of *Corpsing*'s design is the red tinting of the page edges so that the whole of the outside of the book is of one colour.

Here, then, are four books published within the space of four years. Linking them together might seem a rather arbitrary procedure: although all are by British men, the authors are at quite different stages in their writing careers (a first, second, third and sixth book respectively), and the novels come in two different paperback formats (two As and two Bs). Other visual similarities might link the books, though, such as the use of colour and image on the covers of *The Book of Dead Authors* and *Corpsing*, where the white and yellow text of the former turns into a glitzier silver and gold on the latter. Rather than attempting to prove the existence of such a hypothetical mini-genre, though, this is an examination of the ways in which the paratext functions alongside the text in the creation of publishing categories, which these four books illustrate mutually and cumulatively.

The short blurbs given on the back cover of each book, in their paraphrases of the text itself, give one of the clearest juxtapositions of text and paratext, and of the material book's role in its own marketing. The summary of the text for the paratextual copy necessarily curtails the plot, emphasising some aspects whilst hiding others. This is particularly important for the crime plot, where crucial plot elements should not be revealed. The extent to which blurbs also include generic indicators or comparisons with other texts is important, particularly when taken alongside review extracts and biographical information. The full cover copy of each book is contained in Appendix 1.

The blurb for *The Book of Dead Authors* opens with an incident that occurs towards the beginning of the novel, as the first of the murderer's victims encounters the murderer, an 'alluring stranger'. 'Sex and violence', as the *Mail on Sunday* extract on the front cover puts it, are already united in the first sentence, while the second sentence pre-empts the killer's future actions by foretelling a whole sequence of murdered authors, along with positing a motive: revenge. The next paragraph gives an idea of the public impact of the killings, leading up to the cliff hanger of the final sentence. The copy actually gives away much of the bare bones of the plot, as indeed does the title, leaving the reader to wonder more at the motive and, perhaps, the specific nature of sex and violence to be found within the text. What is emphasised within these two short paragraphs above all else, however, is the specifically *literary* nature of these crimes and their reception. The first victim 'turn[s] the page on the last [...] chapter of his life'; the murderer's motive is a 'narrative of revenge'; the crimes are 'instalment[s]'. The 'serial' killer is one through whom a meta-(crime)-fiction promises to be created. Here, murdering is also authoring, and the text is represented as a knowing narrative, a crime novel that acknowledges its fictionality, and that makes an appeal to literariness. This appeal to the *cleverness* of the text connects it to generally perceived attitudes towards crime fiction: when hierarchies are drawn of the mass-market genres, crime fiction is at the top. *The Oxford Companion to English Literature* (2000) entry on 'Detective Fiction' summarises these preconceptions, saying that, 'The fact that it is a popular form that engages the mind rather than the emotions has always given it a degree of respectability: to be seen reading a [Dorothy L.] Sayers or [Ruth] Rendell is very different from being seen reading a Barbara Cartland or an Alistair Maclean.'[23] The cultural assumptions that give rise to genre hierarchies are naturally open to question – why, after all, should a work of art be regarded more highly because it appeals to the head rather than the heart? – but it is clear that although the blurb for *The Book of Dead Authors* does not balk at making its appeal through representations of sex and violence, it also makes a more cerebral claim for its text.

The review extracts used on the paperback edition of Rees's novel accentuate the elements of sex and violence as well as introducing a sense of the text's humour. It is possible that they were chosen in order to emphasise this interpretation of the text, but given that only three quotations appear, with none in the prelims or inside covers (unlike all three of the other novels), it is more likely that these were the only three reviews positive enough to be quotable – the peritext performs a sifting of the public reception to the book, censoring unflattering or inappropriate commentary. The publishers' blurb complements the reviews, so that as well as giving a more specific indication of the plot it also gestures at its literariness. The format chosen (B) for this edition of the book confirms such a reading of the publishers' representations. Alex Hamilton, in a note to his Fastsellers chart in the *Guardian*, explains the distinction between the two formats, 'A: smaller-size paperbacks, usually "mass market". B: larger-sized paperbacks, usually "middle- to highbrow" and following hardback or C-format publication.'[24] Headline, by publishing the novel in B format and on the more literary Review imprint, represented *The Book of Dead Authors* not as straight crime, therefore, but as a more upmarket and literary title. It is nonetheless quite prepared to appeal to voyeuristic tendencies, and to the titillation of sex and violence. Taking a new, young writer (as evidenced by the biographical note), the publishers situate the novel in a crossover position through these various paratextual indicators. Rees the writer is thus portrayed as 'the creator of this most unusual murder mystery'. Author and character are conflated in the promotional gambit as the text is put across as both a murder mystery and more than a murder mystery.

The blurb for *The Houdini Girl* also gives away an element of the crime plot – the 'mysterious death' of Rosa – but begins in a more metaphorical way, ostensibly introducing the main character (and narrator), but also suggesting underlying themes of the text. The mystery – and crime, if there is one – is represented through the filter of the relationship between Rosa and Brandon, a magician. The concern is not so much her disappearance but the frailty of human relationships, and their capacity for deception and illusion. The centre of the narrative is thus presented as Brandon's quest for the truth, where the nature of his profession rebounds upon him with dramatic irony. This metaphor, yoking magic with mystery, also links both character and quest to the role of the writer. Rees is allied to his murderous protagonist, but Bedford weaves the magic web of fiction: author as magician. The review extracts used on the covers support this reading of the text, emphasising Bedford's talent, the 'magic' or 'magical' aspects of his writing and, on the front-cover quotation, its circus-performative magic, as a 'high-wire act of a book'. The extracts on the first page of the prelims confirm the acclaim of the cover reviews, but they also add another element. Out of the eight quotations, four use the generic marker 'thriller'. It is qualified with such adjectives as 'stylish', 'intelligent', 'witty' and 'humane', but is striking in its recurrence. Whilst emphasising more philosophical themes, the review extracts also create a generic paratext for the novel that links it, though with a superlative status, to a mass-market genre. The review extract used on the second front cover, calling the novel 'This year's *Captain Corelli's Mandolin*', is an unusual example of marketing by analogy, as neither textually nor in terms of author biography does *The Houdini Girl* bear any relation to *Captain Corelli's Mandolin*. Rather, this is an example of a publisher referring to the word-of-mouth popularity of *Captain Corelli's Mandolin*, in the hope that it can be repeated.

There is a distinction between the crime novel and the thriller, however, and so the generic markers for *The Book of Dead Authors* and *The Houdini Girl* might seem to be ushering the books towards different categories. Nevertheless, there are thematic similarities between the two books (and between the two genres), not least in the foregrounded issues of sex and violence referred to in the cover copy of both. Moreover, and perhaps more interestingly in an analysis of the publishers' paratexts, the cover copy of both negotiate descriptions of genre, plot and themes, claiming both titles' inclusion within and elevation above genre formulae. These negotiations of design and format are nonetheless handled differently in each book. Whereas *The Book of Dead Authors* is B format, *The Houdini Girl* is the more traditionally mass-market A format, but with a cover design that signals its genre in a less straightforward way. The peepshow effect of the cut-out cover enforces a voyeuristic position on the reader at the threshold, one that is bound up with the themes of illusion and deception suggested by the cover copy. The position, though, is one more redolent of sex and mystery than violence. The copy and design make it less clearly categorisable – an indication, perhaps, of it belonging to the 'literary' genre – but its format, as well as some of the review extracts, suggest its affinity to the thriller. If the cover copy, design and format of Rees's book suggests his is a crime text with literary pretensions, Bedford's indicates it is a literary one packaged into the thriller market.

From an initial glance at Thomson's *The Book of Revelation*, neither the cover design nor format links it to the genres of crime or thriller. The object that hangs from the top of the front cover is not a body but a light bulb, an image striking in its starkness but not suggestive of any genre allegiance. The title and front cover quotation are equally enigmatic. The book may be 'exceptional' and 'perfect', but no indication is given of the genre of book of which it is a superlative example. It is published in B format. All these signals might suggest that the genre this book fits into is that of the 'literary' novel. The back cover augments this impression with an instance of marketing through author reputation. *The Book of Revelation* is cited as being 'from the bestselling author of *Soft* and *The Insult*'. It is not Bloomsbury's intent to create a reputation and market location for Thomson, but to reassert and expand an existing one. The publishers' copy, however, indicates how *The Book of Revelation* might in fact be allied to the other three books. It summons the language of mystery and crime to depict the central scenario of the novel: a man 'abduct[ed]' and 'imprison[ed]' by 'three strangers'. The sudden mysterious insertion of strangers into a successful artist's life has parallels with the publishers' copy on *The Book of Dead Authors*; its tropes of suspense are not dissimilar to *The Houdini Girl*'s strapline, 'Sometimes, when the lady vanishes, she stays vanished'. The consequences referred to at the end of the copy also, as in Bedford's book, proffer some analytical thoughts about the narrative (in *The Houdini Girl* 'betrayal, exploitation and violence are not simply part of the act', and in *The Book of Revelation* the 'consequences [...] are both poignant and highly disturbing'). Much of this similarity is to do with the necessarily concise structure of cover copy writing, which typically proceeds in the order (1) event (or scenario), (2) consequences, and (3) analysis. Such structures derive, of course, from the plots themselves – they are in part mini-plot summaries – and it might be said that the common structure is due to a common theme in literature: the disruption of normal life by an unusual event or stranger(s).[25]

A link is forged between Thomson's novel and the two previous ones, then, in generic terms, declared in the paratext. *The Book of Revelation* includes a healthy parade of review extracts that extend from the front and back covers right through the first four pages of the prelims. An array of genre possibilities are put forward here, from 'a true chiller' (*Guardian*), to 'the Sadean and Freudian genre' (*The New York Times*), to a 'literary crime novel' (*Times Literary Supplement*), to 'an unsettlingly dark vision, coupled with the elements of a thriller' (*Sunday Express*), to one of 'the small number of classic books about sex' (*Literary Review*), to 'part thriller, part meditation' (*Image*), to 'a twisted, pornographic tale of obsession' (*Face*), to 'a slick, modern-day Promenthean [sic] parable' (*Latest*), to 'erotica' and 'a serious and impressive novel' (*Sunday Times*), to 'bear[ing] comparison with the greats' (*Independent on Sunday*), to 'fable' (*New Statesman*), and again to 'thriller' (*Minx*). This variety of critical responses and the generic positionings suggested by the review extracts is the prevailing marketing characteristic of *The Book of Revelation*. It is conveyed as a novel with multiple taxonomic possibilities. Yet the jumble of taxonomic possibilities imply its adherence to the non-generic genre of the literary novel, at least until, as the back cover prompts and as one of the review extracts suggests ('if he's not yet recognised as one of our finest contemporary novelists, he soon will be' (*Daily Telegraph*)), Thomson is well-enough known to constitute his own brand.

The blurb on Litt's *Corpsing* departs from the structure deployed by *The Houdini Girl* and *The Book of Revelation* in favour of a more immediate description of a key narrative event: the shooting of the narrator's ex-girlfriend. It may hint at the narrative's development but does not express any analysis. The themes that are foregrounded are again of sex and violence, expressed here in the most overt way, as the bullet enters 'gorgeous, slightly-famous Lily [...] two inches below her left breast'. The blurb offers no time for reflection or encapsulation, but instead relies on vivid images. As with *The Book of Revelation*, the review extracts reveal a selection of generic statements about the text. It is a 'thriller' (*Mirror* and *Times Literary Supplement*), 'hard-boiled fiction' (*Big Issue*), and a 'conceptual, knowing, very metropolitan thriller' (*Sunday Times*). Two quotations refer to a (potential) film version, and hence the novel's filmic qualities. Perhaps one of the most interestingly chosen and placed quotations, though, is the one on the front cover from the *Guardian*, which reads, 'a remarkable crime debut'. *Corpsing* is described through this quotation both generically ('crime') and in terms of the author's career ('debut'). The blurb, design and format all substantiate the former claim, though the slick packaging might suggest that this is crime of a sophisticated, contemporary and urban nature, rather than a traditional mystery set in a sleepy village. The epithet 'debut', however, is a less obvious paratextual construction of Litt's novel. For *Corpsing* is not the work of a first-time novelist, but the author's second novel after *Beatniks* (1997), and his third publication after the short-story collection *Adventures in Capitalism* (1996).[26] *Corpsing* is not a debut novel but a debut *crime* novel, which through sleight of hand is presented as the first shot of a new crime writer. This sleight of hand is not a deceit, though, because Litt's two earlier works are mentioned in the author biography. Nonetheless, through the choice of this quotation, and the packaging, Litt is situated within the market as a crime novelist. Litt's entry into the crime genre has been an exercise in the repositioning of a writer's career, from a literary niche to a literary/crime crossover. Litt changed publisher from Secker & Warburg to Hamish Hamilton for the publication of *Corpsing* – a moment for both the author to reassess his career and for the new publisher to consider how to package and market their new acquisition, something which Hamish Hamilton appeared to have carried out through the paratextual negotiations.[27] Of all the four books examined here, Litt's name is the most prominent on the front cover. For readers new to Litt, he is presented as a new crime writer. For readers of Litt's earlier work, *Corpsing* is one point in his career trajectory. There is a slyly simultaneous appeal to different reading audiences occurring in the paratexts of the paperback edition of *Corpsing*, where differing levels of knowledge about the author's past career influence the reading experience.

What these four titles demonstrate is how genre definitions are made, at least in part, through the material form of the book. The forms that arise through publishers' decisions about a book's material presentation can sometimes give off conflicting messages – about whether a novel is or is not crime fiction, for example – but can also work towards creating new genre definitions that mix elements from existing patterns.

Such books are hybrids, and the theory of genre that accounts for them is based on the constitutive nature of paratextual activities, as well as contextual factors that affect genre fashion.[28] The placement of these titles in bookshops, to foreshadow the issue of shelving categories explored later in this chapter, is largely within the 'Fiction' section, but occasionally the titles are also – or instead – stocked in 'Crime', thus demonstrating the variability of genre definitions.[29]

Does this then mean that marketing – in its role as the creator of the paratext – is the primary means by which genre is defined? What place, then, has writing, either as the text itself or as the conscious activity of a writer, with models of writing in mind? Behind these paratextual prestidigitations, what is the role of texts and authors, and the processes of literary interpretation and literary invention, denuded from literary paratexts? Opacki, discussing these questions in 'Royal Genres', would throw such notions of the a priori nature of writing and genre definition into disarray:

> Genres do not have unchanging, fixed constitutive features. First of all, because of the 'transformation' which occurs in the course of [genre] evolution. Second – and this is more important in this case – because of the shifts in importance of distinguishing individual features of structure, depending on the literary context of the epoch or literary trend. In the course of evolution, not only does one genre change, but they all do, constituting as they do a context for that genre.[30]

What Opacki's arguments entail is that genre definition is not an absolute but a comparative process. To be specific, what might be perceived as a crime novel at one point (or by one person or community of people) is literary fiction at (or to) another. Genre definition is not controlled by structures but by the perception of prevalent structures at a given historical moment, and as such 'literary fiction', like all other genres, is contextually constituted. Hybridisation is one of the processes through which the evolutionary transformations occur; and the dominant perceptions (which come from, after Stanley Fish, dominant interpretive communities) of the results of such hybridisations determine genre fashion. Calling upon a number of genres to situate a book within the marketplace is not, therefore, simply a profit-orientated manoeuvre, designed to reach the largest possible market, but is illustrative of the processes of genre development and change. The writer can, however, take part in this process of development and change, by styling his or her writing to fit what they perceive to be popular genres in their era (or, in fact, to write in opposition to fashion). The impact of genre evolution on writers' decisions might therefore be the most meaningful textual interpretation of genre in the marketplace, whilst reinterpretations necessarily render texts subject to marketing and the vagaries of material and contextual representation.

Branding

Putting issues of marketing in the publishing industry into historical perspective, Nicci Gerrard comments in *Into the Mainstream* (1989) on the importance of genre categories to contemporary writing: 'The movement towards categorising works of fiction in order to package and market them more appealingly has been one of the major changes in the publishing world over the last two decades.'[31] Writing at the beginning of the period under consideration here, Gerrard also defines the work of 'genre publishing' as 'attempt[ing] to popularise literature through labelling'.[32] This tactic is a form of branding, a way of grouping and hence distinguishing products in the marketplace in order to capitalise on customer experience and perception of products and to maximise their visibility.[33] This market-led approach to publishing is of the sort contested by Allen Lane, in his differentiation of books from the broad mass of consumer products discussed in the previous chapter. Yet Gerrard's statement would suggest that since the Second World War, and particularly in its later decades, books have come to be perceived, and hence marketed, as those other products. How, then, has literature come to be labelled, and what is the place of branding books in the marketing process? What is the relation of ideas of brand to those of genre?

Jo Royle, Louise Cooper and Rosemary Stockdale, in their article 'The Use of Branding by Trade Publishers: An Investigation into Marketing the Book as a Brand Name Product' (1999/2000), began their study with an interrogation of the concept of books as products, noting that 'the perception remains that many consumers still do not identify with the publisher when buying a book, as they would identify with the brand, or product name, when buying other consumer goods.'[34] The belief in books as highly individualised products prejudices book marketing against the possibility of brand recognition, a belief also examined by Alison Baverstock in the opening chapter of *Are Books Different?*[35] Royle et al. set out to investigate how these perceptions might be changing in the contemporary marketplace, and how the tenets of consumer marketing can – and can't – be applied to trade publishing. They debate whether general marketing terms can be applied to publishing, asking the question, 'Does the publisher brand the imprint, the author, the individual book, the series, or a combination of these?'[36] Central to this question is the confused nature of what might actually constitute a publishing 'brand', a question that pays attention to the multiple agencies in the field of publishing and the variety of processes that occur within that field.

The evidence of Royle et al.'s consumer survey would indicate that imprints are, with some notable exceptions (they name Penguin, Dorling Kindersley and Virago), unsuccessful in creating identifiable brands, and thus imprint recognition is 'considerably less common than recognition of an author'.[37] According to their results, whilst '56 percent of book buyers had some awareness of publishers' brands [...] only 4 percent of those questioned thought that the imprint influenced their purchases, although a further 18 percent felt that it was a factor in their buying decisions.'[38] Although the gradations expressed in their survey are woolly (the exact difference between imprints influencing and being a factor in buying decisions is unclear), it is nonetheless apparent that imprints do not, for the main, play a large part in consumers' consciously stated decisions. The effect of less consciously appraised elements of imprint recognition is not discussed by Royle et al., however, because it is not linked to the processes of branding. Their formulation of the power of branding depends upon overt labelling and conscious recognition:

> Once brand identification has been achieved, companies can then add value to their brands, beyond the purely functional aspects of the product, to increase the power of the brand image [...] The powerful brand then promotes a social or lifestyle image with which the consumer identifies, as can be seen with brands such as Nike, Levi's, and Mercedes-Benz.[39]

Therefore, less consciously appraised elements that accrue to imprints are perceived as lacking in the capacity for 'add[ed] value' and hence are not true elements of branding. Such elements, however, are vital in genre definition, and are considered in greater detail in the next section on imprints. The effects of marketing through imprints to the intermediary of the trade are also glossed over, although it is mentioned that HarperCollins is a 'particularly strong brand with the retailers, but not with the consumer'.[40]

The major alternative discussed in the essay as a branding possibility is the author, who is named in Royle et al.'s consumer survey as 'the single most common reason for buying a book'.[41] The tenor of such findings is substantiated by bestseller list evidence. Royle et al. indicate the dominance of 'brand name authors' in the *Publishers' Weekly* 1997 lists; Alex Hamilton's assertions about the recurrence of established authors in his yearly Fastsellers charts demonstrate the same trend.[42] As Wernick theorises in 'Authorship and the Supplement of Promotion', 'authorial name is *promotional capital*'.[43] The way to achieve marketplace visibility thus seems tautological, as it is *already* to be a big seller for a previous book or books. Royle et al. support their argument with a comment from a *Bookseller* article to the effect that 'concentration in author sales' is attributed to the '"power of the author's brand. It is doubtful that the same [...] books would have sold as well if they had not been by a star author."'[44] Several factors might lead to such a conclusion. The first is the most obvious: that consumers will be drawn to books by authors they have already read. The second is that publishers will support authors with an established audience with continuing marketing support, and hence success breeds success. Thirdly, the publishers, booksellers and media will be working within established parameters: the author and his or her work is known, and hence there are obvious patterns for representing them to consumers. All these factors may contribute to the 'add[ed] value' of the author as brand name.

The author, however, does not brand the product only by lending a name to it, but by that name being incorporated into an array of paratextual strategies. The presentation of the name of the author on the cover of the book is an example. On one level, the letters that constitute the author's name have the straightforward role of informing the potential reader who the author is. Yet materiality once again intervenes: the letters are designed, however minimally or unostentatiously. It must be decided if the author's name will figure more or less prominently than the title, or in parity. The practical consideration of the length of title and author plays a part (Toby Litt's short and bookish name no doubt contributes to its prominence on *Corpsing*), but the privileging of the author name through either its greater size or visibility, or both, on the cover of a book becomes an indication of the importance of the author brand to the book's marketing. Along with the author name may also be further paratextual clues to the brand-seeking consumer. Royle et al. talk about the 'consistent image' that publishers create for some brand-name authors, nominating John Grisham's 'marbled jacket design' and Iain Banks's 'black and white textured surface' as examples.[45] Louis de

Bernières is another author treated to 'consistent' design, as the cover artist used for the paperback of *Captain Corelli's Mandolin*, Jeff Fisher, was commissioned to redesign de Bernières' backlist in a similar style. Thus de Bernières' novels make their branded appeal to consumers not solely through the assertion of the author's name, but also through a design recognition built around the author, as Angus Phillips explores in his article 'How Books are Positioned in the Market', which also considers how jacket design contributes to and signals market segmentation by its appeal to a variety of niche audiences.[46] Branding delivered through design can be crucial in the establishment of the writer's oeuvre, rather than a perception of their work as a collection of disparate titles – a factor which arguably contributes to the author's (potential) canonisation.

Attendant to this type of author-name branding is authorial fame. However, it also has an impact on the branding of lesser-known writers, as Royle et al. suggest, through their interviewee Victoria Singer, of the Marketing Department of Virago Press:

> for lesser-known authors we often make an association with well-known authors when marketing them. For example, we use front cover reviews by brand name authors, or give them similar, recognisable jacket designs. This exemplifies the extent to which author design and packaging is integral to the brand, as the reader is able to make an immediate association, not just for a single author's titles, but for others throughout the publisher's list.[47]

Endorsement is an overt form of association. '"Similar, recognisable jacket designs"' make a less overt appeal, though the associations they make may not be any more subtle. The first edition hardback publication of Paul Johnston's debut novel *Body Politic* (1997), for example, with its stylised black and white image of the Edinburgh skyline, seems a very conscious echoing of the designs used on the jackets of Johnston's more famous fellow Scottish novelist, Iain Banks.[48] The rash of covers employing the *Captain Corelli's Mandolin* artist, including books by William Dalrymple and Amanda Craig, also use a form of association.[49] Given the variety of books with Jeff Fisher cover designs, it is perhaps not the specific genre in which *Captain Corelli's Mandolin* might be placed that is being called to mind, but rather the success that it stands for, as with the review extract on Bedford's *The Houdini Girl*. Through such imitative design literary fashions can become apparent, though the extent to which these fashions are sustained textually is less immediately clear. Fisher's ubiquitous cover designs demonstrate that publishers do not

necessarily imply textual similarity but rather are signa
sense of the reading satisfaction it will provide, and the ma
hopefully give them.

Cover design, therefore, indicates branding strategies in the publishing industry.[50] Brand images, particularly author brand images, work towards creating associations in readers' minds which may or may not be related to formal similarities in texts. Branding – in the form of design – thus promotes material analogies. The book is used as a vehicle to express certain interpretations of and aspirations for the book, which may in fact be contradicted by textual readings. The assertion of generic and cultural categories through branding is consequently a negotiation with the various systems that assert meaning. Branding asserts its meanings through alliance and association, with endorsement and cover design as two of its key tools. What an account of publishing representations viewed through the prism of branding might fail to do, though, is consider the other paratextual as well as textual means by which literature is constructed in the marketplace. This might well have something to do with the problematic issue of what a publishing brand might actually be, as Royle et al. indicate in their conclusion:

> trade publishers are becoming increasingly aware of the need to consider brands and brand image in their marketing strategies, but the problem of fitting the practicalities of book publishing to the theory of marketing concepts remains a difficult one.[51]

The varieties of possible publishing brands – imprint, author, individual book, series, or a combination of these – suggest that concepts of genre cannot always account for, or be indicated through, branding. Branding is a marketing concept which does not always fit snugly into the institutional and cultural structures of the publishing industry and its products. Literary fiction imprints might be thought of as particularly averse to branding, given that literary fiction is not largely published to formulae or in series. Imprints, however, are an important marketing structure within the publishing industry and so their role in genre negotiations and the making of literature is explored next.

Imprint

Michael Legat, in *An Author's Guide to Publishing*, discusses how choices might be made about imprint, brand and genre (if a writer is in the comfortable position of being able to choose):

> To some extent the question of which publisher to choose may become a little easier if certain of the people who work in publishers' marketing departments, who are growing in power and influence [...], are correct in predicting that one of the future aims of publishers will be to establish themselves as brand names. By this they mean that publishing houses will attempt to become known for publishing certain genres of books. Some brand names already exist – Mills & Boon, the premier brand name for romances, is the perfect example, and there are numerous other firms which are noted for particular categories of books. This concept, incidentally, also ties into the idea of 'niche publishing'.[52]

Legat's conjunction of brand and genre, and how an author's work might best be supported in a publishing context through its association with the brand leader in the genre field, asserts the importance of imprint, or the publisher's 'brand name', in marketing. But to what extent is Legat's vision of imprints in a marketing-led future becoming reality? How does such a vision vary from market sector to market sector? And how is the publishing of literary fiction in particular affected by imprint?

The most visible impact of imprints upon literary publishing – indeed upon UK publishing as a whole – is not that of marketing, but as the kind of living archaeology discussed in Chapter 1. Tracing the transpositions of these imprints as they go through series of mergers and acquisitions is one way of constructing publishing history. As *Marketing Literature* concentrates on the representations made by marketing, however, publishers' imprints fit into the investigation more properly by way of the cultural values they transmit and the material states they inhabit. In this context, then, the relevance of imprints, though not disassociated from their histories, is in their role in creating cultural categories.

As Royle et al. assert in their report, however, imprint only achieves brand value in occasional cases, and much more readily in some sectors than others. In the industry analysis *Book Publishing in Britain* (1999), the possibility of publishing brands is addressed by the question, 'what guarantees the position of consumer publishers in the value chain?'[53] The market sectors where brands are seen to predominate (text-based reference, travel guides, out-of-copyright literary classics, exam revision guides and instructional publishing) and sometimes work effectively (home reference, egg-head series publishing, genre fiction, hobby reference, anthologies) are set in contrast to other sectors, particularly the general trade sector. Branding is perceived as 'not relevant to 80% of consumer book publishing. In most areas of consumer book publishing it is the name of the author, the subject matter or the design of the book which catches the customer's eye.'[54]

Exceptions can be found to this rule, of course, particularly by the brand-leading imprints referred to in *Book Publishing in Britain*. A reader might, if pushed, name some fiction imprints, among which is likely to be Penguin, whose early entry into paperback mass-marketing, as well as its branded designs, gave the company a flying start in the imprint recognition stakes. Faber and Faber's illustrious literary history and poetry imprint still stands for something, though whether its fiction inspires greater recognition than a host of other fiction imprints is debatable. The distinctive green-jacketed Virago Modern Classics held their sway over sectors of the reading public for a while. In the late 1970s and 1980s, Picador was taken as the standard for serious, innovative literary fiction, so much so that the (then) new Pandora imprint at HarperCollins modelled itself on Picador's lines. Gerrard wrote of Pandora that 'The fiction list, which in the past has been unplanned and without its own distinctive character, will under Kate Figes apparently take on a clear identity: "We want contemporary, exciting, international and provocative novels; we think of ourselves as a Woman's Picador."'[55]

These comments suggest that there is a gendered discourse connected to some imprints. Virago became well known for its feminist stance.[56] The emphasis towards male writers during Picador's ascendancy was so pronounced that when Peter Straus moved to Picador as its publisher in 1990, he encountered 'a general idea that Picador couldn't (and shouldn't) publish women writers', as he put it in interview. By the end of the 1990s the prejudice had been turned on its head, with the two biggest selling authors on the list being Helen Fielding and Kathy Lette.[57]

Generally, however, imprint name, particularly within literary fiction publishing, is not a means by which publishers can make a direct appeal to the potential reader. It can nonetheless be crucial in the determination of genre and from thence to the formation of cultural categories. Part II investigates a specific instance – via *American Psycho*, one of Picador's publications – of how imprints can be formative in the creation of cultural categories. This chapter makes general points about how, despite the evidence to suggest that it is not a key consideration in reader choice, imprint is nevertheless incorporated into marketing.

Kirsty Fowkes, while an editor at Hodder & Stoughton, stated in interview that the publisher's imprint functions as a 'collusion' between the publisher, the media and the bookselling trade.[58] Unlike a member of the reading public, who is not involved in the industry and has neither much knowledge of, or concern with, industry structure, a newspaper's literary editor or a head office bookseller will have a much stronger idea of imprint orientation and reputation. Newspaper reports of literary prizes frequently tot up the long- and shortlisted total achieved by particular imprints, and de Bellaigue uses the number of shortlistings by imprints in order to argue for the continuing quality of publishing under conglomerate rule.[59] The imprint is then not so much a brand as a signal sent down the chain of 'push' marketing and publishing intermediaries.[60] This system is in some ways a convenient shorthand, so that a newspaper's literary editor will more likely commission a review of a new Picador novel than one from its mass-market paperback imprint stablemate, Pan (both these are Macmillan imprints). The genre classifications established through bookshop design also draw on this shorthand: books from crime imprints will be shelved in the crime section. In its most extreme form, such signals can be prejudicial, a means by which media and trade opinion is coerced by the paratext. The case of *American Psycho* is an example of where the collusive properties of imprint were undermined as the reviewers perceived a mismatch in text and paratext.

Even earlier in the publication cycle, imprint plays a part in the submission process, whereby agents carefully select, through the predilections of both the editor and the imprint, where to send their clients' manuscripts. The networks that individuals within the industry form are influential here, but so too are the positions they take, so that, for example, when the agent David Godwin was dealing with the script of Arundhati Roy's *The God of Small Things*, he sent it out to about six publishers, whom he termed 'the obvious ones'.[61] Godwin thought it important that the book be viewed as literary, and consequently be published by a literary imprint, but he was also concerned for it not to be in the shadow of Salman Rushdie at Jonathan Cape or Vikram Seth at Orion. When the agent and author are in the advantageous position of being able to choose their publisher, imprint is a key consideration in asserting genre. An agent might want to contravene the 'obvious' imprint collusions. An example is that of Alexandra Pringle, who sold the rights for Lucy Ellmann's *Man or Mango* (1998) and Ronan Bennett's *The Catastrophist* (1997) to Headline Review.[62] According to Pringle, 'some people did suggest [I] was mad to sell [...] to Headline

Review, because it was known as a mass-market company', an attitude she puts down to 'snobbery'.[63] Headline is known as a mass-market company though its imprint Headline Review, on which Rees's *The Book of Dead Authors* was published, is a relatively young and developing literary list. 'Snobbery' – an over-dependence on the hierarchy of cultural categories – indicates how literary value is created and sustained through collusion, and how it can also be circumvented, and made anew for both promotional and cultural effect.

Collusion, then, is the way in which imprints are used by industry insiders, in order to assert genre and signal value judgements through the chain of intermediaries. Imprint's role is performative, and the collusion between publishers and other industry workers that it instigates functions as a way of constructing value and sustaining categorisation. These values and judgements are not directly communicated to a more general readership, but mediated. The browser in the bookshop, and the newspaper reader, will have the collusive values of imprint communicated to him or her indirectly.

The communication of perceived imprint value is joined by a more peritextual mediation of genre and value. How books look is reliant to a large degree on the imprint on which they are published. Format and design can be crucial in determining genre, as this chapter has argued, but, reciprocally, imprint can be crucial in determining format and design. Peter Straus, in an article discussing 'Format' (1996), states that 'variable formats are aimed at different sections of the market and are also used to underline the change and development in a writer's career'.[64] One of the examples he uses is that of Joanna Trollope, 'the B-format sensation of 1992'.[65] Black Swan rethought the packaging of her front and backlist, bringing the paperbacks of her novels out in B rather than A format, thereafter achieving commercial success and also, in the longer term, critical acclaim. The B format package began, Straus writes, as an attempt by the new imprints Picador and Abacus to differentiate themselves in 1972 from 'the mass-market norm of Pan, Penguin, Panther and Fontana'.[66] This process of differentiation is both one of appealing to new or different markets, as in the case of the 'Crime Boys', but also of staking value claims and of elevating a title from one level in the perceived hierarchy of genre to another.

What the imprint of a book tells a reader about the genre of the text, then, depends on the position of the reader within the publishing field. Given that, within general trade publishing, imprints do not frequently function as brands, readers should be split into groups of industry insiders and outsiders, or those with a greater or lesser knowledge of the structure of the industry, the history of its imprints, and the sorts of book each is known for publishing. The collusion mentioned by Fowkes demonstrates how imprint works as a signalling device without developing conscious brand recognition. The communication of such messages to a potential reading public then occurs through mediating agencies, such as bookshop design and literary prizes, the subject of the final two sections of this chapter.

The bookshop

In the bookshop, through the spaces of bookshop design, the customer comes face to face with the 'conscious' component of genre, to use Duff's terminology. A snapshot analysis of the layout of three high street chain bookshops in Oxford – Blackwell's, Borders and Waterstone's – and one small independent, The QI Bookshop, provides examples of the genre taxonomies of the publishing industry.[67]

All three chain bookshops are similar in keeping their fiction stock in or towards the front section of their ground floors. In Waterstone's, even before the division of titles on the ground floor, the majority of books have been placed elsewhere: children's books in the basement, for example; literary studies, poetry and biographies on the second floor (along with a café concession); and computing and popular science on the third. Blackwell's – which has different shops for music, art and locally-themed books – has a large downstairs room with travel and academic books. On its first floor, it also features a café concession, dictionaries, languages and linguistics. On the second floor are history and rare books, while the third floor carries a selection of second-hand books. Fiction shares the ground floor with children's books. Borders, which has two large floors, has its stock of music and videos/DVDs on the basement floor, along with its children's section, cookery, sport and gardening. The ground floor also has a café, a Paperchase concession, an extensive selection of newspapers and magazines, and history, religion, philosophy and science.

The ground floor of Waterstone's is almost, but not exclusively, devoted to fiction. It has sections for Fiction, Crime, Classics, short story anthologies, Fiction in Translation, the Hardback Chart and the Paperback Chart, Crime Bestsellers, Essential Reading, New Books, sections entitled Oxford Recommends and Fine Writing – Trust Us…, and a seasonal display for Man Booker Prize Longlist titles. It also has a number of tables with selections of sale and 3 for 2 books – the types of promotions discussed in Chapter 1.

Moving around the ground floor of this particular shop, confronted by these arrangements, the customer receives an impression of the output of the publishing industry subdivided into various categories: fiction; classics; crime (these last three subdivided alphabetically by author); short stories (subdivided by publisher); books recommended by the retailer; the book (fiction or non-fiction; paperback or hardback) that sells well (subdivided into descending order). This last is the category that is the most contextual of all, being in no way dependent on the book's contents (though the contents may, of course, have contributed to the sales success).

Blackwell's divides its stock along similar but still different lines. It has separate sections for Fiction (with pre-1945 fiction on the first floor), and also for crime, science fiction and graphic novels. There are separate hardback sections for the first three of these categories. It also has separate shelves for Blackwell's Bestsellers, Books of the Month, Staff Choice Fiction, Signed Copies, Oxford Novels, Prize Winners and Shortlists (as well as a Booker Prize Longlist display), Audio Books and separate bays for the individual authors J. R. R. Tolkien and C. S. Lewis.

Borders has yet another system of categorising its work. It does not divide its fiction into hardback and paperback shelving, but rather has them mixed together alphabetically by author surname. However, it has further sections of shelving devoted to wider categories of 'genre' fiction than either Waterstone's or Blackwell's has: in addition to crime and science fiction, it also has horror and romance. Like the other shops, it has a series of tables featuring a range of promotional offers (3 for 2), as well as tables with new paperback and hardback fiction. It also has, on the survey date, Bestseller, Borders Oxford loves... and Brand New for Autumn shelving.

The impression of publishing industry categories received by a customer walking around Waterstone's would be furthered by visiting Blackwell's and Borders, although the differences between the categories in the three shops might begin to confuse. For there are a jumble of categories here. Some, like the bestsellers, rely on contextual characteristics. The short story anthologies arranged by publisher in Waterstone's are both contextually (through the cultural institutions and business organisations that produce them) and materially (through the placing of the imprint logo on the book itself) defined. Crime or romance novels, although equally bound in a web of contextual and material concerns (imprint placement, cover design, and so on), might more readily be said to be categorised textually, through a satisfaction of the structural demands of the crime or romance plot. A confusion of categories in the bookshops, however, means that a particular title could cross the shop floor, and find an alternative section of shelving in which to be placed. The novels of Alan Hollinghurst, for example, could be found in the fiction or paperback section or, perhaps, if there were one, in a gay and lesbian writing shelving.[68] Here, a variety of elements allow different attributions: the 'literary' nature of the texts; the sexuality of the author; the sexuality of his characters. Shop shelving might thus be thought of as the physical manifestation of a series of Venn diagrams, with Hollinghurst situated at the crossover of 'Gay writers', 'Gay subject matter', and 'Literary fiction'. Further categories could be adduced: 'Writers over the age of 40'; 'English writers'; 'Novels set in Belgium'. The categories could become more and more abstruse – or rather less obviously ordered along the lines of most chain and independent bookshops. The QI Bookshop, also in Oxford, for example, presents a very different proposition to the browser. As well as being tiny compared to the square footage of the chain stores, the shop is categorised in an original way which consciously pulls away from the more standard ways of ordering books, although it does have a QI Bestsellers table, and shelving sections for Prize Winners and Book Club Classics. It has shelving categories such as The Good Life, Modest Proposals, The Sea, Ice, Books about Books, Lives, Secret Lives and Relations. Sorted under these categories are both fiction and non-fiction, with the linkage between the shelving and the individual book not always being readily apparent. Its shelving policy marks it out from the chains, and encourages the potential reader to browse and to ponder the links between categories and individual titles. Niche bookshops such as QI are a reminder that layout – and categorisation – could be done entirely otherwise. The Travel Bookshop in London's Notting Hill, for example, categorises its stock by geographical location, mixing travel guides with other non-fiction, poetry and novels.[69] Hollinghurst's novel *The Folding Star* (1994), then, could slot into the 'Belgium' subsection of 'Europe'.

This jumble of taxonomic possibilities, these overlapping or incompatible categories, are reminiscent of Borges's Chinese encyclopaedia, summoned by Michel Foucault to preface *The Order of Things: An Archaeology of the Human Sciences* (1966).[70] Of the publishing industry, it might be asked, what are these categories, and what are the knowledge systems from which they derive? What happens to our understanding when the categories are physically placed side by side, as they are on the shop floor? Foucault's analysis of the aphasiac, 'consistently unable to arrange' coloured skeins of wool into a coherent pattern, is the end result of categorial uncertainty, in which 'the sick mind continues to infinity, creating groups then dispersing them again, heaping up diverse similarities, destroying those that seem clearest, splitting up things that are identical, superimposing different criteria, frenziedly beginning all over again, becoming more and more disturbed, and teetering finally on the brink of anxiety.'[71] The metaphor of the sick, aphasiac, mind might seem an extreme one to apply to the publishing industry, but its image of taxonomic disruption pushed towards 'the brink of anxiety' is not inappropriate, given the increasing number of books produced and hence the continual reinvention of genre categories of post-war publishing. The image of sickness, however, is a negative diagnosis of the sort discussed in the Introduction, one that certainly underpins many accounts of the industry. Rather than enter such evaluative debate, this chapter moves on to another of the ways by which communication with the potential reading public is conducted – literary prizes.

Literary prizes

The previous elements examined as factors affecting genre are closely connected to the book trade's activities. Literary prizes are one of the wider agencies involved in book marketing, and are not, on the whole, initiated, let alone controlled, by publishers. Nonetheless, prizes still play a crucial role in the interaction between genre and the marketplace, and are one of the forces that come to influence notions of cultural value and literariness. Ostensibly, what every book award might claim to do is to recognise and reward value. A corollary part of this mission is, then, the promotion of the winner or winners: literary prizes can bring relatively unknown writers to public recognition, enhance the reputation of already established authors, turn the attention of the media to books, and so support the consumption of literature generally. As such, the role of literary prizes is already more complex than as an index of literary achievement, and they have a broad range of motivations and implications.[72] Moreover, awarding a prize to a book acts not only to indicate value, but also to confer it. Value is thus doubly constructed in the realm of literary prizes. Yet even before the role of literary prizes in constituting notions of value is assessed, and the contingent nature of value examined, the organisational structures of prizes suggest how they contribute to genre definition and literary categorisation. requirements for each prize provide the key to this. The Booke example, 'aims to reward the best novel of the year written by a British or Commonwealth author'.[73] The novel must also be originally written in English and published by a UK-based publishing house. The definition that the prize gives is to do with national and regional identity, and also the market through which the novel has been published. This definition has contributed to analyses of the Booker Prize as promoting postcolonial writing from within the context of UK cultural imperialism.[74] What is of greater direct impact on the definition of genre, though, is the first part of the description: 'the best novel'. This may seem at first glance to be an absolute definition (within the already circumscribed entry requirements), but by placing it alongside the entry requirements of other prizes its function with regard to genre becomes apparent. A brief survey of the 'Prizes and Awards' section of the *Writers' and Artists' Yearbook* yields, among others, a list including the Boardman Tasker Prize (for the best book 'concerned with the mountain environment'), the Arthur C. Clarke Award (for 'best science fiction novel'), the Betty Trask Award (for the best first novels 'of a romantic or traditional nature'), the Crime Writers' Association 'Daggers' (for best crime writing), the Encore Award (for 'best second novel'), the Lichfield Prize (for the best novel 'based recognisably on the geographical area of Lichfield District, Staffordshire'), the Saltire Scottish Book of the Year (for the best book by 'any author of Scottish descent or living in Scotland, or for a book by anyone which deals with the work or life of a Scot or with a Scottish problem, event or situation').[75] Some, such as the Arthur C. Clarke and the Crime Writers' Association awards use traditional genre definitions, while others choose quite different categorisations. What these entry requirements do, be they stated in terms of the book's subject matter, genre, or author biography, is to indicate a series of *relative* 'bests'. It is in this comparative light that Booker's definition of 'the best novel' acquires generic implications. For the Booker is awarded to the best non-genre novel or, in other words, the best 'literary' novel. By not naming the category, though, what the Booker does is to confirm the 'literary' novel at the top of genre hierarchies. The phrase 'best novel' equates with 'best literary novel', and so it is implied that the winner of the Booker is better than the winner of the Arthur C. Clarke.

Based on the categories of their entry requirements, literary prizes construct notions of value through their choice of winners. Richard Todd's *Consuming Fictions* is premised on the idea that the Booker Prize and its winners have been crucial in broadening the appeal of 'serious literary fiction' from UK publishers, both in home and overseas (particularly the US) markets.[76] Todd's thesis is that the increasing commodification of literary fiction through the course of the 1980s and 1990s, a development led by the Booker Prize, has had the effect of turning writers to particular themes and treatments of themes:

> the novelists I discuss have worked in an increasingly intensified atmosphere, one in which both the promotion and the reception of serious literary fiction have become steadily more consumer-oriented. How many of even the most interesting postcolonial writers of recent years, for example, are – however subconsciously, with whatever desire to say something new – now responding both aesthetically and commercially to the 1980s as 'the Rushdie decade'? Or – likewise – how many slush-pile literary detective novels with a double historical time-scheme has A. S. Byatt's *Possession* spawned?
>
> Such self-conscious commercial categorization offers a real challenge to today's novelists, agents, publishers and readers.[77]

Todd's claim is an interesting one, though difficult to sustain in terms of textual analysis. The real benefit of his thinking, though, is to suggest how agencies such as literary prizes alter perceptions of success, and thus construct notions of genre and value.

The Whitbread Book Awards are particularly apposite to the question of the interaction of literary prizes and genre because of their idiosyncratic organisation. Unlike the Booker, whose parameters are only occasionally interrogated, and much more often on the grounds of its nationality requirements and its post-colonial eligibility structures, the Whitbread's structure of categories casts its observers into immediate ontological doubt. Since 1985, the Whitbread has operated with five separate category awards, each with its own judging panel, shortlist and section winner. In 1999, for example, the section winners were Rose Tremain's *Music and Silence* (1999) for the Novel Award, David Cairns's *Berlioz Volume Two: Servitude and Greatness 1832–1869* (1999) for the Biography Award, Seamus Heaney's *Beowulf* (1999) for the Poetry Award, and J. K. Rowling's *Harry Potter and the Prisoner of Azkaban* (1999) for the Children's Book of the Year.[78] The final judging stage then pits category against category: biography against poetry, first novel against later novels, a task which must yearly fill the judges with a momentary horror as they scrabble for a critical vocabulary to make sense of such disparate artistic forms. The very idea of having a separate category for the novel and the first novel starts to unravel if the first novel section winner goes on to win the main award, as Kate Atkinson's *Behind the Scenes at the Museum* (1995) did.[79] How are the judges to compare an elegantly slim volume of poetry and a encyclopaedically mammoth life? What, moreover, is a panel to make of a book of poetry that is also heavily autobiographical, such as Ted Hughes's *Birthday Letters* (overall award winner of 1998)?[80] These questions of category – questions which demand the comparison of different genres – are not insurmountable, as the Whitbread judges prove each year. Rather, what the questions do is to foreground the construction of value through genre, enshrining a notion of hybridity in its cross-genre judging system. Bud McLintock of Karen Earl Ltd., the Director of the Awards, believes this echoes contemporary reading practices: 'Readers don't tend to make the distinctions that critics make in their reading habits, and the Whitbread Book Awards reflect this.'[81] The model of a cross-genre reader, choosing his or her reading matter from a variety of types and sources, is in accord with Connor's analysis of post-war reading in *The English Novel in History 1950–1995*, in which he writes that:

> If there ever was a moment in which it could be assumed that readers were identical with the readerships to which they belonged [...it] has given way to a condition in which readers [...] typically have multiple affiliations and participate in multiple readerships and forms of reading. [...]
>
> Positing the existence of interpretive groups, or communities of taste, may be useful mostly in order to help to register the effect of the multiple allegiances which precisely work to dissolve the clarity of such groups.[82]

Connor's reference, by way of 'interpretive groups, or communities of taste', to Stanley Fish's theories, suggests the complexity of post-war reading patterns, something which Delany also asserts in noting the shift from product differentiation to market segmentation. This is precisely the challenge to both the industry and its analysts: to 'register the effect of the multiple allegiances' both in terms of patterns of consumption and the impact on the material product.

The addition of the Children's Book of the Year to the overall Whitbread Awards, discussed in Part II, highlights the dialogue the literary prizes have with genre, the marketplace and its consumers. For while Whitbread's exercise in genre comparison might be thought an experiment that threatens to loose the riotous border-crossing of relativism upon demarcated aesthetic boundaries, it should also be seen as a self-conscious example of the general function of literary prizes with respect to genre. The structure of the Awards is such that the very notion of genre boundaries is contested, both supporting and undermining genre divisions in the promotion of literature and reading.

Literary prizes, then, use literary categorisation, both by confirming and contesting existing categories and creating and influencing new ones. They are integrally involved with the processes of canonisation, both by choosing works to reward and promote, but also by defining the ways in which they are chosen. Genre, as well as being created and reflected by the book itself, by branding, by imprints and by retail practice, is crucially influenced by the interventions of wider agencies, such as literary prizes. In addition to being an integrated and integral part of the publishing industry's business practice, marketing therefore operates via a range of publishing activities and publishing intermediaries in order to represent books and authors in the literary marketplace. In so doing, it actively influences reception, negotiates with genre and constructs and reshapes notions of literary value and taste. Through branding, through packaging, through imprints, through bookshop shelving strategies, and through literary prizes, the marketing of literature works actively to create cultural meanings.

Part II
Publishing Histories

4
Icons and Phenomenons

Introduction

Part II of *Marketing Literature* addresses the publishing histories of a series of high-profile books from the 1990s and 2000s. The case studies are divided into three chapters, in which various different models of success, and aspects of the books' marketing, are analysed in empirical detail, thus illustrating the contemporary literary marketplace, and the marketing activities by which that marketplace is constructed. The books contained within these chapters are all examples of books which have achieved a certain level of fame or notoriety in the marketplace, either through commercial or critical success, or by the discussion they have provoked in the media – their economic, cultural and journalistic capital. All of these books could also be designated to a greater or lesser degree as 'literary' titles, although some are very much situated as 'cross-over' books, including the children's and young adults' books discussed in Chapter 6. The construction of the definition of the literary via the marketplace, though, is part of the argument of these chapters.

This chapter, 'Icons and Phenomenons', investigates two of the highest-profile titles of the contemporary period. Louis de Bernières' *Captain Corelli's Mandolin* (1994) and Martin Amis's *The Information* (1995) both achieved a remarkable level of recognition in the marketplace. Because of this degree of recognition, these books present key case studies revealing not only details of the individual books and authors, but also point towards a broader understanding of the contemporary marketplace, activities within it, and attitudes towards it. Because of the extent to which Amis has already been addressed in scholarly writing, the section on him is briefer than that of de Bernières. The next sequence of case studies is entitled 'Marketing Stories'. The books assessed within it – Irvine Welsh's *Trainspotting* (1993), Pat Barker's *The Ghost Road* (1995) and Arundhati Roy's *The God of Small Things* (1997) – reveal a range of different marketing models and routes to success. The final series of case studies are collected under the title 'Crossovers'. Within this chapter are books which, because of the impact of packaging, imprint, media coverage and literary prizes, have traversed genres and, through these effects of marketing, have seen their value constructed and reconstructed in the marketplace, and their textual interpretations radically influenced as a result. The books are Bret Easton Ellis's *American Psycho* (1991), Helen Fielding's *Bridget Jones's Diary* (1996), J. K. Rowling's *Harry Potter* novels (1997–2007), Philip Pullman's *His Dark Materials* trilogy (1995–2000), Mark Haddon's *The Curious Incident of the Dog in the Night-Time* (2003) and finally David Mitchell's *Cloud Atlas* (2004).

A note about the choice of books: the aim is not to suggest which of these successful books from the 1990s and 2000s will still be read – or even studied – in decades to come. As the Introduction stated, the choice of titles is made not with an eye to the future but to the present and the very recent past, in which all of these books have found a place in the contemporary public consciousness. This place is indicated by their sales success, critical reception and media recognition, as the individual case studies narrate. Their place has also been indicated by the manner in which the titles have come to be mentioned in wider literary, social and political debate; so, for example, *Trainspotting* is cited in debates about Scottish devolution and drugs culture, and *Bridget Jones's Diary* has occasioned a wealth of articles on the nation's demographics and on (post-)feminism. The *Harry Potter* series and the *His Dark Materials* trilogy are frequently cited in debates about children's reading habits and literacy, and the value attached to children's literature. *Captain Corelli's Mandolin* is the bestseller par excellence which is representative of the publishing industry at its most successful, and consumers at their most voracious. The titles discussed in this part are, then, paradigmatic as well as particular successes, and while the case studies of their publishing histories largely begin by establishing local detail, they move towards more general models of literary transmission and reception. A phenomenal book can indicate aspects of the functioning of the marketplace, and its relation to society more broadly, as well, if not better, than a more normative example might. As John Mitchinson writes of bestsellers, 'They are what make our trade interesting to the outside world; they are barometers of public taste, the harbingers of the new and one of the obvious indices of our creativity.'[1] Sutherland reiterates this in his introduction to *Reading the Decades*, seeing the 'popular book' as a 'sociological experiment that has worked', and that the process of looking at bestsellers is 'like running one's fingers over a topographical map of British social history'.[2] Yet as Clive Bloom says in *Bestsellers*, these books are also more than a 'barometer of contemporary imagination', as they are additionally 'part and parcel of a sociological climate that includes an aesthetic dimension and in which the sociological and aesthetic are symbiotically joined, but where neither is reducible to the other'.[3] Nonetheless, each of the titles contained within the chapter could potentially be replaced by another. In the 2000s, Dan Brown's *The Da Vinci Code* has been a phenomenal bestseller. On a more modest scale, Sebastian Faulks's *Birdsong* (1993), another First World War novel, was a notable word-of-mouth success like *Captain Corelli's Mandolin*.[4] Nick Hornby's *High Fidelity* (1995) has been as indicative of the state of contemporary masculinity as *Bridget Jones's Diary* has been of femininity.[5] However, the titles analysed within the case studies are chosen for their varied routes to success and the different models of marketing they therefore illustrate. With his first novel, Irvine Welsh went only gradually from a little-known cult author to popular and critical recognition, whereas Arundhati Roy achieved instant, prepublication fame with hers. Entirely different from the meteoric rise of *The God of Small Things, The Ghost Road*'s success was sealed only after Barker's already lengthy career, as was Philip Pullman's approach to the crossover and adult market after decades of writing for children. Each of these case studies, then, attempts to illustrate a different facet of the making of contemporary writing in Britain, while simultaneously contributing to the overall argument about the impact of marketing on the production, dissemination and reception of literature.

Louis de Bernières' *Captain Corelli's Mandolin* (1994)[6]

On 11 January 1999, an affecting story appeared in the *Independent* newspaper:

> Life has imitated art for an Italian man and a Greek woman who rekindled their wartime romance after more than half a century, mirroring the story in the literary bestseller *Captain Corelli's Mandolin* [...]
>
> The story of Luigi Surace and Angeliki Stratigou began in August 1941, when Mr Surace was sent to the Greek port city of Patras. He met and fell in love with Miss Stratigou, aged 23, and promised to marry her.

> When the war ended, he wrote to Miss Stratigou who was living with her aunt. Her aunt intercepted and destroyed the letters. After three years with no reply Mr Surace gave up.
>
> He married in Italy but when his wife died in 1996 he began to search for Miss Stratigou. She was living in Patras and had never married. On Saint Valentine's Day last year they met and Mr Surace, aged 77, proposed marriage. Miss Stratigou, 79, accepted.
>
> The wedding was to have taken place on 22 December. Mr Surace was unwell and the date was put back. He has partially recovered and everything was set to go ahead in two weeks. Then, unexpectedly, Miss Stratigou fell ill. She died on Saturday. However, Mr Surace has not yet been told.[7]

The tragic history of Mr Surace and Miss Stratigou contains the elements of a romantic classic: a couple separated by war and society, water and time. But the reason for its inclusion in the *Independent* is not for the story in itself, or its reflection of the troubled history of Europe in the twentieth century. Its presence is due to a quite different phenomenon: that of the bestseller. Life is not really imitating art, as the first line has it, but the similarities between two stories – one fiction, one fact – are sufficient to deem Surace and Stratigou newsworthy. Romance and tragedy are powerful forces in themselves, but a quite different myth – that of the bestselling book, and specifically of *Captain Corelli's Mandolin* – is the rationale for reporting the story.

Captain Corelli's Mandolin was initially published in hardback in 1994. In line with the hardback sales of de Bernières' three previous novels, *The War of Don Emmanuel's Nether Parts* (1990), *Señor Vivo and the Coca Lord* (1991) and *The Troublesome Offspring of Cardinal Guzman* (1992), the initial print run was comparatively low – only 1500 copies.[8] Yet by the beginning of 1999, sales had reached one million.[9] In 1997, after the novel had started to sell sensationally well, articles seeking to assess the phenomenon began to appear in the media. Joanna Pitman's article in *The Times* in November 1997 is a key example:

> What most readers want is a good old-fashioned, intelligent story, a really compelling book that, according to Norman Mailer's dictum, might change us a little. There are books like this, plenty of them, but they just need to be dug out from the wordy morass. And a very few of them, the really good ones, have a way of selling themselves that defies the marketing strategies of publishers and booksellers. These are the rare volumes that turn into modern classics.

> So, what is that indefinable quality that makes an apparently unassuming novel a modern classic? For a start, it doesn't need to be specially boxed, packaged, discounted or categorised. It doesn't need helping along with hype and column inches and author interviews. It doesn't have to be marketed like mad and then pushed off the shelves within six months to make way for the next product in the trend. These books sell themselves, and continue to sell.
>
> The key to the success of the modern classic is that you have to be told about it – by the quiet, intimate and mysterious process of word of mouth [...] with a personal recommendation you feel that you're in good hands [...]
>
> A good example is *Captain Corelli's Mandolin* [...] First published in 1995 [sic...] it is still walking off the shelves [...] This book, as de Bernières says himself, just will not lie down and die. But Captain Corelli has never been put through the hype machine. The title has not been pushed with noisy special offers, blazing ads or free mandolin strings.[10]

By introducing the concept of 'word of mouth', Pitman's argument is that bestsellers are created by readers, who read and recommend without being prompted by 'hype and column inches and author interviews'. Her formulation is peculiar: of a book that succeeds *despite* its publishers' intentions and those of booksellers, and which *defies* their marketing strategies. Pitman argues that *Captain Corelli's Mandolin* side-stepped the industry and made its appeal directly to its readership without the intercession of publisher or bookseller. This idea invests in the book an anthropomorphic life of its own, so it can 'walk [...] off the shelves', refusing to 'lie down and die'.

This model of a route to marketplace success is beguiling, but extremely contentious. It is significant that Pitman fails to analyse her own contribution, and that of the media more broadly, speaking as if her intervention were a commentary existing outside of the marketing process, and that her article, and articles such as hers, have no impact upon a book's public profile. This may be a more subtle marketing than the sound of mandolin strings, but – in the broader definition of marketing – it is happening nonetheless. If the very arguments that attempt to explain a phenomenon do not take account of their own contribution to that phenomenon, how reliable can they be?

If Pitman's assessment of the media's marketing contribution is flawed, it would be sensible to be cautious of her assertion that the publishers did not market *Captain Corelli's Mandolin*. Indeed the publishing history of the book recounts a rather different version of events. De Bernières' three previous novels had not been runaway successes, although he had begun to attract a critical reputation. Nicholas Best, for example, in the *Financial Times* in July 1991, wrote a prescient review of *Señor Vivo and the Coca Lord*, asking, 'When are people going to take notice of Louis de Bernières?... He is sharp, funny, engaging and British.'[11] De Bernières' inclusion in *Granta*'s *Best of Young British Novelists* in 1993 was another sign that his writing had been noticed by the literati – certainly no hindrance to a career.[12] However, the sales profile of his first three books did not foretell the future that lay ahead of *Captain Corelli's Mandolin* and, in the normal course of events, the effort and budget allocated by Secker & Warburg's marketing department would have been minimal. This is the expectation drawn upon in Pitman's article, but the actuality is somewhat different.

Secker & Warburg decided to put in place a substantial marketing campaign for the novel, which included London tube advertising, point of sale material including posters and postcards, dumpbins and T-shirts, and an author tour.[13] Undertaking any of these promotional activities would underline a commitment to the book. In combination, they suggest a concerted effort. As Geoff Mulligan, Louis de Bernières' editor, claims, the publishers were 'determin[ed]' to get the hardback into the bestseller lists.[14] The other vital element of the campaign was 'a widespread proof mailing'.[15] One of the most effective but hidden marketing tools, bound copies of uncorrected proofs are used by the publisher to persuade booksellers and the media to read the book several months in advance of publication. It is here that the word-of-mouth chain extends beyond the publishing company. The chain, though, is more calculated than the serendipitous discovery depicted by Pitman. Personal recommendation is influential, but bookseller recommendation is invaluable, made as it is by the opinion formers of marketing communications. The effectiveness of this form of marketing stems from its protracted approach: not from publisher straight to consumer (as with advertising), but via the intermediary of the bookseller. For the potential reader, there seems less 'hype' in this approach than with direct consumer advertising, and more quality control, via the filtering process of the supply chain. This is an example of push rather than pull marketing, which achieves a seeming authenticity of recommendation where the more obvious direct to consumer marketing cannot. (The disruption posed to this more 'authentic' recommendation is compromised by bookseller and publisher co-promotions of the sort discussed in Chapter 1, which is one of the reasons why bungs have proved so contentious.)

Perhaps the most telling exhibit in the early publishing history of *Captain Corelli's Mandolin* is its sales presenter.[16] Produced by marketing departments, sales presenters are largely used for selling books to booksellers and other customers (for example librarians and wholesalers, but not individual readers). While their copy must be read with an awareness that the statements made (e.g. 'massive press, radio and TV coverage'; 'set to be one of 1994's bestsellers') describe ideal, not actual, situations, they do give a strong indication of the level at which the company's marketing for the book is pitched.[17] Sales presenters, moreover, are only produced for a few of the books a company publishes in a given month, and the one for *Captain Corelli's Mandolin* was a lavish affair – eight sides of full-colour A4. The wording of the first page immediately contests Pitman's notion that the book was sold only by unprofessionalised reader recommendation, by directing its question '"Can YOU recommend a really good book?'" at the bookseller. Over the page, the copy then reads, 'BOOKSELLERS are recommending it' (plus an endorsement from a bookseller), and 'WE'RE recommending it'. The copy is an unequivocal declaration of the book's appeal, and the proposed method of transmission of that appeal. Further booksellers are then exhorted to 'recommend it', with the added bonus of 'The Mystery Shopper Competition', which although not quite at the level of 'free mandolin strings', is not far off:

> During April, in each of our five sales regions [...] a mystery shopper will be visiting stores asking booksellers to recommend a good book.
>
> For everyone who recommends *Captain Corelli's Mandolin* there will be a personally addressed signed copy of the book and the chance to enter a draw for first prize of a holiday for two in Cephallonia [the island setting of the novel].[18]

The novel is thus the target of *induced* word of mouth, a chain consciously catalysed by the marketing department. And although the popularity of *Captain Corelli's Mandolin* may not be wholly explained by the activities of Secker & Warburg's marketing department, it does not *defy* it. The sales trajectory was also strongly pushed by a BBC Radio 4 *Book at Bedtime* slot in July 1997, a BBC 2 *Bookmark* television special in August 1998 and a major feature film released in 2001. The image of an unmarketed book which received no assistance from booksellers or the media is far from the truth.

The point of this is not to accuse Pitman and other media commentators of a policy of misinformation about *Captain Corelli's Mandolin*, or similar titles. Journalists would not necessarily have seen the sales presenter, nor had access to Secker & Warburg's marketing plans. Nevertheless, the assumptions made could have been easily substantiated or disproved by consulting the publisher. This could be dismissed as lazy journalism, fitting semi-facts to half-baked theories, which then contribute to the marketing of the book itself. Of course, the version of events related by the author's editor should no more be taken as absolute verity. It is not hard to see why a media claim that a book succeeded despite its publishers' intentions would rile the publisher. To counteract the myth of a book making its appeal directly to readers it would be tempting to posit another, of a visionary publishing company and the power of marketing to sell books. Yet marketing rarely achieves its end so spectacularly, and even if the campaign for *Captain Corelli's Mandolin* was particularly strong, the result of over a million copies sold is out of all proportion to expectation. What this case study suggests is rather an understanding of the book's publishing history that lies between myth and counter-myth, taking something constructive from each. For no matter how successful Secker & Warburg's campaign to induce word of mouth was, the birth and development of the bestseller-to-be was laboured and nurtured elsewhere. But where, and how?

Peter Silverton, in a more thoroughly researched article about *Captain Corelli's Mandolin* in the *Observer* of 27 July 1997, tried to combine anecdotal evidence and a more theoretical approach:

> There was no Martin Amis-level media blitz, but its publishers did give *Corelli* a respectable start in life – posters, promo T-shirts, bookshop dumpbins and a launch party at Lemonia, a smartish Greek restaurant [...]
>
> word of *Corelli*'s romantic sweep [got] around [...] Well, where exactly *did* it get around? And how? And from who to whom? And did they buy their own copy?
>
> It is surprising how little companies know about the people who buy their products. Oh, they know the basic demographics – age, sex and income breakdown – and they might know how to separate their potential customer base into such marketing categories as Early Adopters and Late Majority.
>
> They might also be able to plot a Bass Curve [which ...] uses a fairly complicated mathematical formula to predict the diffusion of new products. In the equation, m equals the total number of people who

> will eventually use the product, p is the coefficient of external influence (the effect of media coverage etc.) and q stands for the coefficient of internal influence (i.e. 'word of mouth') – the average values of p and q are 0.03 and 0.38.[19]

Silverton is struggling here, and he knows it, recoiling from a quantification of 'p' and 'q', and resorting to personal anecdote to further his argument. He narrates a gossipy set of snapshots of the reading chain, tracing word-of-mouth recommendation to one of its sources. The book passes through at least one reading group, a 'woman's book circle in Clapham', which disseminates it to eight people in one go.[20] Then, returning to a more conceptual standpoint, Silverton produces with a flourish his master theory, of the 'Maven' – an expert, professionalised recommender:

> When it comes to books, Duncan Minshull is a Supermaven. As producer of *A Book at Bedtime*, he chooses 26 books a year for 600,000 Radio 4 listeners to sample at some length. Mr Minshull has just finished broadcasting *Corelli* [...]
>
> There are also fully-pro mavens. Andy Miller, promotions manager of Waterstone's, is probably the most important. He ran the Waterstone's 100 promotion, which listed their customers' choice of the greatest books, on which *Corelli* sat at number 66 [...[21]] When *Corelli* first came out, Mr Miller was a humble bookshop assistant in Waterstone's Kensington High Street branch. He adored the book. 'Customers are always coming to you and asking what they should read. And that's hard – judging their tastes for them. Corelli was like gold dust for us. You couldn't go wrong with it. You could recommend it to anyone with complete impunity.'[22]

Silverton thus shows how 'recommendation' is an example of effective push marketing. He finishes his article with a string of conclusions, which provide some interesting fodder for debate:

> So what does this tell us about how word of mouth works? Five things, most of them quite obvious. One, we generally require two recommendations before we'll sample a book – though mavens count double in this game. Two, the lag is about three months – that is how long it takes for a book to be recommended, read and the recommendation to be passed on. Three – the chain will break at about the sixth or seventh person [...]

> Four, the interaction of lag time and median chain length produces its maximum effect at the two-year point – i.e., for Corelli, now. Five, there is a pronounced female bias – women do have this kind of talk more.[23]

The sex differential of the fifth point is a particularly charged issue, worth further exploration in tandem with theories of the gendering of reading. One of the conclusions of Book Marketing Ltd/The Reading Partnership's *Reading the Situation: Book Reading, Buying and Borrowing Habits in Britain* (2000), for example, was that 'The social aspect of reading [...] shows a clear distinction between men and women. Men are far less likely to discuss the books that they read, to recommend them and to act on recommendations [...] For women, a recommendation from a friend, relation or colleague is one of the chief sources of guidance for choosing books to read.'[24] Though Silverton's tone is light, his theory, then, is one grounded in actuality and based on observation. Yet in the end, although his analysis ably explains *how* the book is disseminated, it does not manage to say why *this* book succeeded, rather than any other. For even in the more perceptive analyses there remains a subscription to a myth of a valiant little book doing battle with market forces. The book has entered the consciousness of the reading public to such a degree that it seems to be 'created' by the readers themselves. This is a reversion to the 'recycled cliché' that Geoff Mulligan sees in the accounts of the novel succeeding without any help from the industry.[25] But whilst clearly flawed, there is an element of this myth that still manages to hold sway, and is perhaps a key to understanding the sales of *Captain Corelli's Mandolin*. The myth of a book appealing directly to its readers means there is a much greater sense of ownership of the text for those readers, who feel they have discovered the book themselves. This is a democratic vision, where the people come to determine cultural success, seemingly without the interventions of industry or the media. The public persona of Louis de Bernières sustains this theory of the book: a self-effacing 'publicity-shy author' who would prefer the book to speak for itself.[26] For the myth of the valiant little book is one that has been crucial to the book's success. It activates a personal and direct communion – a semi-mystical link between the reader and the page, of the nostalgic sort depicted by Sven Birkerts in *The Gutenberg Elegies* (1994), where the 'investment in the topic of reading [...] ultimately originates in the private self – that of the dreamy fellow with an open book in his lap', terminology not far removed from Pitman's description of 'the quiet, intimate and mysterious process of word of mouth'.[27] Whilst the publisher might not claim to have mounted a publicity campaign so clever as to access the readers' private selves, conscripting journalists and booksellers for their propaganda whilst casting itself as ingénue, the myth of a reader's direct access to the book is a potent marketing tool.

There still remains the question of why *Captain Corelli's Mandolin* – rather than any other book – is an appropriate text for 'ownership'. Maybe it has something to do with the romantic sweep of a story in which love endures through war and society, over water and time. A decision was certainly made in the offices of Secker & Warburg to market this book more heavily than de Bernières' previous sales pattern would normally have warranted and, despite the external factors of the author's developing esteem, the text of *Captain Corelli's Mandolin* would have contributed to the decision. A book's contents are undoubtedly an important factor in the book's success, though the diversity of textual appreciation (as indicated by the variety of opinions put forward both by critics and the readers who post comments on Amazon.co.uk's website) suggests that to venture a definitive answer based on the text is a foolhardy enterprise. The varying degrees of success that the novel has encountered in other territories and in translation implies that it does not have universal appeal.[28] What is more, the myth of ownership that developed around *Captain Corelli's Mandolin* sounds a warning to any recourse to a *textual* answer. If a book's success derives to a large degree from its capacity to appeal directly to millions of readers, that appeal must surely be constructed in manifold ways. This is not to deny that textual criticism has a place, but rather to retreat from a gesture of interpretive closure. No one factor can explain the bestseller, and any singularity of viewpoint is doomed to failure. Ownership may be a myth of cultural production that can be used to mystify its processes, but if it incorporates the agencies of text, reader and author, publisher, bookseller and media, as well as the 'whole socio-economic conjuncture', as Adams and Barker put it in their 'New Model for the Study of the Book', it may lay the foundations of a tenable theory.[29] Just as the liberation of a text from authorial intention engenders a proliferation of possibilities for literary meaning, so the concept of ownership – with a variety of owners, be they rights holders, cultural guardians, or consumers – sets free a model of a text's transmission that might yet prove workable.

Martin Amis's *The Information* (1995)

In his analysis of *Captain Corelli's Mandolin*, Peter Silverton drew on a different novel to suggest the disparity between the marketing activities surrounding them. For *Captain Corelli's Mandolin*, Silverton wrote, there was 'no Martin Amis-level media blitz'. He was referring in this comment to the publication of Amis's ninth novel, *The Information*, an event which became a *cause célèbre* in the publishing world of the 1990s, launching its already well-known author into the promotional stratosphere. The subject of Amis's novel was particularly apposite to the marketing activity surrounding it. *The Information* is a story of literary rivalry between two writers and friends, and has scenes and motifs in it, satirically treated, which illustrate directly many of the marketing activities and agencies discussed in *Marketing Literature*: meetings with editors; the book tour; literary prizes. Moreover, for the publication of this book about authorial rivalry, Amis had actively sought out, after leaving his previous literary agent and publisher for new business partners, an advance in the region of half a million pounds. That his previous literary agent was the wife of the novelist Julian Barnes, and that the two novelists had an acrimonious falling out after years of friendship, compounded yet further the journalistic capital accruing to Amis's book.[30]

Even before these events, Amis's name already made frequent appearances in the media. Formerly on the staff at the *Times Literary Supplement*, with a famous novelist, Kingsley Amis, as a father, Amis's publishing career had been closely watched from its early days. *Money* (1984) and *London Fields* (1989), his provocative Thatcher decade novels, were cynical social commentaries on contemporary life in the UK and the US, and the latter caused a severe rift in the judging panel of the Booker Prize.[31] His experimental treatment of the subject of the Holocaust in *Time's Arrow* (1991) also proved controversial.[32] The 'media blitz' surrounding the publication of *The Information* built on this notoriety, and was extended by the financial circumstances of the book, the gossip about its author, and the self-reflective subject of the book's contents.

Indeed, Martin Amis, and this novel in particular, have been thoroughly incorporated into media commentary and academic study of the promotional circuit. A lengthy *New Yorker* article entitled 'The Literary Life: A Very English Story' set out the background to the deal, and reactions to it among the literary establishment, some of the most vehement of which came from the novelist A. S. Byatt.[33] The financial arrangements – although not that notable in terms of large corporate salaries in other industries – were in stark contrast to the more typical authorial wage discussed in Chapter 1. The negotiations, as the *New Yorker* explored, were held in the glare of a very public spotlight, and when a deal was eventually struck with HarperCollins, much derision was expressed at the valuation of the work. The acquisition of Amis for HarperCollins's list was generally viewed as a sign of misguided vanity on both sides of the deal. Rumours circulated that Amis wanted the money in part to fund expensive dentistry work, in addition to setting himself above his peers as a highly paid literary writer. From the publishers' point of view, the deal was seen as an indicator of the cultural capital they hoped would accrue to their list by the acquisition of Amis, despite potential economic deficit.[34] HarperCollins, it was generally assumed, would never make any money from the deal, and Amis, though with the advance money safely banked, had built up an insatiable – and possibly unsatisfiable – level of expectation about his forthcoming work. (*The Information* was not a complete sales failure, however: the hardback edition appeared at the top of the *Sunday Times* hardback fiction best-seller list in its first week of publication (2 April 1995), and remained in the top ten for a further seven weeks until 21 May 1995.) Nonetheless, the reviews that greeted the publication of *The Information* found it hard not to attempt a measurement of the contents of the book against its advance, and to find the former falling far short of the latter. That the story of *The Information* was one of literary rivalry and jealousy increased yet further the weighing up of the book in monetary and artistic terms, as Moran, Delany and Gardiner all explored in, respectively, *Star Authors*, *Literature, Money and the Market* and ' "What is an Author?" '[35] Gardiner describes in some detail the promotional campaign for *The Information*, which included London tube posters, postcards distributed through London wine bars and restaurants, *Information* T-shirts for Dillons retail staff and a neon sign site in London's Piccadilly Circus. Such promotional hyper-activity was undoubtedly summoned by the high advance spent on the book. In these promotional activities, in the media attention paid to Amis's personal life, and in the large advance, Gardiner sees *The Information* as typifying the late twentieth-century 'shift in emphasis from author production to author promotion', in addition to making explicit, through the 'actualis[ation]' of Bourdieu's 'concept of value' in this deal, the equation between literary value and money.[36] Amis also exemplifies much of the discourse around author branding in the promotional circuit. In 'Martin Amis on Marketing', an article principally about Amis's *Money*, but which touches on *The Information* and Amis's literary career more generally, Daragh O'Reilly discusses the 'novelist as brand', seeing 'Martin Amis' (rather than Martin Amis) as the 'text': a 'web of textual meanings, a contested site, a sign constructed socially, by himself, his publisher, and his readers'.[37]

Amis's *The Information*, then, is an archetypal example of the promotional circuit in the contemporary literary marketplace, with the self-reflexivity of the novel's contents increasing the tendency for it to be seen in this way. As a very high-profile case, *The Information* overtly sets the scene for some of the more subtle and less well-known examples of the marketing of literature. Amis's novel is indicative in explicit ways, given the media and academic discussion of its cultural and economic worth, of the construction of cultural, economic and journalistic capital within the field of contemporary British fiction. Moreover, *The Information* is, as Gerald Howard comments, 'a prime postmodern instance in the dizzying circularity with which the book's whole publication saga mirrored its themes of venality and authenticity' – the paradigm of promotional circuit paradigms, in other words.[38] The cynicism with which many critics approach the literary marketplace was exacerbated by the book's contents, and the questions that Amis posed within his text about value were to be repeated by the paratextual appearance of it within the marketplace, both before, during and after its publication. Just as part of the 'story' about *Captain Corelli's Mandolin* was its apparent lack of marketing, so the 'story' about *The Information*'s hyper-marketing reflects back and forth – 'the dizzying circularity' to which Howard refers – between its text and marketplace contexts.

5
Marketing Stories

Irvine Welsh's *Trainspotting* (1993)[1]

In an optimistic frame of mind about the publishing industry and the state of the novel, the journalist James Naughtie envisioned, in the pages of the *Daily Telegraph* in 1998, a journey north:

> I can't prove it by scientific means, but I'm sure of this. If you wander down the corridor of a train travelling, say, from London to Edinburgh on a Friday afternoon and take note of what the passengers are reading you will get a pleasant surprise. I'd be prepared to bet that the quality of fiction being devoured – and the quantity – is better than it was a couple of decades ago, and much of it is being read by youngsters.
>
> In other words, when I hear the familiar anguished cry about the death of the book I refuse to believe it. There is every reason to be optimistic.[2]

Five years earlier, the publication of Irvine Welsh's *Trainspotting* portrayed a quite different southbound expedition. Renton, Sick Boy, Begbie, Spud and Second Prize are all aboard the night-time National Express, clutching an Adidas bag full of prime Colombian brown. In various states of inebriation, intoxication and drug-induced paranoia, they sweat out the hours before their arrival at Victoria Coach Station, their heroin haul (more or less) intact. The 'Edinburgh consortium' are on their way to a meeting with Pete Gilbert, a London-based dealer who 'convert[s] the smack into hard cash'.[3] The deal struck, the others go out to hit Soho and shoot pool, whilst Renton stays back at the hotel. In a flash of opportunism he takes the cash, leaves the hotel, and heads off to a new life in Amsterdam, knowing he can never return 'to Leith, to Edinburgh, even to Scotland, ever again'.[4]

Shortly after the publication of *Trainspotting*, Welsh also left Scotland, but for Amsterdam, and with cash of a different kind in his pocket: from the royalties of his novel. Despite the similarities in biographical detail, though, this is not to suggest that Renton is Welsh's fictional alter ego, but rather that this section of *Trainspotting* offers some illuminating parallels between the conversion of smack into hard cash and the processes of *Trainspotting*'s publication. The novel's text is an allegory of its own marketing context.

Welsh describes the drugs deal in some detail:

> Gilbert was a professional who had worked in drug-dealing for a long time. He'd buy and sell anything. For him, it was strictly business, and he refused to differentiate it from any other entrepreneurial activity. State intervention in the form of police and courts merely constituted another business risk. It was however, a risk worth taking, considering the supernormal profits. A classic middle-man, Gilbert was, by nature of his contacts and his venture capital, able to procure drugs, hold them, cut them and sell them to smaller distributors.
>
> Straight away, Gilbert clocks the Scottish guys as small-time wasters who have stumbled on a big deal. He is impressed however, by the quality of their gear. He offers them £15 000, prepared to go as high as £17 000. They want £20 000, prepared to go as low as £18 000. The deal is clinched at £16 000. Gilbert will make £60 000 minimum once the gear is cut and distributed.
>
> He finds it tiresome negotiating with a bunch of fucked-up losers from the wrong side of the border.[5]

Gilbert is primarily concerned with business, putting 'entrepreneurial activity' before anything else, including his anti-Scottishness. He is the man who will, 'by nature of his contacts', make many thousands of pounds by the deal. If this deal is an analogy for *Trainspotting*'s publication, a profoundly hard-nosed economic exchange between the text's original authorial creator and its publishing intermediaries becomes apparent. For if the heroin sold by Renton and his consortium is configured as a metaphor for the book sold by Welsh, the drug-dealer/publisher figure looks not only entrepreneurial but exploitative.

The publishing history of *Trainspotting* can fit this analogy. The very first extract of Welsh's work-in-progress appeared in 1991 in the anthology *Scream, If You Want to Go Faster (New Writing Scotland 9)*.[6] Further sections appeared in the South Queensferry Clocktower Press publication *Past Tense: Four Stories from a Novel* in April 1992.[7] The edition of 300 was, according to the publisher Duncan McLean, 'our slowest seller'.[8] Kevin Williamson's first issue of the Edinburgh magazine *Rebel Inc.* in May 1992 included another extract.[9] This passage of *Trainspotting* from one publisher to another is the beginning of a chain that prepared the novel for its big journey south, passing, like the heroin, from hand to hand.

Welsh was eventually taken on by Secker & Warburg, after sending *Trainspotting* to McLean's editor at the company.[10] Secker & Warburg acquired the volume rights for a minimal sum – certainly much less than Gilbert's £16 000 – and rumoured to be closer to £1000.[11] As a business decision it was inspired, and eventually would afford a much higher return than Gilbert's £60 000 – though the street value of the novel could not have been calculated as accurately as that of the heroin. The habitual risk of UK publishing is not the intervention of the law, but the possibility of public indifference, minimal sales and loss rather than profit: 'market censorship', to use Schiffrin's terminology in *The Business of Books*, rather than legal sanction. With the benefit of hindsight, however, the acquisition was a shrewd entrepreneurial move, a tiny investment that would procure a huge return.

The subsequent publishing history is one of growing success – the 'cut and distribut[ion]' of the novel, so to speak. Critics stood up and took note. Some were outraged; others impressed; all were aware of a new voice of great vitality. Welsh and *Trainspotting* began to be mentioned in general discussions of literature, and brought up as a point of reference in reviews of other novels. The novel was acclaimed for its visceral representation of Edinburgh as AIDS and heroin capital of Europe, and its energetic vernacular usage. The transition of *Trainspotting* to the stage in 1994 and then to the screen in 1996 assured yet more column inches, many more sales and eventually a sequel, *Porno* (2002), featuring characters from *Trainspotting* ten years on.[12]

Spearheaded by Welsh, Scottish literature became fashionable, and a perceived 'literary renaissance' was heralded. Authors including Alan Warner and A. L. Kennedy were cast as part of this putative renaissance, and at times the London-based media seemed in danger of homogenising their literary output in pursuit of a perceived trend which arguably effaced the longer literary history and precedents of Scottish writers.[13] This kind of representation by nationality is a publishing equivalent of colouring by numbers. It might find its origins in the quick-pitch necessary for marketing the idea of a book (e.g. 'C is A crossed with B', or 'If you liked X, read Y'), but representing writing primarily through the writer's regional, national or ethnic origins forecloses interpretive horizons, and locks authors and their work into stereotypes, as the case study of *The God of Small Things* later in this chapter also illustrates. While putting forward theories and histories of national literature is by no means a redundant enterprise, locking authors and their work into stereotypes (even if those stereotypes change over time) is at best reductive and at worst ethnocentric.

Welsh's Scottishness, however, was not the only theme drawn on in the novel's marketing and reception. *Trainspotting* also began to be viewed as a novel representative of a predominantly youth-based counter-culture. Dubbed 'the poet laureate of the chemical generation' by *The Face*, Welsh came to symbolise a literary movement that chronicled the worlds of clubs and drugs, and appealed to those involved with them.[14] Welsh's promotional readings in clubs heavily influenced this perception of him as taking literature out of the library and onto the dancefloor. His writing appealed to readers who were disaffected or excluded by the customary output of the mainstream literary establishment – 'non-readers', as Robin Roberston, Welsh's editor, classified them in interview. The counter-cultural appeal of *Trainspotting*, however, to judge by the excitement of the reviewers, meant that more 'traditional' readers were also attracted to Welsh's writing and its window onto an underworld.[15]

The conscription of Welsh into the marketing process of this 'genre' (which included both fiction and non-fiction) demonstrates how marketing functions by endorsement, inclusion and implication. *Disco Biscuits* (1997), for example, a volume of short stories subtitled 'new fiction from the chemical generation', had Welsh at the head of its list of contributors.[16] Endorsements by Welsh feature on other authors' covers, leading one bookseller to comment in the press that a section in the shop could be devoted to his recommendations.[17] Cover designs and typography, even jacket copy, were created to echo the styles used on editions of Welsh's novels, in an attempt to associate the successful branding of Welsh with other aspirant writers.

It is in this way, to extend the analogy between *Trainspotting*'s publishing and its text, that marketing could be seen to operate as a neo-colonial force. It seeks to extend into new territories – in this case that of the group of non-readers, or readers attracted by books detailing alternative lifestyles – by appropriating their discourse. The use of a discourse that seems to speak these readers' own language is an immeasurably clever cultural ploy. The readership becomes complicit in its own surrender through its desire to be seduced. This is a reverse assimilation: not imposing culture upon the colony but allowing it its own in return for economic exchange. All industrialised cultural production might be seen to function thus, with the microcosm of *Trainspotting* bringing the whole system into sharp relief by its contrast of Scottish press and English publisher (McLean seeing the Clocktower Press 'not [as] a commercial, money-making venture, but a cultural intervention'; Williamson describing *Rebel Inc.* as 'kicking back against the literary mainstream').[18] The absorption of the counter-culture into the mainstream becomes a way of reaching new markets. This journey, with happy, beaming customers ('youngsters' particularly, as Naughtie has it) tucking into their literary fare, is a one-way ticket for the coins in their pockets and purses into the publisher's coffers.

Welsh's public persona – which he initially strived to develop through effacing his yuppie, property-dealing days in the 1980s and Heriot-Watt MBA in the 1990s – slots into this paradoxical but effective system of absorbing the counter-culture.[19] Several years after the publication of *Trainspotting,* Welsh describes the impulse behind its writing:

> It was listening to a fellow MBA student from the Home Counties and a middle-class Glaswegian student telling me about what kind of a city Edinburgh was that made me think about its image. That image, that of the middle-class, festival city, was at worst a lie and at best perversely one-sided. Yet it had a hegemony over all the other images of this urban, largely working-class but multi-cultural city. Other realities existed, had to be shown to exist.[20]

This emphasis on a culture hidden under the conventional image of Edinburgh is a vision most intensely fulfilled in the section of the novel entitled 'The First Day of the Edinburgh Festival', which was first published in the *Scream, If You Want to Go Faster* anthology.[21] Renton, prematurely abandoning his self-imposed treatment for heroin addiction, takes opium suppositories. The unfolding of the plot has Renton dredging the toilet of the local bookies in stomach-churningly graphic style, then realising 'it wis the first day ay the Festival'.[22] Throughout the media reception to *Trainspotting,* it is this scene – with its explicit portrayal of a desperate junkie juxtaposed with the image of Edinburgh as the middle-class cultural capital of Scotland, the city of the Festival – that occurs most often.[23]

The paradox, then, is that the initial ideological intent that Welsh describes, and that the text upholds, is conscripted to facilitate the mainstream publisher's enterprise. Alan Freeman's analysis of the currency of drugs and the individualism in Welsh's representation of dealing in his essay 'Ghosts in Sunny Leith: Irvine Welsh's *Trainspotting*' (1996) illuminates this paradox:

> Drug culture enacts the glamour of the outsider, the anti-hero beloved of modern Western culture, the imaginative antidote to bureaucratic circumscription. Yet the image of the anti-hero is closely related to the proliferating modes of representation in commodity culture. Far from being free, this modern individualism is a product, a commodity bought and sold, and the anti-hero is both consumer and consumed, a signified dispersed within the grammar from whence it emerges.[24]

Freeman is referring specifically to the anti-heroic role of the drug dealer, but in his connection of this false myth of individuality to consumer society, his argument can be extended to encompass a reading of the publishing history of *Trainspotting*. Here is a novel sprung from the margins – the Edinburgh schemes, the small outsider Scottish press – but appropriated by mainstream culture. Individualism and counter-cultural impulses turn into 'product, a commodity bought and sold'. Here is Welsh as drug-taking anti-hero, an author who knows his material because he's lived it. In obediently naughty media-friendly mode Welsh hangs out with rock stars, takes drugs, gets drunk, abusive and thrown in jail.[25] He is a consumable marketing dream and, in the high sales that *Trainspotting* went on to achieve, a publisher's bankrolling bad boy. The interpretation that Freeman makes of the drug dealer's role, then, is a refinement of the analogy set up at the beginning of this case study. The dealer is no longer simply the publisher, but representative of a wider set of cultural forces, the figure who exploits and is himself exploited. He is the glamorous outsider who attracts non-readers by his incorporation at the heart of the capitalist system. This is a model of cultural production that sees the producer having only to swallow a small pill (and a cheaply-acquired one, at that) to experience profit-expanding vistas. Where potential profit is involved, it is possible to view cultural production as an exploitation of texts, readers and writers, even if it is a less controversial publishing venture, such as the introduction of a new crime series to the market, for example, which attempts to corner or expand a section of the market.

Some points that this model of cultural industry suppresses are worth making, though. Welsh will have earned much more than his initial advance in royalties, for example, and his London-based editor is actually Scottish. These points could be turned on their heads to fit the model, but that is the intrinsic problem with it. It insists on a framework of power positions of unequal economic exchange, of coloniser and colonised, global conglomerate and small press, London and Edinburgh, publisher and author, even author and text (Welsh exploiting his own work in order to access the financial reward that a broader readership will grant him). Ultimately this is an antagonistic way of looking at the structures of publishing, and additionally, it repudiates any belief in literature's potential to transform the market. To return to the text of *Trainspotting*, it is worth remembering that Renton rails against the self-indulgent masochism he perceives in his compatriots, declaring that:

> It's nae good blamin it oan the English fir colonising us. Ah don't hate the English. They're just wankers. We are colonised by wankers. We can't even pick a decent, vibrant, healthy culture to be colonised by. No. We're ruled by effete arseholes. What does that make us? The lowest of the fuckin low, the scum of the earth.[26]

To subscribe to colonialism, even as the protesting subordinate partner, is, Renton implies, to uphold the system. To view publishing as an exploitative force similarly perpetuates the dichotomy. The analogy provided by the Edinburgh consortium's journey has parallels with the publication of *Trainspotting*, but ultimately the venture is not at all the same. So it is important to be able to separate – while never forgetting the links – the internal impulses of the text from the external methods of its transmission, and to see the difference between where the money goes and where the books go, between profit and culture. To perceive a system of cultural production, in other words, that is founded on a principle of transition: of books into products; of products into cash; but also of the potential change literature, the market and readers can undergo.

Where does that leave James Naughtie, then, in his anecdotal stroll down the aisle of the London–Edinburgh train? He diagnoses, to reverse Renton's words, a 'decent, vibrant, healthy culture', both a pleasing quantity and quality of fiction being read. This is an idealistic vision, but also, in its context, a revealing one. Naughtie is writing as one of the year's judges for the Carnegie Medal for children's literature, which the previous year had been awarded to the controversial but celebrated fiction *Junk*, by Melvin Burgess (1996).[27] That a novel about heroin use could be lauded by a prestigious literary award as the best book for children of its year is surely in part a consequence of the metamorphoses enacted on the market by *Trainspotting*. The market's readiness to adapt might develop from its pursuit of profit, but the end result is a constant process of revivification. If publishers were not to seek new territories – of subject, of genre or of readers – the market would stagnate and the voices of doom would declare once more the death of the novel. For just as publishing is not only a process of station management, but can also lay new tracks and buy new trains, so books can turn not only into hard cash but also, maybe, into gold.

Pat Barker's *The Ghost Road* (1995)[28]

In 'Hype, hype hurrah!' in the *Observer* in August 1995, Nicci Gerrard previewed major novels still to be published in time for entry into that year's Booker Prize. Pat Barker, whose *The Ghost Road* was due the following month, is presented by Gerrard as standing somewhat away from the 'hype'. Gerrard writes that her 'reputation as a novelist has steadily grown over the last decade, and with her trilogy about the horrors of the trenches she has reached a quiet eminence.'[29]

It is this quality of 'quiet eminence' that makes *The Ghost Road*, in comparison to many of the other books discussed in Part II, the least outstanding. Not the least outstanding in literary terms: indeed, some might contend that Pat Barker's is the most obviously 'literary'. Rather, despite winning the Booker, *The Ghost Road* is the least outstanding because it is much less of a visible publishing phenomenon. That *The Ghost Road* is the third novel in a trilogy – following *Regeneration* (1991) and *The Eye in the Door* (1993) – gives a clue as to why the publishing history appears to be less phenomenal, as does the knowledge that *The Ghost Road* is Barker's seventh novel.[30] While Irvine Welsh might always be best known for *Trainspotting*, Louis de Bernières for *Captain Corelli's Mandolin*, and Helen Fielding for *Bridget Jones's Diary*, and while Arundhati Roy announced the forthcoming publication of a second novel a decade after her first, Pat Barker's seventh novel is much more clearly part of a continuing career trajectory.[31] The structure of a career such as Barker's means that the mechanisms of hype are much less apparent, and that no one novel can be taken as representative of the oeuvre. Beginning her career before the age of EPOS it took some time for her career to be established, as Richard Knight regretfully refers to in Chapter 1. The age of the author (both in years and in career terms) also forces a different perspective on her writing: one that, if the author is fortunate, might lead her to be viewed as a 'real' writer, one not forced into the limelight by large marketing budgets and a pretty face, but rewarded for literary esteem and the steady accretion of cultural value. (The obverse of this situation is the writer on whose work the perspective becomes so oblique that their work is scarcely visible at all. For every Pat Barker there are a legion of authors who started their careers in the early 1980s only to encounter diminishing advances and audiences in the course of the later 1980s and 1990s, the 'painful soundlessness' mentioned in Chapter 1.) It is therefore problematic to contain *The Ghost Road* within the bounds of a single book-based case study. The case study of a single book can no more encompass an entire career than a survey of the career can explain the intricacies of the publishing history of a single book. However, this case study, by stretching its remit a little to bring in elements of her career, depicts a history of *The Ghost Road* that also makes some suggestions about the broader career. As this is essentially a book-based case study, though, it begins with the book itself.

The Ghost Road was published in September 1995, the third in a trilogy of novels set during the First World War, in which Barker mixes fictionalised historical figures (including the poets Siegfried Sassoon and Wilfred Owen, and the psychologist and anthropologist William Rivers) with invented characters. *Regeneration*, the first volume, was not originally intended to be part of a sequence.[32] The tripartite structure, however, was well established with the publication of *The Ghost Road*, and the reviews that greeted the final volume drew as much on its status as the third of a trilogy as a discrete text. *The Ghost Road* was hence judged by the standards of its predecessors and assessed as part of a larger literary endeavour. Peter Parker, for example, in the *Times Literary Supplement*, saw it as 'a startlingly good novel in its own right. With the other two volumes of the trilogy, it forms one of the richest and most rewarding works of fiction of recent times.'[33] In the *Sunday Times*, Peter Kemp commented that, 'With The Ghost Road, she brings to a harrowing and heartening close a fictional enterprise that is a magnificent addition to our literature of war.'[34] The largely positive reviews were soon affirmed by the announcement of the Booker Prize shortlist (consisting of novels by Barker, Justin Cartwright, Salman Rushdie, Barry Unsworth and Tim Winton), only a few weeks after the publication of *The Ghost Road*. Rushdie's *The Moor's Last Sigh* (1995) was the clear favourite, and the phrasing of many of the press reports announcing Barker's win dwelt on Rushdie's loss, with the outcome configured as one of a provincial Northern woman over a cosmopolitan member of the literati.[35] For others, including Mark Lawson in the *Sunday Times*, the result was neither unexpected nor incomprehensible. Lawson thought *The Ghost Road* was the 'Best novel of the year [. . .] which only bookmakers and fools thought a surprise Booker winner'.[36] Barker herself was phlegmatic about possible success. Interviewed before the shortlist was announced, Barker wearily claimed to '"know, intellectually and in my bones, that it's just three lemons in a row."'[37] Barker's fruit machine analogy says much about the vagaries of book prizes and their judging procedures, and even more of their deleterious effect on authors awaiting their results. Yet to dismiss the winner of a major prize as a recipient of mere good fortune is not a sufficient analysis. To forgo a more rigorous examination of the implications of winning the Booker would be to ignore the undeniable impact it can have on an author's career, as the discussion of literary awards in Chapter 3 emphasises.

In terms of Pat Barker's career in 1995, the award of the Booker to *The Ghost Road* appeared as its crowning moment. Indeed, awarding the prize to the final volume of the trilogy had a greater resonance than awarding the first volume might have had. For although officially given to a single book, *The Ghost Road*'s Booker win very much consolidated the status of the entire trilogy, and thus of Barker's reputation. This is not to say that the judging panel broke the rules of the prize by unfairly comparing a whole trilogy against single volumes. Whether or not this did happen is bound up in the intricacies of the judging process – a process difficult to separate from gossip and rumour in its semi-public, semi-private dealings.[38] Ultimately what is more interesting – and more enduring – is the symbolic value of the award in its recognition of Barker's achievement. This recognition then retrospectively orders what came before, becoming the point from which interpretation develops. The award of the Booker would mean that an enlarged readership would be introduced to Barker's writing with her seventh novel. For these new readers – even if they were to some degree aware of what came before – their experience of Barker starts with *The Ghost Road*. The reading experience is influenced by Booker approval, which in turn conditions reaction to the rest of Barker's writing.

Francis Spufford, interviewing Barker for the *Guardian* after the award of the Booker, discussed the progression of her career and the implications of the Prize:

> In [her books, she] says, she looks for the direct words that bring a thing home, with a lurch of realisation, or a burst of black humour. Was this something she had deliberately picked up on from the period [of the First World War]? 'Oh, I think you can hear that tone just

as much in the voices of working-class women today. It's a point of contact between the first half of my career and the second. When the prostitutes are talking to each other in *Blow Your House Down* I said it was "trench humour" – without knowing I would write about trenches later.' [...]

There are many other such points of contact and convergence across her work. Despite the three war novels' deep immersion in masculinities, they represent, as she says when asked about perceptions of her career, 'very much a female view of war'. (She's rueful at the suggestion she detects in some of the Booker coverage that she's turned to a major subject 'at last'.)[39]

Laying to one side for a while the issue of whether her success was founded on a change of subject, the 'points of contact and convergence across her work' that Spufford draws attention to indicate how a literary career structure can be modelled. Barker herself subscribes to the model, seeing her writing dividing into '"the first half of my career and the second"', with the '"trench humour"' of the first half finding meaning in the trenches of the second. The exoneration given by the award of the Booker inevitably focuses attention on the *Regeneration* trilogy, and so meaning in Barker's oeuvre is patterned retrospectively. Hence, even though Barker states that the '"trench humour"' was present from her early work onwards, and was what she was writing about all along, it is a hard claim to sustain through the rush of backward Booker momentum.

An account of the award of the Booker demonstrates how her career came to be constructed through the lens of the prize. As chair of the Booker judges in 1995, George Walden made the customary speech announcing the winner before launching a critique of contemporary writing:

So what of the state of our literary culture? When you read first-rate prose, like that of *The Ghost Road* by Pat Barker, sometimes you feel you are snatching illicit pleasures on the sly.

[...] so few of the Booker entries tackled modern England. Are our writers, by their silence, making a point? Is there something wrong with England? Why do they shy away from us? Do we give off a bad smell, like old vegetation?

The flight from the present is becoming a sort of general phenomenon. If the past is another country, then we are facing a sort of mass emigration. Nostalgia is becoming our heavy industry.[40]

Although Walden's praise separates Barker's work from the 'mass emigration', his condemnation of the 'escape into the past', as he also termed it, would seem to tar all historical fiction with the same brush.[41] The refuge of historical fiction, he claims, is artistically degenerate in its refusal to address contemporary issues.

Walden's condemnation of the appeal of historical fiction is more a piece of Booker polemic – the need to find something controversial for the TV cameras and report writers – than the result of a carefully researched study. However, the question of how a genre (in this case historical fiction) might come to appeal to writers and also to readers, and the implications that the appeal might bear for the cultural health of a nation is a reasonable area for debate. Rather than broadening the debate here, though, this case study sites Barker's trilogy in the genre of fiction about the First World War.

Writing fiction about the First World War is not, it goes without saying, an enterprise new to the 1990s. Hugh Cecil, in *The Flower of Battle: British Fiction Writers of the First World War* (1995), catalogues earlier practitioners, some of whom had seen active service during the hostilities. The motivation behind his own critical work is highly relevant to more recent novelists' interest in the First World War. Cecil's study is constructed not as an act of nostalgia but of historical record, which gathered information and resources before the death of its subjects.[42] Geoff Dyer, in *The Missing of the Somme* (1994), published shortly before Cecil's work, is similarly explicit in referring to the need to record the memories of the dwindling population of First World War soldiers:

> Constantly reiterated, the claim that we are in danger of forgetting is one of the ways in which the war ensured it would be remembered. Every generation since the armistice has believed that it will be the last for whom the Great War has any meaning. Now, when the last survivors are within a few years of their deaths, I too wonder if the memory of the war will perish with the generation after mine. This sense of imminent amnesia is, has been and – presumably – always will be immanent in the war's enduring memory.[43]

Dyer's argument is perhaps more subtle than Cecil's. The 'sense of imminent amnesia' he perceives in historians' attempts at remembrance is more than an act of catching memories before they are consigned to the grave. Rather, it premises the act of remembrance in the present, and the material on which it works as mediated solely through the present moment. Thus literature as well as memory is a shaping force. Dyer argues that our current understanding of the war is influenced to a great extent by Sassoon, Owen and other war poets – some of the major fictionalised characters of Barker's trilogy.[44] To set this 'sense of imminent amnesia' and the coping strategies that are performed to prevent it against George Walden's criticism of 'nostalgia [as…] heavy industry', is to cast the production of fictional material dealing with the war as a thought-provoking, structurally complex act against it as a financially advantageous but artistically flawed one. Nostalgia for the trenches might seem an unlikely explanation for the popularity of portrayals of the First World War. Nonetheless Keith Miller, in the *Times Literary Supplement*, tentatively suggests that a form of nostalgia is indeed at work:

> War, as William Tecumseh Sherman once famously observed, is hell. And just as the predicament of the damned has inspired generations of poets, so the literary appeal of war endures, with the tender, melancholy First World War novels of Sebastian Faulks and Pat Barker currently battling for window-space against rather blunter reminiscences. Our appetite for such books may seem ghoulish, but perhaps it stems from a perverse nostalgia.[45]

Given that by 2002, BBC2 programmers were airing *The Trench*, a reality TV show based on life in the trenches, 'perverse nostalgia' seems not too far off the mark. Pat Barker, responding to Walden's charges of a headlong flight from contemporary reality by English novelists in his Booker polemic, argues her position. The *Times Literary Supplement*'s diary column took up the debate:

> Speaking on *The World This Weekend* (Radio 4) on Remembrance Sunday, [Barker…] specifically rejected George Walden's charge of 'nostalgia'. Her interviewer, James Cox, put the charge about the remembrance of war to her again: 'There are those who say, yes, this is nostalgia, this is looking to the past, this is typical old Britain, remembering past glories, past victories. We should be looking forward.' Barker rejected it eloquently: 'I think what we found out about human beings on the battlefields of the First World War and in the death camps of the Second World War is something that we stop remembering at our peril – because we are the same people.'[46]

As a defence against Walden, Barker portrays herself and others occupied in an act of remembrance, a meditation on human nature. The more complex transmogrifications that her fiction enacts on the First World War were forgotten in the heat of literary debate.[47] This case study does not, however, defend Barker's – or any other author's – right to produce historical fiction, but rather examines how these debates construct its appeal, and interact with genre fashion. The construction of the appeal of First World War fictions as one of active remembrance and a reminder of our common humanity is perhaps too idealistic a view of cultural production to fend off its more cynical critics. However, a *Guardian* editorial that appeared close to Remembrance Sunday in 1995 calls on Barker's work to support its analysis of the fascination with war:

> Even those who find the military commemorations of November 11 distasteful should be careful not to disparage this powerful popular impulse. The wish for silence and peace are deep longings, and there is heightened awareness of the wars of the 20th century as moments of great loss, exemplified recently by Pat Barker's prize-winning novels. Whatever the wellsprings of this modern feeling may be, they have little or no connection with triumphalism or parades. The need for the silence comes from our own collective experience, and should be supported in every way.[48]

The reference to Barker is a flattering one, in its use of her work to support an argument about the appropriate form of response to past conflict. It does not, though, ask where the 'powerful popular impulse' and 'the wellsprings of the modern feeling', come from, or pay any heed to the debate about the place of the culture industry in this response to war. Jason Cowley, in an article in the *Sunday Times* two years later, attempted to juggle these concerns, with reference to literary works including those of Geoff Dyer, Pat Barker and also Faulks's *Birdsong*:

> When Sebastian Faulks, in the late 1980s, began telling friends that he planned to write a novel about the first world war, many were incredulous.
>
> Who wants to read about that, they seemed to say. Or, as one colleague bluntly put it, when Faulks mentioned that he was accompanying veterans on a trip to the battlefields of the western front: 'I couldn't think of anything more boring.'
>
> [...] nowadays, writing about the first world war has assumed the exaggerated dimension of a publishing 'boom' – something that is

> reaching a crescendo as we prepare for the 80th anniversary of the armistice of November 11, 1918. Far from being forgotten, the Great War, it seems, is in danger of being over-remembered, our response to it distorted and overdetermined by a heady brew of historical revisionism, cultural nostalgia and commercial opportunism.[49]

Cowley's definition of new writing on the First World War errs on the side of cynicism, but it nonetheless affords thorough analysis. The 'historical revisionism' in particular refers more to Cowley's review of non-fiction, including Niall Ferguson's *The Pity of War* (1998), Lyn MacDonald's *To the Last Man: Spring 1918* (1998) and John Keegan's *First World War* (1998), but the dual thrust of 'cultural nostalgia and commercial opportunism' links directly to fiction, in which 'the war has emerged as a compelling subject', as he phrased it.[50] By plugging into the collective consciousness, his argument claims, writing on the First World War simultaneously tugs at our purse-strings. This cynical turn of Cowley's analysis is tempered by his own visit to the battlefields, where 'It is consoling to believe that no amount of opportunistic publishing can ever erase such peculiar grace', as he put it.[51] Nonetheless, the accusations of a 'publishing boom' and 'opportunistic publishing' pull no punches. How far, his argument asks, is publishing success due to choice of subject? What is the cultural value of books that join an opportunistic bandwagon that travels to commercial gratification via the trenches? How can a topic be seen one year as 'boring' (as Faulks's near-sighted colleague had it) and immensely popular only a few years on? These broader questions of genre fashion were addressed in Chapter 3. The narrower concern of artistic integrity in the face of commercial viability is one that is central to a reconstruction of Pat Barker's career.

Barker's first novel, *Union Street*, was published in 1982. Narrated by seven working-class women in a Northern industrial town, it was the novel Barker was encouraged to write in preference to the unpublished middle-class novels of manners she had previously been engaged in writing.[52] *Blow Your House Down*, Barker's second novel, continued in a similar vein, focusing on a group of prostitutes menaced by a serial killer. Well-received but of limited sales success, Barker's early work came to be inextricably associated with her publisher, Virago. Newspaper articles recording the history of the publisher frequently mention Barker as one of its authors, even after she had moved to Viking.[53] Barker was typified, in the words of Paul Taylor in the *Independent on Sunday* in 1991, as 'specialis[ing] in gritty feminist sagas'.[54] Barker talked about the impact of this typecasting to the journalist Catherine Bennett in an article about Virago for the *Guardian* in 1993:

> 'I wanted to try a different position in the market, I also felt I was getting terribly labelled, you know – working class feminist Virago author, and I think to be identified with a particular publishing house to that extent is not perhaps a very good thing for a writer.'[55]

Barker's analysis of her own predicament, where her writing is so clearly identified with the publisher, is strongly based in market terms. To be labelled is to curtail interpretation of a writer's texts, and also to deny him or her sectors of the market. Barker's desire to '"try a different position in the market"' was an attempt to prevent stereotyping of her work, both in terms of its meaning and its potential audience. Clare Alexander, the editor to whom Barker eventually moved at Viking, defines the situation that the author was previously facing as 'ghettois[ation]'.[56] While Alexander places herself and her company in a positive, emancipatory role (freeing Barker from the ghetto) and hence hers is not a disinterested definition, she nevertheless suggests a useful model for understanding this stage of Barker's career. Lionising Viking and demonising Virago is not the point, however. Rather, it is to assess how contextual as well as textual factors – such as placement on an imprint – contribute to a book's reception in the marketplace.

Pat Barker's move to Viking and its paperback imprint Penguin went along with an altered subject matter in her novels. The first book that Alexander was involved in publishing was the paperback edition of *The Man Who Wasn't There* (1989; paperback edition 1990).[57] This marked, in Alexander's words, a 'turning point', focusing on the vivid imaginative life of a twelve-year-old boy in the 1950s, whose mother claims his absent father was a pilot shot down in the Second World War.[58] A male protagonist, albeit one surrounded by female relatives and friends, was a fictional departure for Barker. Her wholesale defection to Viking was then accomplished with *Regeneration*. With this novel, Barker moved from writing 'gritty feminist sagas' to documentary fiction with a largely male cast and a subject – the First World War – that seemed worlds away from her earlier work.

Talking about this development, Alexander affirmed that 'after *The Man Who Wasn't There*, Pat Barker quite consciously decided to write something about men, and also war, knowing that it would have a greater impact, and indeed with *Regeneration* the male critical establishment did take note [...] in a sense *Regeneration* was a gauntlet thrown down: a challenge to critics to reassess her reputation.'[59] The subsequent critical reception to *Regeneration* gives substance both to Alexander's claims and Barker's understanding of her relationship with Virago. Paul Taylor, who noted Barker's specialisation in 'gritty feminist sagas' in his review of *Regeneration*, went on to say that 'this book represents an admirable extension of her range'.[60] For Justine Picardie in the *Independent*:

> Pat Barker is best known as a feminist writer, and for her gritty tales of working-class women's lives in the north of England. Her new novel, *Regeneration*, therefore comes as a surprise: it enters a very masculine world [...]
>
> One might say that Pat Barker has herself emerged from a kind of chrysalis, from the ghetto of being a 'women's writer', perhaps? The result is an austere and very fine novel.[61]

The language used by the critics, mentioning the 'extension of her range', a 'surprise' entry into 'a very masculine world', indicates that they are watching a career in transition. The most readily discernible element of this transition is in a changed subject matter, moving from 'female' to 'male'. The transition is applauded, even if Picardie's praise is somewhat warily based on the premise that what Barker is doing is breaking out of the ghetto and escaping the tag of ' "women's writer" '. Indeed, Barker's novel after *The Ghost Road, Another World* (1998), moved Virago author Michèle Roberts to note reproachfully in her *Independent on Sunday* review that, 'It's as though masculine concerns and experience really inspire Barker now, offering a new world to explore, bigger and brighter than the conventional feminist sphere, one that lets her get going and spread her wings.'[62] At the time of *The Ghost Road* itself, Kate Kellaway – a critic who was also on the judging panel that awarded the Booker to Barker – develops an idea of this stage of Barker's career as 'male' in a stylistic rather than subject-led manner:

> If I had read *The Ghost Road* without knowing who had written it, I'd have sworn the author was a man. Not because of the subject [...] but because of the tone, the dry control, the use of irony as emotional camouflage, the minimal visual effects and the dispatch of the narrative. And because Sarah, the most significant woman in the novel, although sketched with skill, is given no time to herself.[63]

As with Taylor, Picardie and Roberts, Kellaway has presuppositions about what is meant by women's writing and men's writing, about what technical and emotional attributes typify them, and about their range and focus. The construction of preconceptions about writing, particularly when built upon gender divisions, will always be controversial. A controversial publishing development in the 1990s that had gender divisions in writing at the top of its agenda was the institution of the Orange Prize, a challenge to the Booker with its all-female nominees and judges. The first award was made in the year following Pat Barker's receipt of the Booker, causing the *Times Literary Supplement*'s diarist to comment satirically that, 'Thus any woman who feels that she should have won last year's Booker Prize instead of that notorious war-writer, Mr Pat Barker, has been given another chance.'[64]

An analysis of Barker's career that claims that its later, more successful stage is due to it moving into a 'male' sphere, would soon run into theoretical and ideological quagmires, with its reliance on stratified ideas of 'male' and 'female' writing. In the limited space of a newspaper article, the analysis inevitably tends towards oversimplification. Such oversimplifications make the author 'rueful', to return to Barker's interview with Francis Spufford, most particularly in the implication that she has not only turned to 'male' writing but also to 'major' writing '"at last"'. It is interesting that amongst the reviews for *Regeneration*, one of the few less positive accounts, in the *Financial Times*, displays a greater understanding of the continuity the novel represents rather than the discontinuity: 'Nothing wholly convinces – yet Pat Barker's concerns here are not a step away from those of her earlier novels about working women around Teesside: vulnerability, illusions about manliness, the attitudes and prejudices across the class spectrum which still define English culture.'[65]

A writer could claim a myriad of reasons for shifts in subject choice and career orientation, and the question, 'Where do you get your ideas from?' must dog any author. Barker is no exception: an autobiographical explanation for her interest in the First World War could be found in her upbringing by her grandparents, though the underlying themes explored in the trilogy are continuations of her existing interests: gender, class, sexuality and memory.[66] But the coincidence of Barker's change in subject matter, her change of publisher and her career trajectory suggests a less organic development, and a more strategic act of market positioning. If, as Alexander asserts, Barker was 'quite consciously' throwing down the gauntlet, it was a ploy that had the industry, the media, and the Booker Prize judges eagerly picking it up. Barker's ambivalent feelings towards the construction of her success are akin to that of her character Billy Prior to his status in the army as a working-class officer. Barker is elevated from her origins, from the feminist rank and file, and given new powers and new responsibilities (which include a widened appeal to men, if it is assumed that 'male' subjects will attract male audiences). Research conducted on behalf of the Orange Prize and published in 2000 would seem to support this assertion. Orange surveyed a representative sample of readers to discover male and female attitudes towards cover design:

> Overall it seem[s] to be clear that books written by men are likely to appeal to both men and women, while those written by women are likely to appeal mainly to women. In other words books written by women have to work harder to sell to men than books written by men do to sell to women.[67]

Interestingly, however, Barker's *Regeneration*, which was one of the 20 titles used in the survey, was one of only two that 'significantly more men than women wish to read'. By stepping over the boundaries of the ghetto, it would seem, new market possibilities arise.

Mark Lawson, quoted earlier in this case study, named *The Ghost Road* as the 'Best novel of the year', and described it as a 'brilliant piece of gender and historical ventriloquism'.[68] At a textual level, Barker uses ventriloquism to give voice to male characters, both imagined and real-life, and to a historical period. In terms of publishing history, ventriloquism could be seen as the process by which Barker enables herself to occupy different market positions, and to access new audiences. Ventriloquism is then a metaphor for how fiction finds its voice in the marketplace. Thus, the case study of *The Ghost Road* articulates how Pat Barker and her career come to speak for our beliefs about war and history, historical fiction and literary value, gender definition and cultural achievement. Reading and interpretation – by critics and by judges of literary awards, by professionals and by 'ordinary' readers, by women and by men – become an active process of speaking, but a speaking mediated by the contingencies of text and context in the marketplace.

Arundhati Roy's *The God of Small Things* (1997)[69]

In the Acknowledgements to her 1997 Booker prize-winning novel *The God of Small Things*, Arundhati Roy thanks, among several others, 'David

Godwin, flying agent, guide and friend. For taking that impulsive trip to India. For making the waters part.'[70] David Godwin is Roy's London-based agent, and a central figure in the book's success. After reading the manuscript of *The God of Small Things*, he decided to fly to India to woo Roy as a client. Godwin takes up the story in the pages of the *Independent* some days after *The God of Small Things* won the Booker Prize:

> Her novel arrived one morning, sent to me via Patrick French [another client], and when I read it I was overwhelmed. So I got on a plane to India, and Roy met me in Delhi, very wary of me. I spent a weekend with her, brought the book back here, and it's been a fairytale story. Even as a publisher, I never had a book that sold this sort of numbers – 600 000 copies in hardback worldwide.[71]

Godwin's account reads with the simplicity of a fable. The transition from 'I was overwhelmed' to 'I got on a plane' has a narrative logic that, even with the ease of modern-day intercontinental travel, belies an unusual act, the one that had Roy describing Godwin as her 'flying agent'. Godwin formulates the ensuing journey of the novel into the world as a 'fairytale', in which he could well be cast as the fairy godfather.

For this is a novel whose publishing history is as fairytale-like as any story that may lie within its pages. Jason Cowley, interviewing Roy for *The Times* shortly after he and his fellow panel members awarded her the Booker, wrote that 'Roy's journey, in less than a year, from putative novelist to global literary phenomenon is almost as magical and unexpected as her fiction'.[72]

Whether the analogy that Cowley proffers between text and context can be sustained is debatable, but, unlike some of the skewed media reports about *Captain Corelli's Mandolin*, his analysis of the publishing history has a greater factual grounding. *The God of Small Things* was intensely scrutinised from the moment of its high-profile acquisition. One of the earliest mentions of the novel in the national press was almost a year before UK publication, by Patrick French in the *Sunday Times* (French, as aforementioned, is another of Godwin's clients, and so his reference to Roy indicates how closely networked, even nepotistic, the publishing world can be). He wrote:

> a cross-caste love-story set against a background of political turbulence in Kerala, [. . .] looks set to be the publishing sensation of the year [. . .] Roy's novel was fought over by nine British publishers

> and has already been hyped in the trade magazine *The Bookseller* as 'heart-stoppingly powerful' and a 'modern masterpiece'.[73]

Later in the year, Marianne MacDonald's *Independent* piece further prepared the pre-publication ground:

> Much excitement this week over the discovery of the female answer to Vikram Seth [...] Roy admits to bewilderment at the frenzied reception to her book [...] Philip Gwyn Jones, editorial director of Flamingo Books, which bought the UK rights for more than £150 000, said: 'It's a masterpiece. It proves that real literary genius will always win through, even on a first book.'[74]

The mechanisms of 'hype' that French mentions – the trade press and literary diary pieces – are triggered by money. Large advances grab headlines and Flamingo's investment, their 'big subcontinental gamble' (as the *Sunday Times* phrased it), marked the publisher stepping into marketing overdrive.[75] Ignoring for a while the starkly ethnic constructions ('female Vikram Seth') and creeping language of colonisation ('subcontinental gamble'), *The God of Small Things* would seem to have had the world at its feet – or in the palm of its agent's hands.

Primed as 'India's Next Big Thing' (as the *Independent* put it), Roy and her novel were also mentioned in several previews in the press at the turn of 1996 and 1997.[76] The opening of the novel was extracted in Granta's *India!* issue of Spring 1997, alongside writings by R. K. Narayan, Amit Chaudhuri and Vikram Seth.[77] Major review attention followed, which in terms of allotted space was not hindered by Roy's 'heart-breaking [...] beaut[y]' (*Sunday Times*) – her photograph made numerous appearances in the newspapers.[78] Although the praise was not unanimous, it was substantial, as the profusion of acclaim reprinted on the paperback edition of the novel makes evident.

With the short-listing and eventual award of the Booker in the autumn of 1997, *The God of Small Things*' miraculous few months reached their climax. Roy had accomplished in just over a year what most writers can only dream of achieving in a career: hundreds of thousands of pounds in advances from global rights sales; worldwide publicity; and the award of the Commonwealth's most prestigious and high-profile prize. In Roy's home country of India, *The God of Small Things* was not only successful in itself but also a stimulus to opening the market, as described by Peter Popham in the *Independent on Sunday* in 1999:

> Picador, whose parent company Macmillan has been in India for nearly 150 years, woke up to the fact that suddenly a large number of Indians were buying books [...] When Seth's *A Suitable Boy* was published in India, it sold only 7000 copies in hardback. 'If it was published now,' says [Peter] Straus, 'it would sell a lot more than that. Arundhati Roy's book has given a new confidence to Indian publishers about the size of their market.' [...]
>
> *The God of Small Things* has altered the landscape, coaxed many more people into shelling out for a literary novel, and opened up new selling channels; Arundhati Roy herself tells of being approached in her car at a traffic light by a hawker offering paper tissues, women's monthly magazines, and a bootleg copy of *The God of Small Things*. (She bought it.) But the problem in India is always the same: infrastructure.[79]

An unmitigated, worldwide success, give or take the perils of piracy and the problem of infrastructure? Every fairytale has its dark side, though, and *The God of Small Things* is no exception. The award of the Booker Prize is habitually greeted with derision from some quarters – scandal being integral to the Prize, as English argues in his work on literary prizes.[80] In 1998 Ian McEwan should have been Beryl Bainbridge. In 1996 Pat Barker should have been Salman Rushdie. In 1995 Graham Swift should have thought up his own plot, rather than borrowing William Faulkner's, just as Yann Martel in 2002 wrote a book a little too similar to one by the Brazilian author Moacyr Scliar. In 1994 James Kelman should have written in polite English rather than obscene Scots. (To refer to only a few of the Booker scandals of the 1990s.) And so the litany of complaint extends to Roy. In the televised post-award coverage the publisher Carmen Callil, who had chaired the previous year's panel, said that, ' "I disliked the book so much. It has got a vulgarity about it that embarrasses me. The writing is execrable." '[81] Even before the final decision, one anonymous 'observer' reported in *The Times* dismissed Roy's selection as ' "compensation for them not putting Vikram Seth on the list last time" '.[82] This commentary heightened the 'subcontinental' references, as did several of the other positive and negative remarks and reviews. In a largely generous and thoughtful piece in the *London Review of Books*, Michael Gorra stated that Roy's style had been 'pawed by Rushdie's', like 'other Indian authors'.[83] Peter Kemp in the *Sunday*

Times saw it as 'considerably derivative from Salman Rushdie [...] this is magic realism as recycled candyfloss'.[84] Adverse comparisons, overlaid with a whiff of plagiarism, were drawn between *Midnight's Children*'s depictions of a pickle factory and *The God of Small Things*' scenes set in 'Paradise Pickles & Preserves'. Valentine Cunningham's *Prospect* article, 'Manufacturing a Masterpiece', whose title more than hints at its cynical take on the novel, was an example of such negative comparison.[85]

Even before the award of the Booker, Roy commented to the *Sunday Times* that ' "People's response to my book is refracted through adulation or hostility" '.[86] Her remark was a telling one. Much criticism of the text grew from comparative analyses: to the size of her advance; to her origins; to her beauty; to other Indian writers. Some reviews were favourable in their comparisons, some detracted, but the majority conformed to this pattern. The reception in India, however, had a different frame of reference. For, as Peter Popham wrote in an earlier *Independent on Sunday* article, Roy 'discovered that success in the West is an ambiguous commodity at home'.[87] The particular cause of offence was Roy's portrayal of a sexual relationship between an Untouchable man and a Syrian Christian woman. According to Simon Barnes in *The Times*, 'Roy's book, adored over here and part of the continuing love affair with the Indian novel, is inevitably the subject of an obscenity suit in India. The fact that this concerns a passage about caste taboo will only inflame the passions higher; Indian hostility, English fascination.'[88] Barnes's delineation of the reaction as 'Indian hostility, English fascination', for all its simplification of complex cultural issues, uses a similar terminology to that employed by Roy: the reading refracted either through adulation or hostility. Blake Morrison's review of the novel in the *Independent on Sunday* exemplifies the adulatory reading in his depiction of the peculiarly British fascination with Indian literature:

> The British traditionally look to Indian novels to provide something exotic yet familiar, and *The God of Small Things*, which features a family of larger-than-life Anglophiles 'trapped outside their own history', doesn't disappoint. The landscape is so lush, so teeming with insect and reptile life [...] so palpably there, that it's likely the novel will do for Kerala's already burgeoning tourist industry what John Berendts's *Midnight in the Garden of Good and Evil* has done for Savannah's.[89]

Morrison suggests that British readings give a holiday-maker's view of a country and its culture, rendering it 'exotic'. This is appreciation as literary tourism – or cultural voyeurism. Jackie Wullschlager, previewing forthcoming novels in the *Financial Times* in January 1998, notes the trend for 'the new genre of sexy eastern novels, written by young Indian and Chinese women with a talent for lush prose, whom every publisher in England has been chasing since the success last year of Arundhati Roy's *The God of Small Things*'.[90] The conjunction of desire and orientalism that Wullschlager comments on is an extreme example, but it is not untypical of the ideology behind more subtle representations.

This conjunction is bound up with the issue of mimesis. As Amit Chaudhuri argued in his 1999 *Times Literary Supplement* article, 'The Lure of the Hybrid', the prevalent Western mode of reception of Indian writing, although frequently celebrating postmodern traits of the polyvocal and the fantastic, or magic realist, paradoxically becomes 'a surprisingly old-fashioned and mimetic ['interpretive aesthetic']: Indian life is plural, garrulous, rambling, lacking a fixed centre, and the Indian novel must be the same'.[91] The tendency is thus, according to Chaudhuri, 'To celebrate Indian writing simply as overblown, fantastic, lush and non-linear'.[92] This is a critical act that 'risk[s] making it a figure for the subconscious, and to imply that what is ordinarily called thinking is alien to the Indian tradition – surely an old colonial prejudice.'[93] It is no doubt this school of criticism that some of Roy's reviewers fall prey to, and subsuming her work into what Chaudhuri sees as an 'old-fashioned' and prejudiced 'interpretive aesthetic'. This is the 'postcolonial exotic' that Graham Huggan identifies as the representational process that 'market[s] the margins'.[94] This instance of marketing by ethnicity is thus not only symptomatic of the publicity machine of contemporary UK publishing, but also the interpretive parameters that it both nourishes and feeds upon.

The example of *The God of Small Things*, then, offers some salutary lessons in the understanding of marketing's construction of literature. In his essay arguing against Anglo-centric constructions of literature, ' "Commonwealth Literature" Does Not Exist' (1983), Rushdie writes:

> One of the rules, one of the ideas on which the edifice rests, is that literature is an expression of nationality. What Commonwealth literature finds interesting in Patrick White is his Australianness; in Doris Lessing, her Africanness; in V. S. Naipaul, his West Indianness [. . .][95]

Literature as the expression of nationality, nationality as the emphasis of marketing: the relationship of author, ethnicity and text thus takes on a curious form. It works by metonymy, each entity eliding the others. The acquisition of the novel is a 'subcontinental gamble', Roy a 'female Vikram Seth', even a 'Goddess of Small Things'.[96] Beautiful, exotic author. Sultry Keralan landscape. Lush, descriptive prose. This jumble of constructions is indicative of marketing's parasitic processes. To be sure, it does Roy's career no disservice, providing plenty of hooks to hang media interest on and so to reel in consumers. The impact on the author, though, 'bewilder[ed] at the frenzied reception' as MacDonald put it in the *Independent*, with her book and herself manipulated into exotic icons, is a side-effect that could cause more distress, though it could also be argued that Roy is complicit in the processes of marketing.

Another consequence of the 'Commonwealth' view of literature derided by Rushdie is the tendency for an author of one country to be compared with compatriots. Nowhere can this be more tangibly seen than in the comparisons drawn between Roy and Rushdie himself. Jason Cowley's description of the group photograph in the Indian Fiction issue of the *New Yorker*, in which both Roy and Rushdie appeared, makes the comparison visually clear:

> It is early summer in London and the *New Yorker* is gathering India's leading novelists in one room for a monumental photograph. What is remarkable about the occasion, apart from the exclusion of any writer not working in English, is the prominence given to Arundhati Roy. She stands at the front of the group, squeezed between Vikram Chandra and Anita Desai, laughing playfully as Salman Rushdie rests a supportive hand on her shoulder. It is as if the older writer, who himself did so much in *Midnight's Children* to redefine the boundaries of the Anglo-Indian novel, is bestowing a special favour on the younger Roy, marking her out.[97]

Here is Roy as the chosen one, crown princess to the throne of Indian fiction. In terms of textual comparison this may be a spurious genealogy, but in marketing terms it is a felicitous adoption. What happier event could there be than the birth of a daughter to the king, drawing a direct line of inheritance from Rushdie to Roy?

With Cowley's depiction of Rushdie's paternalistic gesture, the elder Indian writer might seem destined to become Roy's second fairy godfather. However, this family relationship is fraught with difficulties. Rushdie is configured as the patriarch to whom all other Indian writers must defer, the 'godhead', as Chaudhuri ironically puts it, 'from which Indian writing in English has reportedly sprung, revivified'.[98] This is a new hierarchy of exactly the sort Rushdie argues against in

'"Commonwealth Literature" Does Not Exist'. Yet the structures that lead fiction into the marketplace seem incapable of resisting the representational forces of marketing that are exerted upon novels and their authors.

Rushdie's role in Roy's fairytale, moreover, threatened to transmogrify from godfather into ogre. The ogre is a figure of danger, of course: the inevitable comparison that would be made between *The God of Small Things* and Rushdie's oeuvre is one that any first-time novelist might find menacing. But the ogre is also a means for the heroine to prove herself: a battle in which, if Roy comes out well, she can scramble on the stunned body of Rushdie and his admirers to storm the bastion of the literary castle.

The feud that consequently developed between the two writers, if separated from the inevitable gossip, rumour and egotism, seemed to be connected to the ideology of representation, and specifically to the concept of the exotic. In his interview with Roy, Peter Popham wrote:

> Despite these anxieties [of the court case and personal slurs], she is not planning to leave India; in fact, the attacks are one of the reasons this seasoned controversialist is pleased to stay put. 'The wonderful thing about writing in this country is that it's not a clubhouse activity, you are involved in something that touches lives, it's really touching life and setting up arguments and staking your claim to territory.'
>
> The abandonment of their homeland by all India's other prominent writers puzzles and saddens her. 'If it was one or two or three writers who lived outside, one wouldn't question it – what I don't understand is why in that photograph in the Indian issue of the *New Yorker*, 11 of the 12 writers [she was the 12th] live outside. I find it hard to understand why they don't live here [...]
>
> 'I can't imagine being able to live anywhere else as a writer.'[99]

Roy represents India as a real place, not the 'imaginary homeland' that Rushdie writes of from his position of exile and 'physical alienation'.[100] So when critics begin to debate the similarities between *The God of Small Things* and *Midnight's Children*, there is much more at stake than the originality of a metaphor or two. Jason Cowley, an emphatic Roy supporter, takes up the argument:

> Salman Rushdie, though praising her verve and ambition, is disappointed by her refusal to describe India as exotic [...]

> For Rushdie, in unhappy exile in London, India is [...] an exotic land of magic and extremes. As a result, his work is resplendent with [...] gimmicks of magic realism. But for Roy, whose work is grounded in the actual, there is nothing remarkable about India. To her reality is magical.
>
> She says: 'When I was in America I went on a couple of TV shows with Rushdie. And he said, (she borrows the voice of an officious schoolmaster) "The trouble with Arundhati is that she insists that India is an ordinary place". Well, I ask, "Why, the hell not?" It is my ordinary life. The difference between me and Rushdie begins there.
>
> 'I don't want Brownie points because I'm from India. My book doesn't trade on the currency of cultural specificity, even though the details are right.'[101]

Although trading on the currency of 'cultural specificity' is something Roy says she wants to avoid, the ungenerous critic might hint that she is point-scoring by claiming that she lives nearer the pickle factory. Roy's position of speaking and writing from within her home country, a contemporary India, is at once an aesthetic and political ideology. Jack O'Sullivan, writing in the *Independent*, debates these ideas:

> The Booker shortlist, announced this week is, in many ways, nothing but the same old story, the one about the Irishman, the Indian and the Antipodean, who seem perennially to be among the favoured few. So this year the likes of Roddy Doyle, Salman Rushdie and David Malouf step aside for fresh ranks of compatriots, namely Bernard MacLaverty, Arundhati Roy and Madeleine St John [...]
>
> *The God of Small Things* is [...] unlike the classic Indian novel in English, which typically appeals to Anglo-Saxon fantasy about an exotic land. Roy has set the novel in the lush landscape of Kerala in south-west India, but she does not pander to traditional orientalism in the way she presents Indian society. There is a distinctive autobiographical tone as she looks at the Syrian Christian community in which she grew up [...] And so it reflects how her society is racked by conflicts between the energy of modernity and the demands of existing tradition. As the plot unfolds you see these issues played out against a very real, up to date world of bill boards, radio jingles and pop music.[102]

Roy, here, is not at all 'exotic', despite an inauspicious beginning as the subject of a joke about positive discrimination. O'Sullivan manages to hold apart the more habitually conflated 'lush landscape' and its effect on prose style. Roy escapes from the ties of traditional orientalism (which O'Sullivan implicitly attributes to Rushdie by naming him at the beginning of the piece), telling, instead a more real story, 'distinctive[ly] autobiographical' and hence 'deeply moving'.[103]

Rushdie's advocates might want to disagree with the construction of him as pandering to orientalist fantasy, but what is most relevant to the debate in publishing terms is O'Sullivan's attempt to get under the skin of marketing and explode the myths it creates about identity and genealogy. What it prompts most usefully is an analytical model of publishing that can encompass both text and context. It is a model that is aware of the processes of marketing, and so enables itself to combat more effectively its most lurid fantasies. It is also a position from which the inalienable fact of the UK and US's domination of the production of English-language fiction – which forces books to travel from their non-Anglo-Saxon homes if they are to achieve widespread cultural impact – might be assessed. To define this structure as colonial or neo-colonial, as with the example of *Trainspotting,* may not be the most productive definition. *The God of Small Things'* publication in India, which pre-dated those in the UK and US by several months, created success on its own terms rather than those imposed by London and New York.[104] The perception that Straus and Popham have of a changing Indian market is one they believe to be partially wrought by *The God of Small Things.* The 'alter[ation to] the landscape' is dependent on infrastructure – the external conditions of production and distribution – as well as economic stability, something that one novel cannot hope to achieve by itself. The achievement, however, of *The God of Small Things* stems from the collaboration between text and context, and understanding the inter-play between the two is a way of mapping both cultural and commercial success. The location of that success will be found not in a single, flying visit, but in a concerted, concentrated narrative; an epic of the making of writing in the marketplace.

6
Crossovers

Bret Easton Ellis's *American Psycho* (1991)

Bret Easton Ellis's novel *American Psycho* was published in the UK by Picador in 1991. The subject of the novel, his third after *Less Than Zero* (1986) and *The Rules of Attraction* (1988), became infamous. In summary, it catalogues in frequently banal and occasionally lurid detail the life of Patrick Bateman, a Wall Street yuppie whose narrative is packed with the details of designer clothes, modish restaurants, and the torture and dismemberment of his (mostly) female victims.[1] Ellis is an American writer, but the publishing history analysed here is principally of the UK publication and reception of his third novel. Nonetheless, it is worth noting the pre-publication trouble that the book ran into in the US. A report from *The Times* dated 19 November 1990 picked up the story:

> A full-scale storm erupted in Manhattan's literary village last week when Simon and Schuster, the publishers, decided to scrap the book just as it was about to be sent to the shops, on the grounds that it was just too shocking. Writers cried 'censorship', denouncing the publishers for caving in to the pressure of Paramount Communications, their new corporate owners [...]
>
> With advance publicity like that it took about a microsecond for Ellis to find a new publisher courageous enough to issue the book.[2]

The *Independent on Sunday* maintained *The Times*'s cynical tone in its report the following Sunday:

> The end of the *American Psycho* saga turns out happy for all, depending on your point of view. Its original publishers are now the

> dians of taste; Mr Mehta [head of Knopf] is the saviour of f expression; and Mr Ellis is even richer.[3]

A [illegible] months before its appearance in the UK, a monumental literary scrap had developed in the US, in which the values of decency and taste were pitted against freedom of speech and the seeming intervention of corporate owners. The *Independent on Sunday* neatly set up Simon & Schuster and Knopf as chief representatives of these opposing values, whilst *The Times* cannily points out the increased publicity the controversy would create. The fight over the book took place on the battlefield of imprint identity. Simon & Schuster's decision to cancel publication seemed worryingly influenced by 'their new corporate owners', while Knopf seized the chance to publish a book that would declare its imprint Vintage to be at the publishing vanguard. With the publication of *American Psycho*, imprints are the arena in which artistic and moral judgements fuse with business opportunities. It was indeed ironic that a book whose protagonist's day job in 'mergers and acquisitions' is converted into the sinister night-time 'murders and executions' itself seemed to fall prey in the US to corporate takeover, only for it to be rehabilitated by Knopf's acquisition.[4] When reviews of *American Psycho* began to appear in the UK press on the book's publication in April 1991, it was clear that the novel would be contentious on the eastern side of the Atlantic as well. The *Sunday Times*'s jocular 'review of reviews' gives a flavour of the reception that greeted the book:

> Bret Easton Ellis [...] was given a right going over in the back of the van. The literary police showed no mercy. [...] Andrew Motion in *The Observer* let fly with 'Extremely disgusting – not interesting-disgusting but disgusting-disgusting.' [...] Joan Smith in *The Guardian* went for the personal approach: 'If it reveals anything, it is only a glimpse of an author who chose to sit in his apartment thinking of unoriginal ways of torturing women.' [...] Jon Wilde in *Blitz* went berserk: 'American Psycho is the most poisonous, hideous slime ever to emerge from a hole in the name of literature.'[5]

In addition to giving an overview of the reviewers' reactions to the ethics and aesthetics of *American Psycho*, the *Sunday Times* went on to detail the more paratextual side of the debate:

> Leaving the bloody remains of Ellis twitching on the floor, critics turned on the book's publisher Macmillan, who also published

> *Dirty Weekend*. According to [...] the *Daily Telegraph*, *American Psycho* demonstrated 'the thoughtless and irresponsible misogyny of contemporary publishing', while the literary editor of the *Sunday Express* [...] in a brief paragraph which will have mystified those of his readers unaware of this great literary controversy, attacked 'the once reputable house of Macmillan' for publishing two novels which he then declined to name.[6]

For these two detractors from the *Daily Telegraph* and the *Sunday Express*, what is at stake is the reputation of a publisher and the institutions of publishing at large. The publication of this one book is perceived as reflecting badly on its publishers and the publishing industry, an extension of text to context. Indeed, an imprint is given shape and meaning by the books of which it is composed. The history of Picador on Macmillan's website reveals that *American Psycho* was an important part of the imprint's process of self-identification, one of their 'dynamic and distinctive paperback originals'.[7] Just as Knopf's publication of *American Psycho* in the US was at least in part an exercise in self-promotion, so the UK publication of the novel brought the media spotlight to Picador, and allowed it to generate self- and external definitions as a provocative, contemporary imprint.

Yet the effect of an imprint becoming defined through its publications can also be considered in reverse. What was the impact, in other words, of *American Psycho* being published by Picador? Suzanne Moore, in an article from the *Independent* after the furore on publication had died down a little, considered the question:

> The sheltered literary Establishment managed some silly posturing [...] over [...] *American Psycho*, failing entirely to recognise that this sort of thing had been written about for years in what they dismiss as genre fiction. Suddenly, however, content has gone out of the window as all talk is of technique and literary merit which are hauled on as though they emanated magically from the chosen texts. But, surely, great literature is not just great by itself. This greatness has been created by argument, discussion, interpretation. It *is* the job of the defenders of classics to have to defend them routinely, to explain to us why dead authors be given posthumous [...] peerages as literary lords.[8]

Moore, by identifying that the true nature of *American Psycho*'s provocation lay not in its content but in its placement upon a particular publisher's list, also makes the salient point that behind the furore was the desire to control the processes of cultural accreditation. In 1991, Picador had already gained its reputation as a publisher of upmarket literary writing. For *American Psycho* to be published on this list was perceived as a statement of the novel's literary worth. The novel was proffered not as 'genre' fiction but as 'literary'. As Moore points out, by the standards of horror fiction, *American Psycho* was not particularly shocking. But by those of the literary novel – or, arguably of the 'literary establishment' that polices the definition of the literary novel – it was extreme, and hence vilified. Peter Straus confirmed this from the vantage point of 1999, saying '*American Psycho*, which was published by Picador, could have been done as straight horror on Pan and wouldn't have been noticed by the media. As it was published on a literary list, with the publisher implying by its inclusion on the imprint that it was good writing to be taken seriously, it aroused interest and was attacked.'[9] What the critics, and indeed some bookshops which refused to stock the book, were doing in criticising *American Psycho* was not responding to the contents of one book, but actively patrolling genre boundaries and commenting on the decision of a 'literary' publisher to publish the book. When Ellis, and by extension Picador, are 'given a right going over in the back of the van' (in the words of the *Sunday Times*), this is evidence of the cultural arbiters at work. *American Psycho*'s shock value was not in the text itself, but in its imprint placement. The general public, although not necessarily aware of who the publisher of the book was, would have received an interpretation of the text that was mediated by the critics' reaction to its imprint. As Straus has also remarked, 'The perception of a book can completely alter according to the decisions made by the publisher about its packaging and placement.'[10] The reaction to *American Psycho* was not, then, a 'pure' critical judgement, but one based on paratextual and contextual relativism, in which the book was actively constructed by marketing activities and marketplace reactions. The publishing history of *American Psycho* illustrates the disturbances caused by genre-crossing. By placing a novel with elements of horror on the list of a literary publisher, Picador shaped reaction to both the novel and itself.

Helen Fielding's *Bridget Jones's Diary* (1996)[11]

Posted on the 'Customer Comments' section of the Internet bookseller Amazon.co.uk are, among others, these two views of *Bridget Jones's Diary* and its protagonist:

> [1] This is about as funny as being stuck in a police cell.

> Bridget Jones should be shot, and Helen Fielding let off with a caution. This is unrealistic, unfunny, uninteresting, unoriginal pap. The editor should also be shot for allowing this weak, angsty, old hat creation to grace our bookshops. What a relief that Bridget Jones is too sad to find a partner and we're spared any genetic reproduction on that front. I wonder, is Ms Fielding aware that a movement known as feminism occurred this century. Please, no more of this rubbish.
>
> [2] Yes, yes, yes. I am quite aware that this is not the most liberated of portrayals of the inner workings of a woman's mind. No doubt strident feminists are at this very minute burning the book and it's [sic] author in effigy. But come on girls, which one of us can honestly say you haven't thought along the same lines as Bridget at least once? I would not consider myself a slave to my need for emotional fulfilment, or see it as tied to my finding a bloke but I can see where Bridget is coming from. None of us wants to end up dead, half-eaten by an Alsatian. This is a tender, funny and inspiring book. It certainly made me laugh.[12]

These two responses to the novel use the same frames of reference to opposing effect. In terms of the readers' respective attitudes to the novel's perceived humour and relation to reality, the first reader finds it 'unrealistic, unfunny, uninteresting', while the second appeals to fellow female browsers to admit that none 'can honestly say you haven't thought along the same lines as Bridget at least once', and freely admits that it 'made me laugh'. Both refer to Bridget Jones's situation as a single girl to indicate either a personal affinity or anger about the portrayal of a social type. Both also mention feminism to express their reactions. Within these two diverging reader responses, then, are the suggestions of a debate that calls not only upon questions of literary value but also of literary fashion and form, empathy and audience appeal.

According to Peter Straus, the term 'Bridget Jones' is one that might well enter the lexicographical domain in the way that 'Catch 22' has, a belief confirmed by media commentary on the novel.[13] Cherry Norton, for example, writing in the *Sunday Times* in 1998, used Bridget Jones to support her argument, describing, 'The thirtysomething woman with the ticking biological clock, unable to find a suitable man, [who] has [...] become a social stereotype typified by Bridget Jones, the character invented by the writer Helen Fielding.'[14] Katharine Viner in the *Guardian* also debated the 'phenomenon of the singletons' ('singleton' being Bridget Jones's and her friends' terminology for themselves as unmarried thirty-somethings) even sooner after the publication of the novel:[15]

> The urge to label this particular group of women began with the Bridget Jones figure: the woman who works in the media, drinks too much, smokes too much, weighs herself three times a day and desperately wants a boyfriend. [...] The idea has become something of a publishing sensation and not just for Fielding [...][16]

Viner's analysis of the 'media phenomenon', and its 'urge to label' a perceived social grouping notes that it develops alongside 'a publishing sensation'.[17] Bridget Jones moves from her initial context to acquire an appropriated life as the signifier of a popular archetype. This is an interactive process, with the media and publishing in a sometimes symbiotic, sometimes parasitic relationship. Therefore, to venture an answer to the question, 'Who (or what) is Bridget Jones?', is not only to explore the publishing history of one of the bestselling novels of the 1990s, but also to analyse the relationship of publishing with the media, and with society at large.

Bridget Jones made her first public appearance in the pages of the *Independent* on 28 February 1995.[18] This was no innocent debut, though, but a development of a fashionable mode of journalism: the first person confessional. Helen Fielding, a staff journalist at the *Independent*, was asked by the Features Editor to write a confessional column of a type practised by, among others, Zoë Heller in the *Sunday Times*, Kathryn Flett-Flanagan in the *Observer* and Anna Blundy in *The Times*.[19] Written by relatively young female journalists, these columns detailed the day to day events of their authors' lives, placing a particular emphasis on relationships. The basic tenet of this journalism was to promote a form of truth mediated through weekly or monthly doses of public display. Entertainment combined with voyeurism, and the personal testament, with its glimpses of the minutiae of the columnists' lives, elevated the mundane into performative record, through the intermediary of the authorial persona.[20]

Fielding's ironic riposte to her commission was to invent a character, 'Bridget Jones', rather than a persona. This persona informed the column's reader each week of her fluctuating weight, calorific intake, and cigarette and alcohol consumption, and diary-format musings on London life for a single thirty-something woman. The transition of the journalistic mode from artfully-composed fact to a fiction strongly based on reality enabled Fielding to be more extreme in her caricature, as Fielding herself explained in an interview in the *Daily Telegraph*: '"If you write as yourself, you can't help but want people to like you. If you write as somebody else, you can be honest about the secret, stupid shameful things you really think"'.[21] The column was intended as a spoof, but also paradoxically allowed her to present Bridget Jones's life more 'truthfully', Fielding noted, without the inherent self-censorship of an authorial persona. The subsequent appropriation of Fielding's character as a social archetype by others – particularly other journalists such as Norton and Viner – exemplifies the versatility of the creation. Bridget Jones is taken out of the column (and later out of the book) in order to express opinions that may or may not be substantiated by Fielding's writing. That Bridget Jones is thus appropriated demonstrates that there is a confusion between what the readers of the column or the book might believe it to be saying and what commentators on the context believe is happening in society at large. One example of this confusion between textual and the various contextual frames is evident in the journalist Julie Burchill's description, in an interview in the *Sunday Times* in 1998, of an encounter with Fielding:

> 'I think all that stuff is so sad. People who like that book are pathetic, but Helen Fielding is like that. The first time I met her she said, "My biological clock is ticking", and I said, "Why don't you turn it off, then?"'[22]

It is possible that Fielding is as concerned as Bridget Jones to find a partner and have children, but character and creator are not one and the same. Critical theory's problematisation of authorship and intent should at the very least ring warning bells about juxtaposing the opinions of character and creator so unproblematically, as indeed Burchill's own ironic journalistic persona should also indicate. The complex relationship between Fielding and Bridget Jones should serve to indicate an equivalent complexity in the relationship between Bridget Jones and the women she is supposed to represent. The jumble of author, character and media-perceived social phenomenon is undoubtedly one that eventually contributed to the 'publishing sensation', but it also makes it difficult to extricate one version from another, or to mount a prosecution or defence of Bridget Jones, or her Diary, along either literary or sociological lines. Her transition from the newspaper column protagonist to a character in a novel further complicated her identity, as the publishing history of the book shows.

Picador published Helen Fielding's first novel, *Cause Celeb* (1994), to some critical acclaim but no great sales success.[23] After struggling to deliver a second novel, which she was contractually bound to do, Helen Fielding began to formulate – in collaboration with her agent Gillon Aitken and editor Georgia Garrett – what was to become *Bridget Jones's Diary: A Novel*.[24] Bridget Jones's move from column to book was not seamless, however, nor was it an obvious blueprint for commercial success. On being told about the project, the sales team at Picador was reportedly not keen, believing that the book would be a 'poor substitution' for the 'real novel' it had been expecting – an indication both of what the sales reps thought Fielding should be publishing next, and also, perhaps, of what would make a suitable title for the literary Picador imprint. There was also a feeling that newspapers other than the *Independent* 'would not pay it due attention', as it would seem to them a collection of journalism from a rival.[25]

The sales team's initial reserve indicates two things: firstly that the projected *Bridget Jones's Diary* did not match its expectations for a follow-up to *Cause Celeb*, and secondly, that it could not see the intended market for this product. In other words, it found it hard to define the novel. The 'definability' of a book is an essential first step in marketing, and the sales team's caution implied that the generic properties of the novel were either unattractive or too vague. In an article in *The Times* that makes specific reference to *Bridget Jones's Diary*, Joanna Pitman explains the importance of definability: 'The clear-cut genre novel allows booksellers to think in analogies, and that can be a helpful marketing device. Books are, after all, commodities as much as expressions of ideas and imagination, and the more alike they are, the easier they are to sell in large quantities.'[26] *Bridget Jones's Diary*, by not fitting into a 'clear-cut genre', could not be marketed by analogy, and hence a selling pattern was not self-evident. *Bridget Jones's Diary* was not a standard commodity, and despite its close journalistic forebears in the form of the confessional column, was not an obvious publishing success. It is in this way that *Bridget Jones's Diary* is not an obvious 'genre' or 'mass market' novel.

The initial interpretation by the sales team was largely based on a reading of external factors: the belief that a collection of journalism would be hard to sell; that it was not the work the publisher wanted next from Fielding; and that the book had no clear genre definition. Following the production of bound proof copies, however, the readings of the text itself by people within the company began to suggest a different interpretation. Straus noted how proof copies became scarce, and that soon 'everyone in the office began to realise the power of the book'.[27] The early, negative readings of external factors were overridden by colleagues reading the proofs and then remodelling their comprehension of the external factors that would relate to the book's marketing. This, as with *Captain Corelli's Mandolin*, was the beginning of a professionally-instituted word-of-mouth chain, but it is also an example of how a reading of the text itself rather than of its *assumed* marketability, based on existing factors, can reposition the book in the marketplace.

Before examining that repositioning, however, it is valuable to examine more closely the textual transition of Bridget Jones and her Diary from column to novel. Nicola Shulman, in a *Times Literary Supplement* review of the book in 1996, discusses some of the differences:

> Translating a serial into a book has necessitated some changes and reworking of the original material. Unlike a newspaper column, a novel inclines to a conclusion, and to supply that potential the character of Mark Darcy (a rich Human Rights lawyer, originally conceived as a terrible prig) has been reinvented as the Ideal Lover. This, and the suddenly raised chance that a rush at perfect felicity will ensue, has had in turn the effect of exposing Bridget Jones's roots, previously concealed, growing in the unlikely soil of the novels of Barbara Cartland.[28]

The 'inclinat[ion] to a conclusion' is that of the romance plot, indicated here by reference to Barbara Cartland. Bridget Jones in book form is seen by Shulman, then, less as a vehicle for satiric comment on the journalistic construction of truth than as a romantic heroine. In the transition to book form, and taken away from her newspaper context, there is a danger that the irony of Bridget Jones be diminished. It is easier, in other words, to read the completed novel less ironically than the picaresque column, because of its formal concentration on the romance elements.

The resulting blend of irony and romance, with the latter more clearly pronounced in the novel than the column, is a conscious homage by Fielding to Jane Austen's *Pride and Prejudice*. The homage is signalled in various ways, including Bridget's obsessive viewing of a BBC adaptation of *Pride and Prejudice*, the surname of the arrogant but attractive Mark Darcy, and the caddishly flirtatious Daniel Cleaver, who ruins Darcy's first marriage in a parallel to Wickham's seduction of Fitzwilliam Darcy's sister in Austen's novel. The structure of the novel also borrows from *Pride and Prejudice*: the Christmas Day coupling of Bridget and Mark can only occur after an elopement of sorts (by Bridget's mother rather than her sister) is resolved by Darcy. The romance elements threaten to overwhelm the irony, however, as the negative criticism – such as that expressed by the first Amazon.co.uk customer – fails to notice, or find amusing, the satirical standpoint.

Picador attempted to safeguard their author's ironic stance in the transfer to book form by embedding multiple readings in the cover copy:

> A dazzling urban satire of modern human relations?
> An ironic, tragic insight into the demise of the nuclear family?
> Or the confused ramblings of a pissed thirty-something?[29]

The publisher's copy offers interpretations of the novel that vary from the intellectual to the trivial. The placement of question marks at the end of each statement becomes a self-protective act that hints at the novel's portrayal of contemporary society whilst undermining its own pretensions. It puts forward and simultaneously retracts its claims to literariness and seriousness, both inviting and mocking the interpretive act. This self-protective gambit was not an over-cautious one. After a very promising hardback sale (around 60 000 copies), *Bridget Jones's Diary* went on to sell over a million copies in paperback, an undisputed commercial success.[30] Fielding went on to produce a sequel, *Bridget Jones: The Edge of Reason* (1999), and films were made of both books.[31] However, the critical reception to the novel was mixed. Reviews of the novel on its first publication in November 1996 took the book, on the whole, on its own merits, though some already discussed the novel in terms of the media phenomenon of the confessional.[32] The emphasis was on the humour of the work, with, for example, *The Times* calling it 'simply hilarious' and the *Sunday Times* describing it as 'gloriously funny'.[33] In time, though, the critical attention on the novel began to shift, focusing more on the empathetic aspects provoked by the text. Towards the end of Nicola Shulman's early review in the *Times Literary Supplement*, the possibility that the book held for self-identification in a specific sector of consumers is flagged through her *Madame Bovary* paraphrase, '*Bridget Jones's Diary* rings with the unmistakable tone of something that is true to the marrow; it defines what it describes. I know for certain that if I were a young, single, urban woman, I would finish this book crying, "Bridget Jones, c'est moi."'[34] Although distancing herself from such empathy, Shulman predicted that the book's appeal would largely reside there: in the identification it would inspire and the social typing it would stimulate. Indeed, the continuing reception of the book developed along these lines. A little over a year after publication, in January 1998, Catherine Bennett analysed the book and its reception in the pages of the *Guardian*, and her conclusions were firmly based in its capacity to stimulate empathy:

> From the first, features about Fielding's book emphasised reader identification – rather than, say, the author's comic invention – as the reason for its success. Magazines showed women competing for the prize of closest resemblance to a fictional character – '*I'm* Bridget Jones, No, *I'm* Bridget Jones.' And, they predicted, if you hadn't identified with her yet, you would, you would: 'You are very BJ if you... Drink more than you should, smoke more than you should, take up to a day to prepare for a date...'. [...] Somehow, Fielding's dippy hedonist became, as Newsweek proclaimed, 'a heroine for modern women'. [...]
>
> But the mystery evaporates when you finally read the book. As indestructible as Tom or Jerry, Bridget Jones is miraculously undamaged by her intake of wine, cigarettes, and chocolate. None of the acutely observed, nineties insecurities can prevent her living out an impeccable romantic fantasy: a helpless girl's effortless ensnaring of a rich, handsome man. Most shockingly, the saint of single thirty-somethings is not really single at all. Bridget Jones's diary is Bridget Gets Her Man. It's Mills and Boon brought up to date [...] If this explains much about the appeal of '*I'm* Bridget Jones, No, *I'm* Bridget Jones', competitions, it is also instructive for those with high hopes for the New Feminism: forget it.[35]

Once the book has moved from the realm of the review (which *did* emphasise the 'comic invention') to that of 'features' (articles focusing on the book as a social phenomenon rather than as a text) Bennett argues that the appeal to readers is configured as one of identifying with the protagonist. In this reading of *Bridget Jones's Diary*, the 'acute observat[ion]' serves simply to attract and sustain the reader's empathy, and thus any irony is smothered. The romantic resolution of the plot, which Bennett links to those of Mills & Boon, is then used to castigate this construction of its appeal – it is seen as a rebuff to the 'New Feminism'.[36] Bennett's cynical tone is one that suggests she has her reservations about both the book and the 'New Feminism'. A less mannered but similar critical response is contained in an article in the *Independent* in 1998 by the author Bidisha: 'The mega-hit *Bridget Jones's Diary*, for instance, is desperately conservative, despite its humorous presentation

[…] The public like this book because it is deeply conformist (and therefore deeply sexist) in its politics.'[37] In the face of such hostile responses to *Bridget Jones's Diary*, the self-embedded irony of the cover copy seems not paranoia nor whimsy but motivated by a real threat. Moreover, the threat is not solely from the media, but in the responses of non-professional readers. The negative Amazon.co.uk Customer Comment that begins this case study is constructed in exactly the same way as Bidisha's. The book is dismissed as anti-feminist, and the industry that produced it, and the readers to whom it appeals, as conservative and old-fashioned. The underlying accusation is that *Bridget Jones's Diary* is far too similar to the romance genre for comfort, too close to the formal and moral implicits of certain kinds of mass-market fiction. At this point, the attempt to protect the novel through a bit of rhetoric would seem a frail armour. The textual transition of *Bridget Jones's Diary*, with its negotiation between ironic and romantic impulses, a process that hazardously enters the post-feminist fray, is thus one that intersects tellingly with debates about society, and notions of literary value, as well as the publishing history of the book.

Cataloguing more fully the levels of audience response – or indeed an understanding of the demographics of audience composition – would demand a more ethnographic study of readership than can be entered into here. Interpreting the headlong collision of the novel with feminist debate is also a complex area that calls for lengthier exploration, as is the difference between the book's appeal and the media's construction of the book's appeal.[38] In terms of the publishing history of *Bridget Jones's Diary*, however, the import of these responses to the novel is in terms of genre, and the function of the market with regard to it, which returns the argument to Picador's sales team. As described by Straus, the sales team could not at first comprehend the genre in which *Bridget Jones's Diary* was to be placed. Almost two years after the book's publication, in August 1998, an article in *The Times* perhaps indicates why this might be, in the course of a discussion about suitable beach reading:

> Publishers have quickly latched onto the success of Helen Fielding's novel, and the demand for such fare. New novels with Bridgetesque heroines are coming thick and fast this summer, with pages packed with stories of insecure, single twenty and thirtysomething girls, looking for love, better jobs, and well, more exciting lives in general.[39]

The phrases 'Bridgetesque heroines' and the 'demand for such fare' indicate that the reason the sales team found it difficult to pigeonhole

Bridget Jones's Diary was that it was itself the 'chicklit' trendsetter. Bridget Jones becomes not only a term for a certain social type, then, but also shorthand for a certain sort of novel and a certain sort of success. Wanting to replicate the success, the publishers 'latch [...] onto' the genre, recognising, but willing to undergo, a pattern of diminishing returns. The generic comparisons are even explicitly made by publishers wanting to ally their new commodities to the previous success, as the labelling of Mike Gayle, author of *My Legendary Girlfriend* (1998), as the 'male Bridget Jones', exemplifies.[40] Bridget Jones, although a term loaded with its own textual meaning, and that pushed on it by the social commentators, is thus a cipher for the language of publishers' marketing, and a way of configuring genre distinctions.

The source of much of the annoyance about *Bridget Jones's Diary* is in its role in defining this new genre rather than for the novel itself. In the same month as *The Times* article on 'Bridgetesque heroines', the *Guardian*'s Emma Forrest found herself in a publishing hell, where 'There is a sub-genre more horrifying than horror writing, and it's called Bridget Jones's Afterbirth.'[41] Publishers and agents alike show themselves aware of the problematic nature of marketing and even commissioning by analogy. Straus says that 'the similar books in Bridget Jones' wake showed that publishers are like lemmings, going over the cliff and so destroying the genre'.[42] The literary agent Carole Blake, in Joanna Pitman's previously cited article, investigates the workings of genre fashion:

> 'These cycles don't last very long,' says Carole Blake. 'We're still on the look out for really good writers in this genre [of *Bridget Jones's Diary*], because once a few early ones become proven winners, the bandwagon gets going and editors are happy to publish more. After a while, though, the imitators will start to crowd the market. They are seldom as good as the original ones, and so they start weighing the genre down. That's when the cycle moves on to something else.'[43]

The 'cycle mov[ing] on' is an understanding of publishing as a process dominated by genre fashion and a notion of 'original[s]' and 'imitators'. So although *Bridget Jones's Diary* exists in a continuum of romance fiction – with allegiances to Mills & Boon, Barbara Cartland and even Jane Austen – the genre manifestation of which it is the most visible and successful example is one that is new to the 1990s, one of which it is at the vanguard.

In John Sutherland's discussion of bestselling fiction in *Bestsellers*, he debates the shifting nature of the genre of the 'woman's romance':

> with a change in market conditions the most stereotyped forms of popular literature can perform remarkable *volte faces*. Thus woman's romance, against all its aspirin traditions, becomes articulate, radical and sexually aggressive in the 1970s: its assumed generic motto changing from Mills & Boons's 'Books that please' to Marilyn French's 'This novel changes lives' [...] This drastic turnabout in the nature of women's fiction is attributable, I think, to the female reading public – or its trendsetting vanguard – becoming more like the male market for science fiction: that is to say, younger, college-educated and susceptible to 'ideas'.[44]

Writing in 1981, Sutherland had yet to witness the deradicalisation of the market in the 1980s, where the 'woman's romance' was ruled by the 'sex-and-shopping' or 'bonkbuster' novel typified by Jackie Collins's work, proving that the 'female reading public', or at least fiction directed at it, does not move to a consistent political agenda. Yet the analysis of a genre affected by 'change in market conditions' holds true. The novel may change lives, but the shifting desires of readers also shapes novels. Some of the characteristics of a given manifestation might lead it to be viewed, as Bidisha does, as 'desperately conservative', but her analysis – that 'the public likes this book because it is deeply conformist' – pays no heed to how market conditions change and the subtle relationship between what readers want and what the industry produces. The publishing history of *Bridget Jones's Diary* ultimately resides in the extremely clever act of market positioning in which the novel is placed between the 'mass' and 'literary' markets, by appealing to and playing on the conventions of romance fiction, and hence negotiating with readers' expectations of protagonists and plot. For readers looking for romance, Bridget Jones gets her man. For readers looking for satirical deconstructions of a woman cast adrift in a post-feminist world, Bridget Jones's recorded thoughts and deeds are a metanarrative of the lives of the women for whom she is a supposed archetype. Gesturing at both triviality and seriousness, *Bridget Jones's Diary* crosses the borders of existing genres – and assumptions of literary value made of them. *Bridget Jones's Diary*, then, is a paradigm of a type of genre-crossing fiction: a postmodernist and post-feminist publication strategy.[45] For a book to be situated at the interstices of genre definition is to risk its identity at the most basic level – the book may never make itself known to a readership of any size. It is also, however, to do what *Bridget Jones's Diary* has done – to gamble an identity, to suffer appropriation, to be open to variable interpretations – but, in the final analysis, to achieve remarkable market visibility and success, and to begin a new chapter in genre.

J. K. Rowling's *Harry Potter* series (1997–2007), Philip Pullman's *His Dark Materials* (1995–2000) and Mark Haddon's *The Curious Incident of the Dog in the Night-Time* (2003)

This case study addresses not one book or author, but a series of writers and their publications. All of these writers work within the field of children's literature, but their publishing histories reveal their appeal to a broader, adult audience, as well as their appropriation of 'adult' themes and subject matter. Within the period of the 1990s and 2000s, the children's book market benefited from a period of growth, of commodification, and of media attention. This case study concentrates on a small number of the more prominent publications of the period, looking particularly at the ways in which these books have been deemed 'crossover' texts, addressing both child and adult audiences.[46] The books and authors that this case study refers to are J. K. Rowling's *Harry Potter* series, Philip Pullman's *His Dark Materials* trilogy and Mark Haddon's *The Curious Incident of the Dog in the Night-Time*. The shortlisting and award of these authors for various literary prizes provides the particular prism for studying the marketing successes of their books, and the influences of marketing upon the reception of their books.

The children's book market in the 1990s and 2000s, then, underwent a transition from being viewed as underprivileged to being deemed as in a 'golden age'. Philip Pullman, in a short contribution on children's fiction for *The Writer's Handbook*, commented as late as 1999 on the paucity of review space, the lack of marketing spend on children's books, and the less lucrative prize purses of children's literary awards. Put simply, children's literature was taken less 'seriously' than books written for adults.[47] Pullman cites as an example the Whitbread Children's Book of the Year award, which was then worth £10 000, whereas the winner of the adult Whitbread Book of the Year Award won £21 000. In the mid-to-late 1990s, however, there started to be a shift. Julia Eccleshare chronicled this shift in successive annual reports for the US trade publication, *Publishers Weekly*. Eccleshare, who is also the children's literary editor of the *Guardian*, opened her 2004 analysis of the UK children's book market with the following comment:

> The received wisdom about children's books is being challenged. Their hallmark was once a long life in the slow lane. Not so anymore. Children's books are now up front big sellers and the barriers to their success are tumbling down.[48]

Eccleshare went on to cite eight authors in the UK children's market selling at adult levels, including home-grown talent J. K. Rowling, Pullman and Jacqueline Wilson, and US imports Meg Cabot and Lemony Snicket. Sales were undoubtedly being led by the *Harry Potter* series, but others have also contributed strongly to the commercial success of children's books. Jacqueline Wilson, for example, has conducted marathon book-signing events, including one session lasting over eight hours, in which she signed books for approximately 3000 fans.[49] Wilson also overtook the saga writer Catherine Cookson as the most borrowed author from libraries, as revealed in 2004 Public Lending Right figures. Wilson remained in primary position in 2005, and in 2006 loans of her books totalled over two million.[50] Following the success of these leading writers, there was an enormous amount of attention focused on the children's book world, and a consequent raised level of hype in its marketing. More children's authors now have literary agents, an unusual arrangement a decade ago. Large advances are given to children's authors for the rights to publish their properties. The Bologna Book Fair, which concentrates on children's and young adult's books, is a focal point for rights trading and also, more recently, for film scouts to prospect for the hottest children's books to turn into television and movies. Several established adult novelists, including Helen Dunmore and Jeanette Winterson, have also begun writing for children. In 2004 for the first time, A&C Black produced a separate volume for would-be children's authors, the *Children's Writers' and Artists' Yearbook 2005*.[51]

For the children's book market, then, the period of the 1990s and 2000s was a golden age in terms of commerciality and market excitement. Discussion of the period has also, moreover, commented on the content and quality of writing for children, and recognition of children's books in the literary field more generally. Changing perceptions of children's literature outside the world of children's books has included the consecration offered by literary prizes, which has had a particularly strong impact in these cultural shifts. In an earlier *Publishers Weekly* report from 2002, entitled 'A Golden Time for Children's Books', Eccleshare wrote:

> The year 2002 began with the most propitious of omens. Philip Pullman's *The Amber Spyglass*, winner of the Whitbread Children's Book of the Year, then warded off opposition from the other Whitbread winners to take the overall Whitbread Book of the Year Award. It was a first for a children's book and something many thought would never happen. The resulting publicity was sensational. Banner headlines in national papers proclaimed: 'He writes like an angel'; 'Pullman rivals Chekhov'; 'One of the finest writers in Britain today'.[52]

This, then, has been a period in which British children's literature entered a much-vaunted golden age, in which a sometimes undervalued genre proved itself capable of competing with adult literature both in terms of literary consecration and the literary marketplace. Rowling, Pullman and Haddon have all won prizes dedicated to children's books. Pullman's *Northern Lights* (1995), for example, won both the Carnegie and the Guardian Children's Fiction Prize, and Haddon's *The Curious Incident of the Dog in the Night-Time* was the recipient of the Guardian Children's Fiction Prize and the Book Trust Teenage Prize. The first three books in the *Harry Potter* series – *Harry Potter and the Philosopher's Stone* (1997), *Harry Potter and the Chamber of Secrets* (1998) and *Harry Potter and the Prisoner of Azkaban* (1999) – all won Nestlé Smarties Gold Awards. Of greater interest, however, in terms of the crossover nature of these books, and the ways in which marketing activity has affected their reception, is the award of adult literary prizes to children's authors.

The first instance of this is provided by the third novel in the *Harry Potter* series, *Harry Potter and the Prisoner of Azkaban*, and its entry in the Whitbread Book Awards. As Chapter 3 explained, the Whitbread Awards are split into several categories addressing different literary genres: biography, poetry, novel and first novel. The winner of each category award then goes forward to compete with the other winners for the accolade of overall Whitbread Book of the Year, thus forcing the juries to judge different genres alongside one another. The climax of the judging of the 1999 award, which took place at the beginning of 2000, was compounded by an additional factor. After several years of petitioning from those advocating that literature for children be viewed as comparable to literature for adults, and with the added clout of the phenomenal *Harry Potter*, the Children's Book of the Year was once again deemed eligible for the overall prize, from which (as Pullman's article mentioned) it had previously been excluded. (This had been done in order to allow it more coverage, as it was thought that the interest in the adults' prizes obscured the children's winner.) The final decision fell between *Harry Potter and the Prisoner of Azkaban* and Seamus Heaney's poetic rewriting of *Beowulf*. The mechanisms of promotional hype were cranked into a fury of hyperbole: a battle royale between a thirteen-year-old wizard and a thousand-year-old monster-slayer (with a helping hand from an elder statesman of the literary establishment with an impressive prize scalp or two already to his collection).

This clash of David and Goliath – won, on this occasion, by Goliath – provoked a fierce debate on literary standards. Robert McCrum announced in the *Observer* his belief that it was farcical that there should be any contest at all between what he termed 'a critically-acclaimed version of a 3000-line Old English masterpiece and a popularly-venerated contemporary fairytale for articulate ten-year-olds'.[53] The title of McCrum's article, 'Why Eng Lit Smites Pop Culture', makes clear that this was an argument fraught with supposed distinctions between high and low culture and value judgements with regard to audiences. It was apparent, whichever side of the debate the particular critic was on, that from this year the Whitbread Awards had at least made the discussion possible, rather than confining children's books to a literary ghetto. This time the children's book may not have won, but its widely reported runner-up status rendered it a possibility that one day the overall prize might go to the junior competitor.

The third book in Philip Pullman's *His Dark Materials* trilogy, *The Amber Spyglass*, followed in *Harry Potter*'s footsteps in beating a path to the grown-up literary prizes. In 2001, the first year that the Booker Prize longlist was made public (previously it had remained confidential, bar the occasional 'leak' to the press), *The Amber Spyglass* took its place among novels by Ian McEwan, Peter Carey, Nadine Gordimer, Beryl Bainbridge and V. S. Naipaul. *The Amber Spyglass* did not make it to the shortlist stage of the Booker. At the beginning of 2002, however, having already won the Whitbread children's category award, Pullman went on to achieve greater distinction, as Eccleshare reported in *Publishers Weekly*. He won the overall Whitbread Award, in competition with the adult categories, thus surpassing Rowling's achievement two years earlier. For many commentators, this was *the* signal that children's literature was being taken seriously in terms of literary consecration. Boyd Tonkin, the literary editor of the *Independent*, in an article about the vogue for adults reading children's books, suggested that, compared to Harry Potter: 'the more strenuous theological myths spun by Philip Pullman in the trilogy *His Dark Materials* [have] made a passion for current children's writing intellectually watertight – a process crowned by Pullman's victory in the Whitbread book awards.'[54]

Swiftly on the heels of Pullman's success in the Whitbread Awards with *The Amber Spyglass*, Mark Haddon won the overall Whitbread Award for *The Curious Incident of the Dog in the Night-Time*. Haddon's novel was also longlisted for the Man Booker, and that year's Chair of Judges, John Carey, was openly disappointed not to usher it onto the shortlist.[55] *The Curious Incident of the Dog in the Night-Time* has an interesting publishing history in terms of its material manifestations. Haddon was a children's writer, but his new book was published simultaneously as a children's and an adults' book by David Fickling Books and Jonathan Cape, two different imprints of the same conglomerate company, Random House. Haddon's publishers chose to submit him for the novel category in the Whitbread Awards, rather than the children's, and after convincing its category judges it went on to beat the other contenders, including the winner of the children's category, David Almond's *The Fire-Eaters* (2003).[56]

Haddon later went on to win another literary award more usually reserved for adult fiction, the Commonwealth Writers Prize. Ironically, however, Haddon was awarded the Commonwealth Best First Book category prize rather than the Commonwealth Best Book category, despite *The Curious Incident* not being his first publication. It can only be assumed that his previous children's books did not count as 'Books', a sign that – like Toby Litt's reinvention as a crime novelist with *Corpsing* discussed in Chapter 3 – the processes of literary marketing can work in slightly devious ways by effacing the memories of previous books, as well as running counter to the narrative of the children's market in a golden age. Indeed, Haddon's next two publications, a poetry collection and the novel *A Spot of Bother* (2006), were aimed at adults and published only on adult imprints.[57] Nonetheless, it is evident that with the examples of Rowling, Pullman and Haddon, children's literature took on the grown-ups in the domain of adult literary prizes, and even, on occasion, won. In the process, children's writers and their books became more visible, sold more copies, and were consequently taken more seriously.

In order to gain broader recognition, these children's books extended their appeal outside of their traditional markets of children and young adults, and their parents, teachers and librarians. Just as children's books came to be awarded adult literary prizes, so they also found adult readers outside of the usual markets for children's books. As Tonkin's comments suggest, it became fashionable in the 1990s and 2000s for adults to read children's books, a trend led, in no small way, by the *Harry Potter* series. Bloomsbury, Rowling's UK publisher, reacted to and augmented this trend by publishing editions of the series with different covers for children and adults. The editions also had different cover prices, with the adult paperback version having a recommended retail price of £1 more than the children's. (The sales of the children's editions of the books have been much greater than those of the adults', suggesting that many adults were happy to buy and be seen reading the children's version. The adult edition of *Harry Potter and the Order of the Phoenix* (2003), for example, accounted for only 12.5 per cent of first day sales.[58]) Pullman's books were also published by Scholastic in adult editions in the UK, featuring sombre paintings rather than the sci-fi/fantasy influenced covers of the children's versions. The two hardback editions of *The Curious Incident of the Dog in the Night-Time* had different cover designs and copy, but the same price point and text.

In this sense, then, children's books such as the *Harry Potter* series have crossed over into new markets, and are marketed at and read by both children and adults. However, the so-called crossover phenomenon has an additional meaning which is slightly different from children's books that have come to be read by an adult market. Pullman's *His Dark Materials* trilogy and Haddon's *The Curious Incident of the Dog in the Night-Time* are also, arguably, adult books *at the same time as* children's books. The nature of the categorisation is different here: it is not a matter of adults reading children's books, but both adults and children reading a book which could be designated for either audience. Certainly the 'strenuous theological myths' of *His Dark Materials*, its intertextuality and its engagement with religious, political, environmental and moral debates would suggest that the trilogy is a work of great seriousness (although its author would be at pains to argue that children's literature frequently surpasses writing for adults in these very areas). Pullman's initial conception of the trilogy was as '"*Paradise Lost* for teenagers in three volumes"', and it is perhaps here that the books' primary definition should rest.[59] The teenager is, of course, in a 'crossover' position physically, emotionally and sociologically, and books aimed at them should be expected to display attributes that would appeal to both a child and an adult. However, there is also teen fiction, such as the social realist and frequently hard-hitting work of Melvin Burgess, which addresses issues of teenage drug-taking and sexuality in

Junk (1996) and *Doing It* (2003), which has not appealed to the adult market as strongly as Pullman's work.[60] Nonetheless, there are elements of Pullman's trilogy that also strongly suggest that it is a work that develops from the traditions of children's literature: its semi-orphaned child protagonists; its *Bildungsroman* structure; its themes of innocence and experience; its cast of talking animals, witches and other fantastical beasts; to enumerate but a few.[61]

The Curious Incident of the Dog in the Night-Time is more genuinely a title which could be designated as a children's or an adults' book because of its subject matter, mode of writing, and central characters. Its narrative of a teenage boy with Asperger's Syndrome, and his troubled family relationships, is not an obviously juvenile topic. In describing the book's genesis, however, Haddon questioned the crossover description, saying that 'I never intended the book as a crossover novel at all. I wrote it as an adult novel with a teenage protagonist. It was my agent and my publishers who realised it had crossover potential.'[62] It was this realisation that led Random House to purchase the book and publish simultaneously through two of its imprints. David Fickling, the publisher of the eponymous list that produced the children's edition, and also Pullman's editor, has stated that crossover is nothing more than an act of 'professional categorisation' or, in other words, a description of how books are sold, and where they are shelved in bookshops and libraries. Crossover is, to Fickling, 'purely commercial and practical', as sales and marketing teams attempt to maximise exposure for titles by getting them displayed in as many locations as possible. Haddon has stated that it was only with hindsight that this strategy was deemed successful, as 'the same book is reviewed in different places, advertised in different places and, most importantly, placed on two different shelves, and often in two different rooms, in the same bookshop'.[63]

The paratextual nature of such strategies, from the publisher's peritext of the cover and cover blurbs, through to its review coverage, bookshop location and prize-winning potential, have, as Chapter 3 discussed, a vitally important influence on the interpretation, categorisation and reception of literature. The marketing of literature, in other words, has a central role in constructing literary categories and literary value. Literary prizes contribute in crucial ways to marketing literature, and thus are part of the process of constructing categories and value. Although crossover might be deemed a superficial exercise in labelling, the practical ways in which such definitions affect the conditions of book marketing mean that their impact extends from 'professional categorisation', the 'commercial and practical', to the realm of literary value construction. How books reach their child or adult audience, and how they are constructed in the process, is ultimately a question of marketing, in which literature is constructed by and through the marketplace.

Just as the publication of particular books affects the interpretation of publishers' imprints, so the award of literary prizes to particular titles has an impact on the awards themselves and, in considering the marketing of these crossover books it is worth analysing this reverse aspect. English, in *The Economy of Prestige*, notes the 'simply tremendous growth of cultural prizes' in the twentieth century.[64] One of the implications of this has been the increasing competitiveness of book awards, in order to gain and retain sponsors, to attract optimum media attention, and to acquire the leading reputation for their quality of judgement. The 1990s and 2000s in the UK have been a time of particularly strong competition. The Orange Prize for Fiction, the high-profile award for women writers mentioned with regard to *The Ghost Road*, was set up in 1996 specifically in order to redress the pro-male bias in the judging panels and decisions of the Booker Prize. With effective marketing and a prize purse which substantially exceeded the Booker's offering at the time, Orange firmly implanted itself into the prize scene. Booker responded in 2001 by following Orange's own media strategy of making public its longlist in advance of the shortlist and eventual winner, which both Pullman and Haddon duly appeared on. In 2002, however, a greater opportunity was made available to Booker in the form of a generous new sponsor. The Man Booker Prize increased the prize purse to £50 000, bettering Orange's £30 000. The Man Booker International Prize, based on lifetime achievement rather than a single publication, and open to US and writers in translation as well as UK and Commonwealth English-language writers, was also set up in 2005, increasing the exposure of the Man Booker brand.

As a result of this competitive environment, it can be argued that literary prizes have chosen to make awards to children's books not only to recognise the achievements of their authors, and to promote their writing and the genre, but also in order to enhance their own standing. One of the primary reasons for adult literary prizes in paying attention to books by children's authors, this case study contends, is in order to increase their own cultural and journalistic capital. Rowling, Pullman and Haddon had already achieved a certain level of literary acclaim and popularity by the time they were garlanded with adult literary awards, even if the awards then served to extend that acclaim and popularity. It is possible to extend a hypothesis that the juries decided to include these books on their shortlists and longlists, and judged them to be best overall, not simply because of any perceived intrinsic value, but because such decisions were media-worthy, because they were interesting, refreshing choices, and because they would reflect back positively on the prizes and their judges. An analogous example is the widely acknowledged eagerness of the Booker to reward post-colonial writing, as Chapter 3 discussed, thus increasing its own cultural capital.[65] The procedures of judging meetings tend to be kept confidential, and as such evidence to support such a hypothesis is not easy to come by (although archives such as that of the Booker Prize at Oxford Brookes University, mentioned with regard to the case study of *The Ghost Road*, may provide some evidence to researchers).[66] A Frequently Asked Question (FAQ) response on the Whitbread Awards' website about the Children's Book Award, however, hints that this line of argument may have some plausibility. The website reads, 'Whitbread is delighted to have been at the forefront of promoting the importance of children's books within the UK's wide and varied literary tradition.'[67]

Locating itself at the 'forefront' is a deliberate act of self-fashioning. By making its overall award to Philip Pullman in 2002, Whitbread declared itself to be bold and at the vanguard of promoting children's reading and all the values it entails in the multimedia world of the twenty-first century. This is clearly self-promotion, of a sort to which newspapers are also party. Robert McCrum, clearly believing Pullman to be a stronger writer than Rowling, trumpeted the page placement of the *Observer*'s review of *The Amber Spyglass*:

> We have presented our evaluation of his long-awaited, latest novel at the front of this section, just as we might Kazuo Ishiguro, Tom Wolfe or Julian Barnes – ie, like any important adult writer.
>
> We are not under any illusion that this will change the way people look at children's literature, but we do rather fervently hope that it will help to have Philip Pullman evaluated as an important contemporary novelist who happens to write in a certain genre, a significant writer to be spoken of in the same breath as, say, Beryl Bainbridge, A. S. Byatt or Salman Rushdie.
>
> [...] Pullman is simply the most distinguished and probably most talented of a bunch of writers whose work is known chiefly to children and teenagers [...] In this respect, Pullman has suffered critical neglect in the same way that some very successful crime, science fiction and thriller writers have been overlooked by the bien pensant literary commentariat.[68]

The 'fervent' hope of the newspaper may well be to promote Pullman and his writing, but its effect is also to set itself apart from the ironically dubbed 'bien pensant literary commentariat' that would overlook such a talented writer. Thus, the *Observer* simultaneously promotes Pullman and itself, and the reflection of merit is mutual. The impact of a literary institution praising certain writers or genres can also, therefore, be to praise itself.

In his commentary upon the crossover phenomenon, Mark Haddon went on to say that, 'The sudden excitement about "crossover" is not a sign that books have changed but that publishers have suddenly realised that they can market certain books to everyone from the ages of twelve to ninety.'[69] Haddon's rather cynical approach to his own success story reminds commentators on the literary marketplace of its commercial imperatives; the economic capital, in other words, of the publishing industry. Literary awards also operate within this marketplace, even if they might sometimes be believed to have a very different rationale. One final set of literary prizes – the British Book Awards – illustrates this. Haddon, Rowling and Pullman have all been successful in the Nibbies, as these awards are popularly known (due to their prize trophy in the form of a pen nib). Rowling and Pullman both won the Children's Book of the Year category in 1998 (Rowling) and 1997 and 2001 (Pullman). Haddon won the Literary Fiction Award in 2004 (rather than the children's category). In 2000 and 2002 respectively, Rowling and Pullman won the Author of the Year Award, and in 2006 *Harry Potter and the Half-Blood Prince* (2005) won the Book of the Year Award. Again, there is a pattern of the children's authors moving from winning awards designated for the age-group of their core audience, to competing with books for adults and winning more general awards. The nature of the British Book Awards, however, gives rise to further questions about the nature of literary prizes in the marketplace. The Nibbies have been, since their establishment in 1990, the book industry's trade awards, a celebration of that which is already successful. These are not prizes that bring to public prominence little-known books or authors, but on the contrary reward those who have already done extremely well.[70] This is effectively to ask whether literary prizes, in terms of marketing theory, are innovators and early adopters, or part of the early and even late majority.[71] The British Book Awards are dependent on other markers of success – a book's sales, its reviews, its highly marketable author, its other literary awards – and so take these indicators of success to accrue success. The British Book Awards are awarded on promotional merit and external indicators of success, meaning that their decisions tend towards a concentration of awards on a handful of already high-achieving books, an argument that English makes about cultural awards more generally in *The Economy of Prestige*. As celebrations of trade success, the British Book Awards intensify this effect, and also, like the Whitbread website and the *Observer* editorial comment, serve to promote the industry itself.

Literary prizes, therefore, are part of the process of bringing to attention undervalued books, genres and their authors. However, as the example of the award of adult literary and trade prizes to children's books demonstrates, they also have the effect of celebrating what is already successful and of bringing attention to the prizes themselves, thus continually focusing interest on the literary market and its crossover phenomena such as *Harry Potter*, *His Dark Materials* and *The Curious Incident of the Dog in the Night-Time*. In this way, the literary marketplace revives and renews itself through a continual creation and recreation of marketing stories with which to surround, celebrate, and ultimately, sell literature.

David Mitchell's *Cloud Atlas* (2004)

'A remarkable book – there won't be a bigger, bolder novel this year', announced the wraparound band for the hardback of David Mitchell's *Cloud Atlas*.[72] Quoting from a *Guardian* preview article, the publisher's promotional material boldly stated their aspirations for their author's third novel.[73] Mitchell's career provided a very strong pre-history for the publication of his latest book. Both of his previous novels, *Ghostwritten* (1999) and *number9dream* (2001) had been published to rapturous critical acclaim, to which the back cover of the first edition of *Cloud Atlas* bears testament.[74] Sections of *Ghostwritten* had appeared before its publication in the *New Writing 8* anthology (1999), edited by the novelists Lawrence Norfolk and Tibor Fischer.[75] Other writers, including A. S. Byatt, Adam Lively, William Boyd and Matt Thorne, showed their appreciation in the literary pages of the newspapers, and in 2003 Mitchell was included in *Granta*'s *Best of Young British Novelists 2003*, thus following in the footsteps of Martin Amis, Julian Barnes, Pat Barker and Ian McEwan in 1983 and Louis de Bernières, Hanif Kureishi and Jeanette Winterson in 1993.[76] *Ghostwritten* won the *Mail on Sunday*/John Llewellyn Rhys Prize, and was shortlisted for the *Guardian* First Book Award, and *number9dream* was shortlisted for the Booker Prize and the James Tait Black Memorial Prize.

In critical terms, then, Mitchell had been thoroughly taken up by the literary establishment, and – if the promise in the *Guardian* preview was fulfilled – the publication of *Cloud Atlas* would cement his reputation. Part of the reputation that Mitchell had built up was as an inventive, structurally daring writer whose work crossed genre boundaries. *Cloud Atlas* is a novel in a similar vein. Inspired by his love of the narrative playfulness of the postmodern novel, and particularly of Italo Calvino's *If on a Winter's Night a Traveler*, with its series of opening chapters of unfinished novels, Mitchell devised a 'Russian doll' plot structure which incorporated six different narratives of differing period, genre and tone.[77] Each of these narratives (apart from one) is sliced in the middle, so that the first narrative stops halfway through and leads into the next, and so on until the sixth narrative exits back into the second half of the fifth, and the narrative winds its way back to the second half of the first narrative. Each narrative, however, leaches into the next, existing either as a found narrative (a trashy novel submitted to a vanity publisher, for example), or with characters from one making a glancing appearance in another, while themes of predation unite all six narratives together. Far from a conventional realist narrative, Mitchell's pyrotechnics had reviewers rummaging through their critical vocabulary in order both to describe the structure of *Cloud Atlas*, and to express their verdict upon it.

The acclaim was not universal. Some did not like it at all, with the *Sunday Telegraph* purposefully setting themselves apart by stating that its reviewer would not be giving it a 'rave' review like other 'diverse publications', because he found it 'unreadable' and 'impossible to finish'. The reviewer wrote that 'the whole book shouts: "I am so clever that I don't need to entertain you" ' and concluded 'Well, at least we have brought Mr Mitchell's post-modern blockbuster to the attention of our discerning readers.'[78] Some reviews were equivocal, such as those in the *Irish Times* and the *Daily Telegraph*.[79] More normal, however, were reactions which, even if laced with some criticism, were overwhelmingly positive. Reviews in the opinion-forming *Independent on Sunday, Observer, Independent* and *Times* all paid their respects to what one of their number called 'The novel's scale, ambition and execution [which] make almost everything in contemporary fiction look like a squalid straggle of Nissen huts compared with its vertiginous edifice.'[80] Matt Thorne intensified his earlier praise for Mitchell with his statement that, '*Cloud Atlas* is a singular achievement, from an author of extraordinary ambition and skill, setting himself challenges that would drive most authors to madness. For the third time in a row, Mitchell has excelled himself. It is almost frightening to contemplate where he might go next.'[81] While such reviews clearly demonstrate their writers' struggle for the appropriate metaphor to describe Mitchell's writing, as well as a jostle to join the Mitchell praise bandwagon, it is clear that *Cloud Atlas's* author was being feted as one of the best and most exciting novelists working in Britain at the beginning of the twenty-first century.

When *Cloud Atlas* was announced first as a longlisted, and then a shortlisted, Booker Prize title in the autumn of 2004, the commendation offered by the judging panel was very much in line with the novel's critical reception. Mitchell's book swiftly became the bookmakers' favourite, and its sales, which had started to dip slightly after its March publication, were given a big boost, jumping from a slump of only 67 hardback copies a week to 919 a week at the end of October 2004.[82] To the surprise of many, however, and after a reportedly hard-argued judging session, *Cloud Atlas* lost the Booker laurels to Alan Hollinghurst's *The Line of Beauty* (2004).[83] *Cloud Atlas* thus lost out on one of the prime retailing opportunities afforded to literary novels in the British marketplace. However, hardback sales of the book remained buoyant, with a paperback promised for a year after the hardback publication, in February 2005. In December 2004, though, *Cloud Atlas* won another sort of award entirely, as it was announced that it would feature on the second television series of Richard & Judy's Book Club on Channel 4.

Richard & Judy's Book Club is a phenomenon that has managed to repeat the success of Oprah Winfrey's equivalent show in the US. The long-established chat-show hosts decided to add to their formula a televised book club, feeding into the contemporary vogue for group-reading activities, which has been documented in studies such as Hartley's and Long's.[84] In the UK, various media outlets have fed into the trend for more home-spun reading groups, including the *Mail on Sunday*'s *You* magazine hosting a regular book group and BBC Radio 4's Bookclub. Richard & Judy's Book Club took the format to a new level of popularity, leading to its producer Amanda Ross being named in the *Observer* in 2006 – above the chief executives of major publishing companies, the editors of prestigious literary imprints, and the most powerful literary agents – as the number one 'player' in 'the world of books'.[85] As joint managing director of Cactus TV, the production company responsible for Richard & Judy, Ross convinced Channel 4 that the show should include a book club element, and that the British Book Awards, the industry prizes that Rowling, Pullman and Haddon all triumphed at, would be promoted through the show.

The decisions made by Ross, who is primarily responsible for the choice of books on the programme, are eclectic. In the series in which *Cloud Atlas* featured, the other titles were a selection of fiction and non-fiction, including Carlos Ruiz Zafon's literary thriller *The Shadow of the Wind*, Audrey Niffenegger's romantic science fiction novel *The Time Traveler's Wife*, the historical drama *The American Boy* by Andrew Taylor, Justin Cartwright's literary *The Promise of Happiness*, the reading-group based novel *The Jane Austen Book Club* by Karen Joy Fowler, William Brodrick's historical thriller *The Sixth Lamentation*, Jodi Picoult's story of family dilemma *My Sister's Keeper*, Paula Byrne's Regency biography *Perdita* and Robbie Williams' and Chris Heath's co-authored pop memoir *Feel*.[86] The list crosses genre boundaries, mixing – at its most extreme juxtaposition – the account of a celebrity pop star's life with *Cloud Atlas*, arguably a difficult, unconventional, complicated literary narrative. Indeed, Mitchell's novel, and the shortlisted contenders for the Booker Prize, prompted an industry commentator to write that in comparison to Yann Martel's 2002 winner *Life of Pi* (2002), an ' "incredibly accessible story" ', ' "All three favourites [are...] literary novels about subjects without immediate mass market appeal" '.[87]

Ross clearly disagreed about the potential mass-market appeal of *Cloud Atlas* in choosing to feature Mitchell's novel in the Richard & Judy Book Club, and thus effectively placed the book in the mass market. The impact of a book being featured on Richard & Judy is dramatic in sales terms. In its 2006 season alone, it was credited with selling £58 million of books.[88] It was reported that *Cloud Atlas* benefited from a nineteen-fold increase in sales in the two weeks after it was discussed on the television programme, peaking at a sale of just under 30 000 copies in one week alone.[89]

Moreover, when readers had the opportunity to vote for their preferred of all ten titles in the second series, *Cloud Atlas* – which this time would have been unlikely to be the bookmakers' favourite – won. It was therefore awarded at the British Book Awards both the Waterstone's Literary Fiction Award *and* the Richard & Judy Best Read of the Year. In this double award, Mitchell's crossover appeal to both literary and mass markets was sealed and celebrated. Although it could be argued that the Literary Fiction Award is hardly disconnected from commercial impulses – it is after all sponsored by the UK's major book retailer – it nonetheless demonstrates a level of distinction in its categorisation. The Richard & Judy title is both more democratic in its nomenclature of the 'Best Read', and in the way in which it is chosen – by reader vote. Moreover, by considering Mitchell's earlier garlanding by the literary critics and the Booker Prize judging panel, it would seem that in *Cloud Atlas*, the contemporary British book marketplace had found a title which ultimately combined cultural and economic capital, thereby fusing the 'literary' and the 'popular'. A book which in itself crossed numerous genre boundaries in its various narrative styles, thus made an unexpected but seemingly unproblematic transition back and forth between the literary and popular fields, in terms of its market placement. These transitions belied the attitude of the *Sunday Telegraph* reviewer mentioned earlier, in which the seeming postmodern antics of Mitchell were rejected because they were adjudged to be unreadable. The *Sunday Telegraph*'s cosy appeal to its own 'discerning readers' seemed in retrospect extremely ill-judged as readers took to Mitchell's writing in their hundreds of thousands. What the *Sunday Telegraph* did, with regards to *Cloud Atlas*, was to underestimate the reading public and its capacity to take on Mitchell's writing. Indeed, one of the 'diverse publications' the *Sunday Telegraph* was setting itself against, the *Sunday Times*, analysed *Cloud Atlas*'s success as 'intriguing' in its capacity to appeal both to 'the intelligentsia' and the 'mass market', therefore making a more progressive assessment of the reading public and the ways in which literature appeals to it via the constructions of marketing agencies:

> The significance of Mitchell's ability to straddle literary and popular readerships is twofold. It demonstrates a rare gift for storytelling and a ferocious imagination. It also confounds assumptions about dumbing down books for the general public.
>
> 'It says a lot about the fact that the public have been underestimated,' says Giles Elliott, charts editor of *The Bookseller*. 'People are ready to read a lot more than just pulp fiction, especially when recommended. Richard and Judy are in effect saying: "We loved it and we're just simple, honest folk". Word of mouth is absolutely key to building authors.'[90]

It is perhaps no surprise that so much of the book market took Mitchell to heart, because his success is a demonstration of how, in the globalised corporate world of early twenty-first century publishing, complex literary fiction can also sell extremely well, and appeal to a large number of readers, given the forceful interventions of marketing. The publishing history of *Cloud Atlas* is a stirring tale indeed, in which the virtues of the crossover novel demonstrate the workings of the literary marketplace at its most interesting, effective and inclusive.

Conclusion
Writing Beyond Marketing

Through its concentration on marketing as an act of representation, *Marketing Literature* has explored the processes that occur within the literary marketplace. These acts of marketing have – as this book has argued – been the making of contemporary writing, constructing the meaning of literature, representing it in the marketplace and influencing its reception. This exploration has been carried out by conscripting the communications circuit and marketing communications theory, and analysing the negotiation of cultural, economic and journalistic capital. The series of case studies in Part II demonstrate this fusion most fully, and in the case studies' construction of the varying relationships between author, book and reader, and of the broader narratives of publishing history, they indicate the pre-eminent role of marketing in the making of literary fiction. It also confirms the inherent narratability of publishing history noted in the Introduction. This storytelling tendency is evident in the extremes of both the 'lament school' and the cultural optimists, and is intensified by the economic contexts of the 1990s and 2000s: the conglomeration of the publishing industry, the vast market share of a tiny handful of companies, and the money made available for advances and marketing. Publishing history and polemics are never far apart. Yet even with a more measured approach, stories are told, narratives develop, and metaphors of production, reception and consumption arise. And so, just as the activities of marketing represent literary fiction in the marketplace, so the stories told about publishing affect analysis of its past and present and the shaping of its future, whether those stories are told by academics in the hunt for scholarly capital or others agents in the field: publishers, booksellers, literary journalists and critics, book award judges, industry analysts, readers and writers. These multiple agencies in the marketplace thus continue to make and remake contemporary writing, interpreting and reinterpreting texts through a series of paratextual negotiations. These agencies have a profound impact on writers and their work, even as these writers are part of the process of the promotional circuit themselves.

One of the effects of a literary culture in which the role of the author/promoter is constantly foregrounded is, as Lorna Sage has argued, an inscription of 'avatars of the author' as a 'voice on the page', an internalisation of the institutions of publishing and its impact on writers within texts as 'inset "I" figures, tale-tellers, performers'.[1] For some writers this textual negotiation results in overt inscriptions of the authorial life – Amis's parable of authorship, promotion and literary rivalry in *The Information* is the most prominent recent example. Rowling's *Harry Potter and the Goblet of Fire,* the fourth in the series, sees Harry besieged by the investigative journalist Rita Skeeter – a character presaged by the media fascination with Rowling herself. These legitimate concerns about the pitfalls of celebrity and the promotional circuit are not quite where *Marketing Literature* ends, however. Rather, it is completed with a coda that tells one more publishing story – that of Zadie Smith's *White Teeth* – in which the trope of literary celebrity figures large, but also in which a more introspective meditation of space, sound and silence is brought into being. It is one in which authors wrestle back some of their role as literary producers, and in so doing continue to make their own writing through, and beyond, marketing.

Coda: Zadie Smith's *White Teeth* (2000)

At the beginning of 2000, Zadie Smith's *White Teeth* was published. It was an eagerly awaited debut. Before the novel itself was published, Smith's writing had been showcased in major literary magazines on both sides of the Atlantic: an extract from the novel was published in the Autumn 1999 issue of *Granta,* and a short story, 'Stuart', made its way into *The New Yorker*'s 'Millennial Fiction' issue at the turn of 1999/2000.[2] Smith's literary reputation was established by her appearance in such prestigious and high-profile arenas. A pre-publication interview in *The Bookseller* in 1999 indicated further reasons why the novel was so eagerly awaited: the journalist Benedicte Page relates a publishing story of high advance levels, pre-publication hype and publishers' marketing spend – a story very similar to the explosive appearance of Arundhati Roy on the publishing scene, and confirming the prime place of marketing in contemporary publishing:

> Two years ago *White Teeth* was signed up on the basis of a mere 80 pages, for an advance rumoured to be very considerable; its author was only 22 and had started the novel while studying for her finals at Cambridge. Now Hamish Hamilton is backing the book heavily – perhaps inevitably given its investment – but it is clear that in this case the publisher does indeed have a formidable talent to promote.[3]

White Teeth was the subject of a substantial marketing campaign (including a *Bookseller* front cover), leading to widespread media coverage, publication in translation around the world, the award of numerous literary prizes (including the Whitbread First Novel Award, the Commonwealth Writers Best First Book Prize, the James Tait Black Memorial Prize for Fiction and the *Guardian* First Book Prize), an enviably high position in the bestseller charts for both hardback and paperback editions, and in 2002, a Channel Four TV adaptation.[4] Smith, as the author of the book, became a literary celebrity. The story in *The Bookseller* interview of how she began to write the novel while studying for her finals, and her own narrative of her family background and how it connected to her novel in a pre-publication interview in *Publishing News* in November 1999, illustrated her potential as a marketable author.[5] The thrust of the publisher's campaign, as indicated by the *Bookseller* front cover advertisement, was primarily to introduce the *author*. As the main line of the advertisement read, 'In January 2000, Hamish Hamilton are proud to launch a dazzling new literary talent'.[6] The advertisement, which continues on the inside front cover, also features a large photo of the author and a brief, but tantalising, author biography.[7]

In fact, the promotion of Smith as literary celebrity began even earlier, years before publication, and before there was a text to speak of (only the 'mere 80 pages' that was offered to publishers by Smith's agent). The reputedly high advance level, Smith's youth, and also her ethnic origins (with a white English father and a black Jamaican mother), attracted attention to *White Teeth* before it had been completed. The *Daily Telegraph, The Times* and the *Independent on Sunday* all mentioned Smith in articles in December 1997 and January 1998.[8] During the period in which she was actually writing the rest of the novel, then, she had already come to public attention.

Again, as with the case of Arundhati Roy, a marketing synchrony was achieved between the author and her novel. Smith's biographical similarities to one of her characters, Irie Jones, and the setting of her novel in the same area of north-west London that she herself grew up in, compounded by its multicultural theme, led many reviewers of the novel to link Smith's life and her work. Much of the media interest in Smith demonstrates a fascination with details of her background, seeing her, as one journalist rather euphemistically put it, as 'ethnically interesting'.[9] Such dubious blandishments aside, though, it is clear that Smith was a gift to a marketing department: young, intelligent, attractive and opinionated, and representative of a new multicultural Britain. As Sam Wallace put it in the *Daily Telegraph*, 'Zadie Smith is the perfect package for a literary marketing exercise', while Simon Hattenstone in the *Guardian* wrote that 'she ha[s] the fortune, or misfortune, to be the perfect demographic'.[10] Details of her biography, whilst not completely dictating the terms of her first novel's reception, certainly increased her exposure and the nature of that exposure. Smith's subsequent engagement with the trope of celebrity in her second novel, *The Autograph Man* (2002), was revealing of the predicament of the promotable and promoted author. The strains of playing the role of author/promoter thus linked her second book to the self-reflexive tendency in *The Information* and *Harry Potter and the Goblet of Fire*.[11]

Smith's multicultural theme in *White Teeth* led both publishers and reviewers to allude to, or to mention specifically, possible literary influences. A glowing pre-publication quotation from Salman Rushdie was used on the hardback cover of *White Teeth* and in marketing materials (including *The Bookseller* advertisement), and offered a similar patronage extended by Rushdie to Roy. Robert McCrum, reviewing the year's publications in the *Observer* at the end of 2000, commented of *White Teeth* that, 'It's perhaps too early to say exactly how good this novel is, but there's no doubt that it marks an important literary watershed in much the same way as the publication of *Midnight's Children* or [Hanif Kureishi's] *The Buddha of Suburbia*.'[12] McCrum summons two forebears of demonstrable importance to Smith's career: Rushdie in granting an endorsement for her novel (and, whilst not necessarily the structure for her work, certainly a similar, playful, hybridised language use); and Hanif Kureishi for providing a model for a short story by Smith, 'Mrs Begum's Son and the Private Tutor' (1997), from which the narrative of *White Teeth* shows obvious development.[13] A strong argument can be made for the links between Smith, Rushdie and Kureishi: Smith's portrayal of multicultural London is in the tradition of Kureishi's debut novel and Rushdie's *Satanic Verses* (1988), and Smith nods towards Rushdie's controversial novel and the religious tension it caused through a depiction of some of her young Muslim characters travelling to a book-burning in Bradford.[14] Largely, however, these perceived literary allegiances were informed by the similarities in (multicultural) theme and biography, a critical mode that Smith herself dismissed.[15] This is a further example of marketing by ethnicity informing reception. Literary celebrity – the manufacture of the public authorial presence as an adjunct of the marketing process – is central to this.

White Teeth and its author have come to be seen as representative, illustrating themes and concerns of contemporary British society as well as exemplifying aspects of the publishing industry. In an article by Fiachra Gibbons in the *Guardian* in 2001, 'The Route to Literary Success: Be Young, Gifted and Very Good Looking', Smith is touted, along with high-flying peers, as 'cool and fashionable – the most marketable'.[16] In equal measure, such reports revel in these young literary celebrities and express anxiety for an industry that seems to value qualities that come from beyond the text, thus displaying the media's unsettled relationship vis-à-vis the publishing industry. Smith's literary celebrity, built upon the foundations of her youth and her ethnicity, and forged by journalistic capital, was a complement to the critical acclaim and sales success achieved by the novel. Her work came to be seen as an example of the *zeitgeist*, a new, multicultural, multicoloured Britain. This is the Zadie Smith with 'demographics at her fingertips', as Sarah Sands put it in the *Daily Telegraph*, and the vision of optimistic social mixing that is to be found in the pages of *White Teeth* was taken as a blueprint for a new Britain.[17]

Yet the text of *White Teeth* resists such slick definitions. The book's comic demeanour should not belie its portrayal of the sense of alienation and loss suffered by immigrants, and the difficulties, racist attitudes and liberal platitudes that are directed towards them. In *White Teeth*, Smith satirises the liberal schoolteacher Poppy, who supports Samad's plea for more Muslim events to be incorporated into the school calendar, on the grounds that they 'would be so much more ... colourful', tying the events in 'with art work, music'.[18] Poppy's other reason is that she finds Samad attractive, comparing him to the exotic Eastern film star icon Omar Sharif.[19] There is a critique in this satire of how many critics would eventually respond to *White Teeth*, applauding it for the brightly varied environment of Willesden Green. Smith may have presented a largely optimistic view of multiculturalism, but not without also satirising the attitudes that would inform her own reception.

There is, moreover, a cynicism in Smith's portrayal of a supposedly 'Cool Britannia' – one of the synonyms for the 'new Britain' associated with the 'new Labour' government of 1997 onwards – founded on the premise of multiculturalism. Throughout *White Teeth* there is a discourse on the lot of the immigrant that steers away from the xenophobia of the right but also from the liberal platitudes of the left. Smith writes of the rhetoric surrounding this supposedly welcoming 'greenandpleasantlibertarianlandofthefree' into which immigrants step, '[w]e have been told [...] as *blank people*, free of any kind of baggage, happy and willing to leave their difference at the docks.' The narrator of *White Teeth* is extremely sceptical of the vision of 'Mr Schmutters and Mr Banajii [...] merrily weaving their way through Happy Multicultural Land'.[20]

Subsequent novels by other authors, including Monica Ali's *Brick Lane* (2003) and Andrea Levy's *Small Island* (2004), have also entered this multicultural debate.[21] If literature has a role in shaping and informing national identity, the success that these three novelists have achieved is undoubtedly founded on their engagement with issues of immigration and multiculturalism, along with their own multicultural backgrounds. They speak of Britain, of who we are as a nation, and their imaginative engagement contrasts sharply with the ill-informed discourse of the media and all too frequently of politicians with regard to asylum seekers, illegal immigrants, and what they contribute to or take from the UK.

In the grand finale of the novel at the Perret Institute, Smith's commentary on the vacuous signifiers of branding is a plea for the importance of remembering the humanity of individuals, their long histories and how they find and fit into the spaces of the world. Smith articulates this through the juxtaposition of her satire on a new Britain in the consumer style questionnaire through which the Institute is envisioned with the figure of its Polish nightwatchman:

> people can finally give the answers required when a space is being designed, or when something is being rebranded, a room/furniture/Britain (that was the brief: a new British room, a space for Britain, Britishness, space of Britain, British industrial space cultural space space); they know what is meant when asked how matt chrome makes them feel; and they know what is meant by national identity? symbols? paintings? maps? music? air-conditioning? smiling black children or smiling Chinese children or [tick the box]? world music? shag or pile? tile or floorboards? plants? running water?
>
> they know what they want, especially those who've lived this century, forced from one space to another like Mr De Winter (né Wojciech), renamed, rebranded, the answer to every questionnaire nothing nothing space please just space nothing please nothing space[22]

The chapter ends with these unpunctuated words, gesturing towards a form of expression beyond fashion, beyond speech. For set against the noise of the hype surrounding the marketing of the book, and indeed the book's own very attractive loquacity, is perhaps a more unexpected and paradoxical theme: an appeal for calm and the occasional virtues of quietism. This plea for 'a bit of silence, a bit of *shush*', is seen in scenes of momentary union such as that between Irie and her father Archie, on their way to the finale at the Institute, in which the noise of constant conflict gives way to a respite uncommon to their family life, and the hectic narrative of *White Teeth*.[23] This is very different from the trendy multiculturalism that Smith has sometimes been taken as representing.

Within the satire on the new Britain of the Perret Institute, it is also possible to discern a nascent uneasiness, via its interrogation of branding, with the representational forces that (publishers') marketing, rebranding and spin, can unleash. The text – and its author – here attempt to reclaim their own textual and authorial space, a space that offers respite from the proliferating array of marketing agencies. The author is thus granted a voice that is rather different from that of the author/promoter, and yet it is not an unhappy retreat into the 'painful soundlessness' of the underpromoted. Is there, then, an escape from the *mise en abyme* of the promotional circuit, the hall of marketing mirrors? Can there be, contrary to Andrew Wernick's assertion, a space that is '*hors-promotion*', a writing beyond marketing?

Throughout this book, it has been argued that marketing, in its broader definition as a process of representation carried out by a wide variety of agencies, not only influences reception but also constructs meaning. This process is inescapable, though its dimensions change from period to period, and from marketplace to marketplace, thus providing conditions that are more or less congenial to the various agencies in a literary field. Authorial and textual resistance to these conditions can be, and is, made, and thus sanctions the continuing power of both author and text, and indeed constructs at least part of their appeal to readers. Yet these acts of resistance are also acts of representation and of meaning-making, and hence both stem from and are incorporated into marketing. No escape then. As Wernick explains after developing his notion of no *hors-promotion*, this can bring forth a cynicism in the interaction between writers and readers, and all the intermediary agencies involved in the literary field.

Wernick's vision of readerly and writerly cynicism in the face of the market is bleak, yet while authors still struggle to communicate with their readers, despite the quandaries of textual production and the vagaries of textual consumption, their work will continue to provide metaphors of escape and eloquent reminders of humanity's capacity for imagining the world and its systems otherwise. One such is Zadie Smith's FutureMouse, a genetically-modified experiment by the scientist Marcus Chalfen. Marcus's intent is to ' "correct the Creator's mistakes" '.[24] As a metaphor for hybridisation and multiculturalism, and as an incorporation of late twentieth-century anxieties about genetics, FutureMouse is one of *White Teeth*'s less subtle creations. But in the anthropomorphised 'getaway of a small brown rebel mouse' in the very final words of the novel, *White Teeth* provides an interrogation both of humanity's ability to control the future, and, by extension, of any system of meaning to exert its influence.[25] Therefore, *Marketing Literature* will conclude with one final image, one final metaphor for the projected escape of literature from marketing, and, paradoxically, its continual incorporation into meaning-making. Archie, the hapless hero of the novel, bleeding from a gunshot wound that traps him in a complex and circular pattern of history, watches with envy and delight the renegade mouse:

> He watched it stand very still for a second with a smug look as if it expected nothing less. He watched it scurry away, over his hand. He watched it dash along the table, and through the hands of those who wished to pin it down. He watched it leap off the end and disappear through an air vent. *Go on my son!* thought Archie.[26]

Appendix 1

The mark | indicates a line break in the original cover copy.

Emlyn Rees *The Book of Dead Authors* (London: Headline Review, 1998; paperback edition)

Front cover copy:

The Book of Dead Authors
Emlyn Rees

'Sex and violence on every page . . . brilliant' | MAIL ON SUNDAY |

Back cover copy:

'A wonderfully black piece | of gratuitous sex and violence, | funny in a grim way, well plotted, | spooky and in splendidly bad taste' | EVENING STANDARD |

When acclaimed author Adam Appleton opens the door of his | charming Hampstead home to an alluring stranger, he has no idea | that he is turning the page on the last, short and horribly violent | chapter of his life. For his killer, however, it is merely the exhilarating | opening scene in a long and grisly narrative of revenge, as one by one | famous writers come to sticky and wickedly appropriate ends. |

Soon a nation is holding its breath, waiting for the murderer's next bloody | instalment, while terrified authors cower in their Soho clubs, hoping against | hope that they are not about to feature in this appallingly gripping serial. | But the creator of this most unusual murder mystery is no mere hack, and when | the final climax comes, it comes with one last terrifying, heartstopping twist . . .|

'A gleefully wicked tale of the world's | first literary serial killer hunting down | authors and dispatching them in a suitably | grisly manner . . . Pity it's only a novel' | THE BIG ISSUE |

Martyn Bedford *The Houdini Girl* (London: Penguin, 2000; paperback edition)

Front cover copy (1):

THE HOUDINI GIRL
MARTYN BEDFORD

'An exciting high-wire act of a book' | Sunday Times

Front cover copy (2):

'This year's *Captain Corelli's Mandolin*' | VOGUE |

Back cover copy:

Fletcher Brandon is a conjurer, an illusionist, a | master of deception. |

A professional magician, he charms wild, | impulsive Rosa into his life with simple sleight | of hand. But her mysterious death, and the lies | that emerge soon after, force Brandon to face a | painful realization – even the trickster can be | tricked. |

As he delves deeper into the circumstances of | Rosa's life and death, confronting her secret | past, Brandon enters a world where betrayal, | exploitation and violence are not simply part of the act. |

Sometimes, when the lady vanishes, she stays | vanished. |

'A great success, delivering what Bedford | always promised: writing that is nerve- | racking, bold, unusual, stylish, never | complacent and always intelligent' | *The Times* |

'Magical in more senses than one, a novel, | that once started, is hard to put down... a | refreshing and enviable new talent' | *Express* |

'A brilliant read: fast, funny and scary... Sexy | – and magic' | *Cosmopolitan* |

Rupert Thomson *The Book of Revelation* (London: Bloomsbury, 2000; paperback edition)

Front cover copy:

'AN EXCEPTIONAL BOOK... IT IS PERFECT' GUARDIAN

THE BOOK OF REVELATION
RUPERT THOMSON

Back cover copy:

From the bestselling author of | Soft and The Insult |

On a bright spring day in Amsterdam a man goes out | to buy a packet of cigarettes. He is a dancer – | charismatic, talented, and physically beautiful. What | happens next takes him completely by surprise and | marks him for ever. His abduction by three strangers | and his subsequent imprisonment in a mysterious | white room have consequences that are both poignant | and highly disturbing. |

'Intellectually intriguing, viscerally gripping and | emotionally engaging. The only reason you'll put this | book down is to postpone the dreadful moment when | you finish it' Independent |

'An exceptional book... It is perfect... From beginning | to end it is a true chiller' Guardian |

'Gripping, original and intricately conceived and | written' *The Times* |

'Compelling... A truly memorable book, full of insights | into sexuality, and the dehumanisation of a man who | loses everything through no fault of his own' Marie Claire |

'Witty, unsettling, nightmarish, entrancing' | Daily Mail |

'An unsettlingly dark vision coupled with elements of a | thriller... Start reading and you're gripped' | Sunday Express |

'Thomson's new novel bears comparison with the | greats' Independent on Sunday |

Toby Litt *Corpsing* (London: Penguin, 2000; paperback edition)

Front cover copy:

toby litt
corpsing
'a remarkable crime debut...| has all the hallmarks of | a cult book' guardian |

Back cover copy:

'A heart-thumping story- | line of murder, infidelity | and revenge... a grisly, | as well as gripping, | read' *GQ* |

The first bullet entered the body | of my ex-girlfriend – gorgeous, | slightly-famous Lily – two inches | beneath her left breast. We were sitting | at a table in Le Corbusier, Frith Street, Soho. | As the first bullet went into her, I turned to | look at the gunman. Wearing Day-Glo Lycra, | a helmet, mirror shades and a pollution-mask – just like | a bike courier – he had a black and silver gun in his hand. | And he was shooting the woman I still loved...|

'Sexy, full of twists and wickedly funny... By page twelve | you have laughed out loud more than once... Tension, pace | and a sharp wit... Litt writes brilliantly' *Daily Mail* |

'The dialogue is fresh and the pace frenetic... Has "soon | to be a major motion picture" written all over it' *i-d*|

'A genuine page-turner of a thriller' *Mirror* |

'Breakneck narrative... devastatingly | enjoyable... I cannot wait for | the movie' *Daily Telegraph* |

Notes

Introduction

1. J. K. Rowling, *Harry Potter and the Philosopher's Stone; Harry Potter and the Chamber of Secrets; Harry Potter and the Prisoner of Azkaban; Harry Potter and the Goblet of Fire; Harry Potter and the Order of the Phoenix; Harry Potter and the Half-Blood Prince; Harry Potter and the Deathly Hallows* (London: Bloomsbury, 1997, 1998, 1999, 2000, 2003, 2005, 2007); Dan Brown, *The Da Vinci Code* (London: Bantam, 2003).
2. Gérard Genette, *Fiction and Diction*, translated by Catherine Porter (Ithaca: Cornell University Press, 1993; originally published in France in 1991), 1–29.
3. Genette writes, 'Literariness, being a plural phenomenon, requires a pluralist theory that takes into account the various means at the disposal of language for escaping and outliving its practical function and for producing texts capable of being received and appreciated as aesthetic objects', *Fiction and Diction*, 20–1.
4. Steven Connor, *The English Novel in History 1950–1995* (London: Routledge, 1996), 13–27.
5. Connor, *English Novel*, 19.
6. Examples of 1990s literary thrillers include Peter Høeg, *Miss Smilla's Feeling for Snow*, translated by F. David (London: Harvill, 1993; first published in Denmark in 1992); Caleb Carr, *The Alienist* (London: Little, Brown, 1994); David Guterson, *Snow Falling on Cedars* (London: Bloomsbury, 1995); and Lauren Belfer, *City of Light* (London: Sceptre, 1999).
7. Connor, *English Novel*, 19.
8. Bret Easton Ellis, *American Psycho* (London: Picador, 1991); Helen Fielding, *Bridget Jones's Diary* (London: Picador, 1996).
9. Randall Stevenson, *The Last of England? The Oxford English Literary History Volume 12 1960–2000* (Oxford: Oxford University Press, 2004); James F. English, ed., *A Concise Companion to Contemporary British Fiction* (Oxford: Blackwell Publishing, 2006).
10. Thomas R. Adams and Nicolas Barker, 'A New Model for the Study of the Book', in Nicolas Barker, ed., *A Potencie of Life: Books in Society. The Clark Lectures 1986-1987. The British Library Studies in the History of the Book* (London: The British Library, 1993), 5–43, 33.
11. Jonathan Rose's survey of work in the history of the book, 'The History of Books: Revised and Enlarged', illustrates this (in Haydn T. Mason, ed., *The Darnton Debate: Books and Revolution in the Eighteenth Century. Studies on Voltaire and the Eighteenth Century* 359 (Oxford: Voltaire Foundation, 1998), 83–104). More recently Simone Murray also mentioned the lack of more recent studies in her conference paper 'Publishing Studies: Critically Mapping Research in Search of a Discipline', at *SHARP 2006*, The Hague/Leiden, July 2006.

12. A discussion of the durability of contemporary fiction is to be found in Andrew Holgate and Honor Wilson-Fletcher, eds., *The Test of Time: What Makes a Classic a Classic?* (Brentford: Waterstone's, 1999).
13. Studies include Janice Radway's *Reading the Romance: Women, Patriarchy, and Popular Literature* (Chapel Hill: University of North Carolina Press, 1984); Joseph McAleer's *Passion's Fortune: The Story of Mills & Boon* (Oxford: Oxford University Press, 1999); and Eva Hemmungs Wirtén's *Global Infatuation: Explorations in Global Publishing and Texts* (Uppsala: Avdelningen för litteratursociologi vid Litteraturventenskapliga Institutionen i Uppsala, 1998).
14. D. F. McKenzie, in 'Trading Places? England 1689–France 1789)', in Haydn T. Mason, ed., *The Darnton Debate* (Oxford: Voltaire Foundation, 1998), 1–24, encapsulates this split in his question, 'As a matter of intellectual and publishing history [...] are we looking for great books that changed the world, although (or because) they addressed an elite, or for a critical mass of texts that less perceptibly shaped popular opinion?', 18.
15. John Sutherland, *Fiction and the Fiction Industry* (London: Athlone Press, 1978); *Bestsellers: Popular Fiction of the 1970s* (London: Routledge & Kegan Paul, 1981).
16. John Sutherland, *Reading the Decades: Fifty Years of the Nation's Bestselling Books* (London: BBC, 2002), 7.
17. Clive Bloom, *Bestsellers: Popular Fiction Since 1900* (Basingstoke: Palgrave Macmillan, 2002).
18. Paul Delany, *Literature, Money and the Market: From Trollope to Amis* (Basingstoke: Palgrave Macmillan, 2002), 1–16, 172–91, 180.
19. John Feather, *A History of British Publishing* (London: Routledge, 2006; 2nd edn.). Volume 7 of *The Cambridge History of the Book* is in preparation.
20. Stevenson's *The Last of England?* has a chapter on 'A Golden Age? Readers, Authors, and the Book Trade'. Brian W. Shaffer, ed., *A Companion to the British and Irish Novel 1945–2000* (Oxford: Blackwell Publishing, 2005) has a chapter by myself on 'Novelistic Production and the Publishing Industry in Britain and Ireland' (177–93). English's edited volume *A Concise Companion to Contemporary British Fiction* has chapters by Richard Todd on 'Literary Fiction and the Book Trade' (19–38) and by English and John Frow on 'Literary Authorship and Celebrity Culture' (39–57).
21. John B. Thompson, *Books in the Digital Age: The Transformation of Academic and Higher Education Publishing in Britain and the United States* (Cambridge: Polity, 2005). Thompson is currently working on a similar volume treating the general trade sector.
22. Judy Simons and Kate Fullbrook, eds., *Writing: A Woman's Business: Women, Writing and the Marketplace* (Manchester: Manchester University Press, 1998).
23. Simone Murray, *Mixed Media: Feminist Presses and Publishing Politics* (London: Pluto Press, 2004).
24. S. I. A. Kotei, 'The Book Today in Africa', 480–4; Philip G. Altbach, 'Literary Colonialism: Books in the Third World', 485–90, reprinted in Bill Ashcroft, Gareth Griffiths and Helen Tiffin, eds., *The Post-Colonial Studies Reader* (London: Routledge, 1995); Graham Huggan, *The Postcolonial Exotic: Marketing the Margins* (London: Routledge, 2001).
25. Richard Todd, *Consuming Fictions: The Booker Prize and Fiction in Britain Today* (London: Bloomsbury, 1996), James F. English, *The Economy of Prestige: Prizes,*

Awards, and the Circulation of Cultural Value (Cambridge, Mass.: Harvard University Press, 2005).

26. Joe Moran, *Star Authors: Literary Celebrity in America* (London: Pluto Press, 2000).
27. Eva Hemmungs Wirtén, *No Trespassing: Authorship, Intellectual Property Rights, and the Boundaries of Globalization* (Toronto: University of Toronto Press, 2004).
28. Laura J. Miller, *Reluctant Capitalists: Bookselling and the Culture of Consumption* (Chicago: University of Chicago Press, 2006).
29. Stephen Brown, ed., *Consuming Books: The Marketing and Consumption of Literature* (London: Routledge, 2006).
30. Eric de Bellaigue, *British Book Publishing as a Business Since the 1960s* (London: British Library, 2004).
31. McAleer, *Passion's Fortune*; Jeremy Lewis, *Penguin Special: The Life and Times of Allen Lane* (London: Viking, 2005); Elizabeth James, ed., *Macmillan: A Publishing Tradition* (Basingstoke: Palgrave Macmillan, 2002).
32. Diana Athill, *Stet* (London: Granta, 2000); Tom Maschler, *Publisher* (London: Picador, 2005).
33. James, 'Introduction' to *Macmillan*, 1–10, 10.
34. Timothy Garton Ash, *History of the Present: Essays, Sketches and Despatches from Europe in the 1990s* (London: Penguin, 2000 updated edn.; 1st edn. 1999), xix.
35. For more information on the Oxford International Centre for Publishing Studies, see http://www.brookes.ac.uk/publishing
36. Carmen Callil and Colm Tóibín, *The Modern Library: The Two Hundred Best Novels in English Since 1950* (London: Picador, 1999), vii.
37. Simone Murray, 'From Literature to Content: Media Multinationals, Publishing Practice and the Digitisation of the Book', at *SHARP 2002*, Institute of English Studies, School of Advanced Study, University of London, 10–13 July 2002. André Schiffrin, *The Business of Books: How International Conglomerates Took Over Publishing and Changed the Way We Read* (London: Verso, 2000). Other books referred to by Murray include Athill's *Stet*; Jason Epstein's *Book Business: Publishing Past Present and Future* (New York: W. W. Norton, 2001) and Hilary McPhee's *Other People's Words* (Sydney: Picador Australia, 2001).
38. D. J. Taylor, *A Vain Conceit: British Fiction in the 1980s* (London: Bloomsbury, 1989), 1.
39. Connor, *English Novel*, 16.
40. Louis de Bernières, *Captain Corelli's Mandolin* (London: Secker & Warburg, 1994); Martin Amis, *The Information* (London: Flamingo, 1995).
41. Irvine Welsh, *Trainspotting* (London: Secker & Warburg, 1993); Pat Barker, *The Ghost Road* (London: Viking, 1995) and its prequels *Regeneration* and *The Eye in the Door* (London: Viking, 1991, 1993); Arundhati Roy, *The God of Small Things* (London: Flamingo 1997).
42. Philip Pullman, *Northern Lights, The Subtle Knife, The Amber Spyglass* (London: Scholastic, 1995, 1997, 2000); Mark Haddon, *The Curious Incident of the Dog in the Night-Time* (London/Oxford: Jonathan Cape/David Fickling, 2003); David Mitchell, *Cloud Atlas* (London: Sceptre, 2004).
43. Zadie Smith, *White Teeth* (London: Hamish Hamilton, 2000).

1. Publishing Contexts and Market Conditions

1. These continuities are suggested by Simon Eliot in 'Continuity and Change in British Publishing, 1770–2000', *Publishing Research Quarterly*, 19: 2 (Summer 2003), 37–50.
2. Jeremy Lewis, *Kindred Spirits: Adrift in Literary London* (London: HarperCollins, 1995), 3.
3. Andrew Milner, *Literature, Culture and Society* (London: UCL Press, 1996), 100.
4. Giles Clark, *Inside Book Publishing* (London: Routledge, 2001; 3rd edn.), 15.
5. The Bookseller, *Who Owns Whom: Book Publishing and Retailing 1980–1989* (London: J. Whitaker & Sons, 1990); Christopher Gasson, *Who Owns Whom in British Book Publishing* (London: Bookseller Publications, 1998 and 2002).
6. Further measured accounts of the economic situation can be found in Ian McGowan, 'The United Kingdom', in Philip G. Altbach and Edith S. Hoshimo, eds., *International Book Publishing: An Encyclopaedia* (London: Fitzroy Dearborn, 1995), 565–74, and Ian R. Willison's 'Massmediatisation: Export of the American Model?', in Jacques Michon and Jean-Yves Mollier, eds., *Les Mutations de Livre et de l'Edition Dans le Monde du XVIIIe Siècle à l'An 2000: Actes du Colloque International Sherbrooke 2000* (Saint-Nicolas: Les Presses de l'Université Laval, 2001). For more opinionated accounts of the impact on culture of the processes of conglomeration see L. A. Coser, C. Kadushin and W. W. Powell, *Books: The Culture and Commerce of Publishing* (New York: Basic Books, 1982), Thomas Whiteside, *The Blockbuster Complex: Conglomerates, Show Business, and Book Publishing* (Middletown: Wesleyan University Press, 1981) and Ben Bagdikian, *The Media Monopoly* (Boston: Beacon Press, 1983).
7. De Bellaigue, *British Book Publishing*, 13.
8. Gasson, *Who Owns Whom in British Book Publishing* (2002), 88–9.
9. The cartoon was contained within the editorial 'John Murray: Gentlemen Overcome by Arrivistes?', *The Bookseller*, 17 May 2002, 26. See also Boyd Tonkin, 'Lord Byron's Publisher Bids Farewell to Independence', *Independent*, 11 May 2002, 9.
10. Chris Patten, *East and West: The Last Governor General of Hong Kong on Power, Freedom and the Future* (London: Macmillan, 1998).
11. See Derek Jones, ed., *Censorship: A World Encyclopedia Volume 3: L–R* (London: Fitzroy Dearborn Publishers, 2001), 1946.
12. Schiffrin, *The Business of Books*, 103.
13. Clark, *Inside Book Publishing*, 15.
14. De Bellaigue, *British Book Publishing*, 190.
15. Simone Murray, 'From Literature to Content'. The design of Random House's appointments schedule from the Frankfurt Book Fair 2002 does nothing to dispel this idea, featuring an array of over 100 imprint colophons belonging to the conglomerate (Random House appointments schedule, 2002).
16. De Bellaigue, *British Book Publishing*, 3–4.
17. Clark, *Inside Book Publishing*, 15.
18. Carole Blake, a UK literary agent, discusses why the agent (and the author) would find this a desirable business process in *From Pitch to Publication: Everything You Need to Know to Get Your Novel Published* (London: Macmillan,

1999), particularly in the chapters 'Who Sells Where' and 'Selling Other Rights', as does Lynette Owen's *Selling Rights* (Abingdon: Routledge, 2006; 5th edn.).

19. Ian Norrie, *Mumby's Publishing and Bookselling in the Twentieth Century* (London: Bell and Hyman, 1982; 6th edn.), 91–2, 220.
20. Athill, *Stet*, 34.
21. Norrie, *Mumby's Publishing and Bookselling*, 220; *Book Facts 2001: An Annual Compendium* (London: Book Marketing Ltd, 2001), 17.
22. *Book Facts 2001*, 17.
23. *Book Facts 2001*, 17; Alison Bone 'Output Surges 11%', *The Bookseller*, 9 September 2005, 7.
24. Eliot, 'Continuity and Change', 48.
25. Schiffrin, *The Business of Books*, 112.
26. KPMG, *The UK Book Industry: Unlocking the Supply Chain's Hidden Prize*, February 1998. The 1998 report was followed by the further KPMG document, *Tackling Returns*, August 1999.
27. R. E. Barker and G. R. Davies, *Books Are Different: An Account of the Defence of the Net Book Agreement Before the Restrictive Practices Court in 1962* (London: Macmillan, 1966). Alison Baverstock turned this phrase around in her book of 1993, *Are Books Different?; Marketing in the Book Trade* (London: Kogan Page, 1993), in order to question both the practice of retail price maintenance and its broader implications for the cultural and business status of the publishing industry.
28. See Joel Rickett, 'Year-in-View of the Publishing Industry', in *Writers' and Artists' Yearbook 2006* (London: A&C Black, 2005; 99th edn.), 270–3, 271.
29. Rickett, 'Year-in-View', 271.
30. Posy Simmonds, *Literary Life* (London: Jonathan Cape, 2003), 30.
31. Giles Gordon, 'Proper Publishing Goes Bung', *Bookseller*, 25 January 2002, 27–8, 27.
32. Gordon, 'Proper Publishing', 27.
33. Gordon, 'Proper Publishing', 28.
34. Danuta Kean, 'Bungs – Are They Fair Trade?', *Bookseller*, 15 February 2002, 26–9.
35. Kean, 'Bungs', 26, 27; Margaret Atwood, *The Blind Assassin* (London: Bloomsbury, 2000).
36. Kean, 'Bungs', 26, 29.
37. Kean, 'Bungs', 29.
38. Kean, 'Bungs', 28.
39. Kean, 'Bungs', 28.
40. Kean, 'Bungs', 27.
41. Joel Rickett, 'Publishing by Numbers?', *Bookseller*, 1 September 2000, 20–2, 21.
42. Rickett, 'Publishing by Numbers?', 21. Knight refers to Dava Sobel's *Longitude: The True Story of a Lone Genius Who Solved the Greatest Scientific Problem of His Time* (London: Fourth Estate, 1996).
43. An argument explored by Laura J. Miller in 'The Best-Seller List as Marketing Tool and Historical Fiction', *Book History* 3 (2000), 286–304.
44. Winslow Farrell, *How Hits Happen: Forecasting Unpredictability in a Chaotic Marketplace* (London: Orion Business, 1998), 20.

45. *Book Retailing – UK* (London: Mintel International Group Limited, 2000), accessed via http://reports.mintel.com, 25 July 2003.
46. The Competition Commission's inquiry is available at http://www.competition-commission.org.uk/inquiries/ref2005/hmv/, accessed 29 September 2006.
47. Book Marketing Limited, *Books and the Consumer: Summary Report on the Findings of the 2004 Survey* (London: BML, 2005), 21.
48. Steve Hare, *Penguin Portrait: Allen Lane and the Penguin Editors 1935–1970* (London: Penguin, 1995), 7.
49. As reported in Book Marketing Limited, *Expanding the Book Market: A Study of Reading and Buying Habits in GB* (London: BML, 2005), 5.
50. Michael Lane, *Books and Publishers: Commerce Against Culture in Postwar Britain* (Lexington, Mass.: Lexington Books, 1980), 112.
51. Book Marketing Limited, *Expanding the Book Market*, 5.
52. Danuta Kean, *Book Retailing in Britain* (London: Bookseller Publications, 2001), 49.
53. Rickett, 'Year-in-View', 271.
54. Kean, *Book Retailing in Britain*, 48; Liz Bury and Danuta Kean, 'Browser to Buyer, Amazon Style', *The Bookseller*, 7 January 2005, 26–7, 26; Rickett, 'Year-in-View', 271.
55. Chris Anderson, *The Long Tail: How Endless Choice is Creating Unlimited Demand* (London: Random House, 2006).
56. Bury and Kean, 'Browser to Buyer'.
57. Kean, *Book Retailing in Britain*, 5.
58. Thompson, *Books in the Digital Age*.
59. Miller, *Reluctant Capitalists*, 117–39.
60. Iain D. Brown and Jo Fletcher, eds., *Superstores – Super News?: The Report of Fiona Stewart, 1998 Tony Godwin Award Recipient* (London: The Tony Godwin Memorial Trust, 1999).
61. Leon Kreitzman, 'Shop Around the Clock', *Bookseller*, 26 March 1999, 36.
62. Miller, *Reluctant Capitalists*, 117.
63. For a discussion of Borders' entry into Oxford and Cambridge, see Richard Barker, 'A Tale of Two Cities', *Bookseller*, 30 April 1999, 30–2.
64. Feather, *A History of British Publishing*, 102, 140–1.
65. Michael Legat, *An Author's Guide to Literary Agents* (London: Robert Hale, 1995), 14.
66. Suki Dhanda, 'Our Top 50 Players in the World of Books', *Observer*, 5 March 2006, 4–7.
67. Dhanda, 'Our Top 50', 4.
68. Kate Pool, 'Love, Not Money: The Survey of Authors' Earnings', *The Author* 111: 2 (2000), 58–66. In 2007, the Authors' Licensing and Collecting Society (ALCS) produced a report that summarised equally depressing news for writers. http://www.alcs.co.uk/multimedia/pdf2/word2.pdf, accessed 25 March 2007.
69. Cyril Connolly, ed., 'Questionnaire: The Cost of Letters', *Horizon*, 14: 81 (1946), 140–75; Andrew Holgate and Honor Wilson-Fletcher, eds., *The Cost of Letters: A Survey of Literary Living Standards* (Brentford: Waterstone's Booksellers Ltd, 1998).
70. Holgate and Wilson Fletcher, *The Cost of Letters*, 23.

71. James F. English, 'Winning the Culture Game: Prizes, Awards, and the Rules of Art', *New Literary History* 33: 1 (2002), 109–35, 123; Karl Miller, *Authors* (Oxford: Oxford University Press, 1989), 192.
72. Andrew Miller, *Ingenious Pain* (London: Sceptre, 1997); Interview with Andrew Miller, 30 June 2000.
73. Juliet Gardiner, '"What is an Author?" Contemporary Publishing Discourse and the Author Figure', *Publishing Research Quarterly* 16: 1 (Spring 2000), 63–76, 69.
74. Moran, *Star Authors*, 1.
75. See, for example, previously mentioned studies by Moran, Gardiner, English and Frow.
76. As Jamie Hodder-Williams, Sales and Marketing Director, Hodder & Stoughton General Division, explained in interview at Hodder Headline, 13 July 2000. Typically a company will have one 'lead' fiction and one 'lead' non-fiction title a month, along with a handful (c.3–6) of 'supersellers'.
77. Moran, *Star Authors*, 38.
78. Catherine Feeny, '"I Haven't Actually Read Your Book, Catherine..."', *Independent*, 10 March 2000, 6 (World Book Day 2000 supplement).
79. Lorna Sage, 'Living on Writing', in Jeremy Treglown and Bridget Bennett, eds., *Grub Street and the Ivory Tower: Literary Journalism and Literary Scholarship from Fielding to the Internet* (Oxford: Clarendon Press, 1998), 262–76, 264.
80. Sage, 'Living on Writing', 266–7.
81. Sage, 'Living on Writing', 265, 267.
82. English and Frow, 'Literary Authorship and Celebrity Culture', 45.

2. Literature and Marketing

1. Coser, et al., *Books: The Culture and Commerce of Publishing*, 7.
2. Delany, *Literature, Money and the Market*, 97, 98.
3. In 'I Write Marketing Textbooks but I'm Really a Swill Guy', Chris Hackley notes Dag Smith's comment in Patrick Forsyth and Robin Birn, *Marketing in Publishing* (London: Routledge, 1997) to the effect that 'book publishing is still product- rather than marketing-led but argues that this is rapidly changing, at least in the UK industry'. In Brown, ed., *Consuming Books*, 175–82, 178.
4. Q. D. Leavis, *Fiction and the Reading Public* (London: Peregrine, 1979; first published in 1932), 32.
5. Leavis, *Fiction and the Reading Public*, 32.
6. Leavis, *Fiction and the Reading Public*, 163. She refers to F. R. Leavis, *Mass Civilisation and Minority Culture* (Cambridge: Minority Press, 1930).
7. Joan Shelley Rubin, *The Making of Middle/Brow Culture* (Chapel Hill: University of North Carolina Press, 1982); Janice A. Radway, *A Feeling for Books: The Book-of-the-Month Club, Literary Taste, and Middle-Class Desire* (Chapel Hill: University of North Carolina Press, 1997).
8. Radway, *A Feeling for Books*, 9.
9. Rubin, *The Making of Middle/Brow Culture*, xix.
10. John Seabrook, *Nobrow: The Culture of Marketing the Marketing of Culture* (London: Methuen, 2000), 12.

11. John Carey, *The Intellectuals and the Masses* (London: Faber and Faber, 1992), vii.
12. Leavis, *Fiction and the Reading Public*, 19; Geoffrey Faber, *A Publisher Speaking* (London: Faber and Faber, 1934), 29.
13. Richard Hoggart, *The Uses of Literacy* (London: Chatto & Windus, 1957), 193.
14. Hoggart, *The Uses of Literacy*, 196.
15. Hare, *Penguin Portrait*, 237; C. H. Rolph, ed., *The Trial of Lady Chatterley* (Harmondsworth: Penguin, 1961).
16. Rolph, *The Trial of Lady Chatterley*, 17.
17. Connor, *English Novel*, 14.
18. Fredric Warburg, *An Occupation for Gentlemen* (London: Hutchinson, 1959), 118–19.
19. Anne Batt, 'A Book is Not a Tin of Beans…', *Daily Express*, 8 May 1967.
20. Hare, *Penguin Portrait*, 189.
21. Warburg, *An Occupation for Gentlemen*, 14–15.
22. Cited in Hare, *Penguin Portrait*, 263.
23. The Arts Council's decibel initiative produced the report *In Full Colour: Cultural Diversity in Publishing Today* in collaboration with *The Bookseller* in March 2004 in order to assess the extent of the industry's diversity. Its verdict was that there was still much to achieve.
24. Hare, *Penguin Portrait*, 263.
25. Lane, *Books and Publishers*, 77, 112.
26. Doris Stockmann's article 'Free or Fixed Prices on Books – Patterns of Book Pricing in Europe', *Javnost The Public* 11: 4 (2004), 49–64, explores European trends in book pricing and price fixing.
27. Schiffrin, *The Business of Books*, 5–6.
28. Morris B. Holbrook attempts to do so in 'On the Commercial Exaltation of Artistic Mediocrity: Books, Bread, Postmodern Statistics, Surprising Success Stories, and the Doomed Magnificence of Way Too Many Big Words', in Brown, *Consuming Books*, 96–113, but ends up tying himself in knots.
29. Catherine Lockerbie, 'Return of Reading's Red Letter Day', *The Scotsman*, 10 April 1999, 10.
30. English and Frow, 'Literary Authorship and Celebrity Culture', 45.
31. English and Frow, 'Literary Authorship and Celebrity Culture', 45.
32. Andrew Wernick, 'Authorship and the Supplement of Promotion', in Maurice Biriotti and Nicola Miller, eds., *What is an Author?* (Manchester: Manchester University Press, 1993), 85–103, 101–2.
33. Stephen Brown, Anne Marie Doherty and Bill Clarke's self-reflexive *Romancing the Market* (London: Routledge, 1998) is one example. Brown's *Consuming Books* has two chapters that look at books about marketing: Charles Chandler's 'No Experience Necessary (Or, How I Learned to Stop Worrying and Love Marketing)', 167–74, and Chris Hackley's 'I Write Marketing Textbooks but I'm Really a Swill Guy', 175–82.
34. Alison Baverstock, *How to Market Books* (London: Kogan Page, 2000; 3rd edn.); Patrick Forsyth and Robin Birn, *Marketing in Publishing* (London: Routledge, 1997).
35. Forsyth and Birn, *Marketing in Publishing*, 2.
36. See, for example, Sally Dibb, Lyndon Simkin, William M. Pride and O. C. Ferrell, *Marketing: Concepts and Strategies* (Boston: Houghton Mifflin, 2001; 4th edn.), 9.

37. Robert Darnton, 'What is the History of Books?, in *The Kiss of Lamourette: Reflections in Cultural History* (London: Faber and Faber, 1990), 107–35, 111. First published in *Daedalus* (Summer 1982), 65–83.
38. Darnton, 'What is the History of Books?', 112, 113.
39. Darnton, 'What is the History of Books?', 110.
40. Book historians do legitimate their study with the claim that histories of the book are in fact histories of the world – or at least of a particular part of society in a given place and time. As Thomas R. Adams and Nicolas Barker write in 'A New Model for the Study of the Book', in Nicolas Barker, ed., *A Potencie of Life: Books in Society. The Clark Lectures 1986–1987. The British Library Studies in the History of the Book* (London: The British Library, 1993), 5–43, 12, 'for a period of roughly five hundred years the printed book reigned supreme, as a method of recording, communication and storing all that people put on paper: knowledge, ideas, persuasion (political or religious), diversions, etc. Its influence on one or more of these areas touched almost every aspect of what we call western civilization, in ways we still have to discover.'
41. Adams and Barker, 'A New Model', 12.
42. Darnton, 'What is the History of Books?', 135.
43. Darnton, 'What is the History of Books?', 135.
44. Adams and Barker, 'A New Model', 12.
45. Adams and Barker, 'A New Model', 15.
46. Adams and Barker, 'A New Model', 15.
47. Adams and Barker, 'A New Model', 15.
48. Adams and Barker, 'A New Model', 16.
49. Adams and Barker, 'A New Model', 18.
50. Adams and Barker, 'A New Model', 23.
51. Adams and Barker, 'A New Model', 25–6.
52. Adams and Barker, 'A New Model', 38.
53. Adams and Barker, 'A New Model', 39.
54. Pierre Bourdieu, 'The Field of Cultural Production', in *The Field of Cultural Production: Essays on Art and Literature*, translated by Randal Johnston (Cambridge: Polity Press, 1993), 29–73. Originally published in *Poetics* 12/4–5 (1983), 311–56.
55. Leavis, *Fiction and the Reading Public*, 32.
56. Leavis, *Fiction and the Reading Public*, 163; Bourdieu, *The Field of Cultural Production*, 40.
57. Bourdieu, *The Field of Cultural Production*, 38.
58. Bourdieu, *The Field of Cultural Production*, 34.
59. See, for example, Theodor Adorno, *The Culture Industry: Selected Essays on Mass Culture*, edited with an Introduction by J. M. Bernstein (London: Routledge, 1991).
60. Bourdieu, *The Field of Cultural Production*, 30.
61. Bourdieu, *The Field of Cultural Production*, 37.
62. Bourdieu, *The Field of Cultural Production*, 31.
63. Peter McDonald, *British Literary Culture and Publishing Practice 1880–1914* (Cambridge: Cambridge University Press, 1997), 20.
64. Bourdieu, *The Field of Cultural Production*, 30.
65. Bourdieu, *The Field of Cultural Production*, 38.
66. Bourdieu, *The Field of Cultural Production*, 40.

67. Bourdieu, *The Field of Cultural Production*, 39.
68. English, 'Winning the Culture Game', 123.
69. English, 'Winning the Culture Game', 125, 126.
70. English, 'Winning the Culture Game', 127.
71. English, 'Winning the Culture Game', 127.
72. Nicolas Barker, 'Intentionality and Reception Theory', in Barker, ed., *A Potencie of Life*, 195–210, 200.
73. For example, Jonathan Rose's *The Intellectual Life of the British Working Classes* (New Haven: Yale University Press, 2001), Radway's *A Feeling for Books* and Elizabeth Long's *Book Clubs: Women and the Uses of Reading in Everyday Life* (Chicago: University of Chicago Press, 2003).
74. Darnton, 'What is the History of Books?', 122.
75. Darnton, 'What is the History of Books?', 131. Darnton refers in a footnote to Wolfgang Iser, *The Implied Reader: Patterns of Communication in Prose Fiction from Bunyan to Beckett* (Baltimore: Johns Hopkins University Press, 1974), Stanley Fish, *Self-Consuming Artifacts: The Experience of Seventeenth-Century Literature* (Berkeley: University of California Press, 1972) and *Is There a Text in This Class? The Authority of Interpretive Communities* (Cambridge, Mass.: Harvard University Press, 1980), Walter Ong, 'The Writer's Audience is Always a Fiction', *PMLA* (*Publication of the Modern Language Association of America*) 90 (1975), 9–21, and to Susan Suleiman and Inge Crosman's *The Reader in the Text: Essays on Audience and Interpretation* (Princeton: Princeton University Press, 1980) for an overview of reader-response theorists.
76. Robert Darnton, 'First Steps Towards a History of Reading', in *The Kiss of Lamourette*, 154–87. First published in the *Australian Journal of French Studies* 23 (1986), 5–30.
77. Darnton, 'What is the History of Books?', 131; Michel Foucault, 'What is an Author?', in Josué V. Harari, *Textual Strategies: Perspectives in Post-Structuralist Criticism* (London: Methuen & Co, 1980; English translation first published in the US in 1979), 141–60.
78. Foucault, 'What is an Author?', 159.
79. Foucault, 'What is an Author?', 153, 159.
80. Foucault, 'What is an Author?', 160.
81. Darnton, 'First Steps Towards a History of Reading', 181–2.
82. Darnton, 'First Steps Towards a History of Reading', 157.
83. Guglielmo Cavallo and Roger Chartier, 'Introduction', in Guglielmo Cavallo and Roger Chartier, *A History of Reading in the West*, translated by Lydia G. Cochrane (Cambridge: Polity Press, 1999; first published in Italy in 1995), 1–36, 3.
84. Fish, 'Interpreting the Variorum', in *Is There a Text in This Class?*, 147–80, 171.
85. Fish, 'Interpreting the Variorum', 180.
86. The most passionate recent advocate of the traditional canon is Harold Bloom, in *The Western Canon: The Books and School of the Ages* (New York: Harcourt Brace, 1994).
87. Judith Fetterley, *The Resisting Reader: A Feminist Approach to American Fiction* (Bloomington: Indiana University Press, 1978).
88. Including the work of Long's *Book Clubs* and Jenny Hartley, *Reading Groups* and *The Reading Groups Book 2002–2003 Edition* (Oxford: Oxford University Press, 2001, 2002).

89. Avi Shankar, 'Book-Reading Groups: A "Male Outsider" Perspective', in Brown, ed., *Consuming Books*, 114–25, 121.
90. Hartley, *Reading Groups*, particularly in the chapter 'How Groups Talk', 73–101.
91. Chris Fill, *Marketing Communications: Contexts, Contents and Strategies* (London: Prentice Hall, 1999; 2nd edn.), 1. In her essay 'The Bridge from Text to Mind: Adapting Reader-Response Theory to Consumer Research', in *Journal of Consumer Research* 21 (December 1994), 461–80, Linda M. Scott made an interesting attempt to bring together these two sets of discourse.
92. Baverstock, *How to Market Books*, 185.
93. For an example of the impact of literary awards on sales, see 'Winning Prizes: The Sales Effect', *The Bookseller*, 9 July 1999, 19.
94. I discuss this in more detail in my article 'Judging on a Cover: Book Marketing and the Booker Prize', in Nicole Matthews and Nickianne Moody, eds., *Judging a Book by its Cover: Fans, Publishers, Designers and the Marketing of Books* (London: Ashgate, forthcoming).
95. Interview with Erica Wagner, Literary Editor of *The Times*, 1 February 2000.
96. Interview with Robert McCrum, Literary Editor of the *Observer*, 1 February 2000.
97. See Stephen Brown, *Wizard! Harry Potter's Brand Magic* (London: Cyan Books, 2005), for an investigation of this.
98. P. R. Smith *Marketing Communications: An Integrated Approach* (London: Kogan Page, 1998; 2nd edn.), 509.
99. Interview with Robert McCrum.
100. Fill, *Marketing Communications*, 10.
101. Fill, *Marketing Communications*, 33.
102. Fill, *Marketing Communications*, 33.
103. Smith, *Marketing Communications*, 75.
104. Baverstock, *How to Market Books*, 185.
105. Interview with Erica Wagner.
106. Interview with Robert McCrum.
107. Fill, *Marketing Communications*, 23.
108. Interview with Robert McCrum. Fill, *Marketing Communications*, 203–11. He names the demographic, geographic, geodographic, psychoanalytic and behaviouristic, and adds usage, benefit, loyalty and buyer readiness stage.
109. Sage, 'Living on Writing', 272.
110. Darnton, 'What is the History of Books?', 111.
111. Sage, 'Living on Writing', 262.
112. Darnton, 'What is the History of Books?', 122.
113. Interview with Robert McCrum.
114. Caroline Sylge, 'Reviews – Who Needs Them?', *The Bookseller*, 27 February 1998, 26–9, 26.
115. Claire Tomalin, *Several Strangers: Writing from Three Decades* (London: Viking, 1999).
116. Forsyth and Birn, *Marketing in Publishing*, xiii.
117. John Mitchinson, 'Bestseller Genes', *The Bookseller*, 2 April 1999, 24–6, 25.
118. Farrell, *How Hits Happen*, 87.
119. Mitchinson, 'Bestseller Genes', 25.

3. Genre in the Marketplace

1. Darnton, 'What is the History of Books?', 111.
2. Benedetto Croce, 'Criticism of the Theory of Artistic and Literary Kinds', in David Duff, ed., *Modern Genre Theory*, translated by Douglas Ainslie (Harlow: Longman, 2000; first published in Italy in 1902), 25–8, 28.
3. Croce, 'Criticism of the Theory of Artistic and Literary Kinds', 25.
4. Duff, 'Key Concepts', in *Modern Genre Theory*, x–xvi, xiii.
5. Tzvetan Todorov, *Genres in Discourse*, translated by Catherine Porter (Cambridge: Cambridge University Press, 1990; first published in France in 1978).
6. Todorov, *Genres in Discourse*, 18.
7. 'Genres are the meeting place between general poetics and event-based literary history; as such, they constitute a privileged object that may well deserve to be the principal figure in literary studies', *Genres in Discourse*, 19–20.
8. Todorov, *Genres in Discourse*, 19.
9. Boyd Tonkin, 'Historical', in Jane Rogers, ed., *Good Fiction Guide* (Oxford: Oxford University Press, 2001), 62–4, 62. Another account of the re-emerging popularity of the historical novel is provided by Matthew Kneale in 'Re-animating the Past', *Waterstone's Books Quarterly*, Issue 2, 2001, 22–5.
10. Interview with Andrew Miller. Miller's historical fictions are *Ingenious Pain* and *Casanova* (London: Sceptre, 1998). His third novel, *Oxygen* (London: Sceptre, 2001), is contemporary.
11. A. S. Byatt, 'Fathers' in *On Histories and Stories: Selected Essays* (London: Chatto & Windus, 2000), 9–35, 9.
12. Todd, *Consuming Fictions*, 128. A. S. Byatt's *Possession* (London: Chatto & Windus, 1990) won in 1990, Salman Rushdie's *Midnight's Children* (London: Jonathan Cape, 1981) won in 1981.
13. Ireneusz Opacki, 'Royal Genres', in Duff, *Modern Genre Theory*, 118–26, 123. First published in 1963, translated by David Malcolm.
14. Michael Legat, *An Author's Guide to Publishing* (London: Robert Hale, 1998; 3rd edn.), 82.
15. The forthcoming volume of essays edited by Nicole Matthews and Nickianne Moody, *Judging a Book by its Cover*, promises to treat this topic in detail.
16. Gérard Genette, *Paratexts: Thresholds of Interpretation*, translated by Jane E. Lewin (Cambridge: Cambridge University Press, 1997; first published in France in 1987), 1–2.
17. Genette, *Paratexts*, 5.
18. Legat, *An Author's Guide to Publishing*, 181.
19. Legat, *An Author's Guide to Publishing*, 95.
20. Juliet Gardiner, 'Recuperating the Author: Consuming Fictions of the 1990s', *The Papers of the Bibliographical Society of America* 94: 2 (2000), 255–74.
21. Emlyn Rees, *The Book of Dead Authors* (London: Headline Review, 1997); Martyn Bedford, *The Houdini Girl* (London: Viking, 1999); Rupert Thomson, *The Book of Revelation* (London: Bloomsbury, 1999); Toby Litt, *Corpsing* (London: Hamish Hamilton, 2000). Paperback editions are Rees, *The Book of Dead Authors* (London: Headline Review, 1998); Bedford, *The Houdini Girl* (London: Penguin, 2000); Thomson, *The Book of Revelation* (London: Bloomsbury, 2000); Litt, *Corpsing* (London: Penguin, 2000).

22. Gaskell comments that, 'In deciding what and how much to include, the bibliographer must ask himself repeatedly: "What is the purpose of the descriptions? Who really needs each item of information? Can anything be abbreviated?" Only thus can we avoid burdensome and expensive superfluity, and escape the ultimate absurdity of mistaking the means of bibliography for its end, of practising bibliography for bibliography's sake.' (Philip Gaskell, *A New Introduction to Bibliography* (Oxford: Clarendon Press, 1972), 322.)
23. Entry for 'Detective Fiction', in Margaret Drabble, ed., *The Oxford Companion to English Literature* (Oxford: Oxford University Press, 2000; 6th edn.), 277.
24. Alex Hamilton, 'Fastsellers 2000: The Hot Paperbacks', *Guardian*, 6 January 2001, 10 (Saturday Review section).
25. For example, a 1990s novel of an entirely different note, Joanne Harris's *Chocolat* (London: Black Swan, 2000; first published in 1999) has paperback cover copy structured in a very similar way.
26. Toby Litt, *Adventures in Capitalism* (London: Secker & Warburg, 1996) and *Beatniks* (London: Secker & Warburg, 1997).
27. Further details of this are given in Claire Squires, 'Toby Litt', in Michael Molino, ed., *Dictionary of Literary Biography 267: Twenty-First-Century British and Irish Novelists* (Detroit: The Gale Group, 2002), 164–71.
28. David Duff defines 'Hybridization' in *Modern Genre Theory* as 'The process by which two or more genres combine to form a new genre or subgenre; or by which elements of two or more genres are combined in a single work.' 'Key Concepts', xiv.
29. Evidence derived from visits to Waterstone's (1 March 2001) and Blackwell's and Borders (18 March 2003). See note 67 for full details.
30. Opacki, 'Royal Genres', 123–4.
31. Nicci Gerrard, *Into the Mainstream* (London: Pandora, 1989), 116.
32. Gerrard, *Into the Mainstream*, 118.
33. Dibb et al., drawing on Peter D. Bennett, ed., *Dictionary of Marketing Terms* (Chicago: American Marketing Association, 1988), 18, for their own *Marketing: Concepts and Strategies*, 269–70, define 'brand' as 'a name, term, design, symbol or any other feature that identifies one seller's good or service as distinct from those of other sellers. A brand may identify one item, a family of items or all items of that seller.'
34. Jo Royle, Louise Cooper and Rosemary Stockdale, 'The Use of Branding by Trade Publishers: An Investigation into Marketing the Book as a Brand Name Product', *Publishing Research Quarterly* 15: 4 (Winter 1999/2000), 3–13, 3.
35. Baverstock, *Are Books Different?*, 13–29.
36. Royle et al., 'The Use of Branding by Trade Publishers', 5. They refer to Philip Kotler's *Marketing Management: Analysis, Planning, Implementation and Control* (Englewood Cliffs, NJ: Prentice Hall, 1996; 9th edn.).
37. Royle et al., 'The Use of Branding by Trade Publishers', 5.
38. Royle et al., 'The Use of Branding by Trade Publishers', 5–6.
39. Royle et al., 'The Use of Branding by Trade Publishers', 5.
40. Royle et al., 'The Use of Branding by Trade Publishers', 6.
41. Royle et al., 'The Use of Branding by Trade Publishers', 9.
42. Alex Hamilton writes in 'Top Hundred Chart of 1996 Fastsellers', in *Writers' & Artists' Yearbook 1998* (London: A&C Black, 1998), 261–8, 262, that 'Surveyed

over a period, the fastseller lists indicate a rather conservative attitude on the part of buyers. It is not very common for a book to appear in the top 20[...]which has not [i.e. whose author has not] appeared somewhere on the list in previous years [...] Once established on the list, an author has only to turn in a regular supply of similar works to stay on it.'

43. Wernick, 'Authorship and the Supplement of Promotion', 93.
44. Royle et al., 'The Use of Branding by Trade Publishers', 9, quoting from Hugh Look, 'Stars for all the Write Reasons', *The Bookseller*, 10 July 1998, 27.
45. Royle et al., 'The Use of Branding by Trade Publishers', 10.
46. Angus Phillips, 'How Books Are Positioned in the Market', in Matthews and Moody, eds., *Judging a Book by Its Cover*.
47. Royle et al., 'The Use of Branding by Trade Publishers', 11.
48. Paul Johnston, *Body Politic* (London: Hodder & Stoughton, 1997).
49. For example, William Dalrymple, *From the Holy Mountain: A Journey in the Shadow of Byzantium* (London: Flamingo, 1998; paperback edn., first published in 1997); Amanda Craig, *A Vicious Circle* (London: Fourth Estate, 1997; paperback edn., first published in 1996). See Alan Powers, 'Jeff Fisher', in *Front Cover: Great Book Jackets and Cover Design* (London: Mitchell Beazley, 2001), 128–9. Powers comments on Fisher's design for *Captain Corelli's Mandolin* that 'One day soon, students will write dissertations explaining the magnetic attraction of this cover design which, in an age of computer graphics, indicates the power of hand, eye, and paintbrush.'
50. Powers' *Front Cover* offers a variety of such branding strategies in the twentieth century, including Victor Gollancz (22–3), Penguin (30–1) and the more recent Pocket Canons (120–1)
51. Royle et al., 'The Use of Branding by Trade Publishers', 12.
52. Legat, *An Author's Guide to Publishing*, 55. McAleer's *Passion's Fortune* traces Mills & Boon's development.
53. *Book Publishing in Britain* (London: Bookseller Publications, 1999), 15.
54. Brands typified respectively by Oxford, Lonely Planet, Penguin, Letts and Teach Yourself, and by Dorling Kindersley, Modern Masters, Mills & Boon, Haynes and Faber (*Book Publishing in Britain*, 16).
55. Nicci Gerrard, *Into the Mainstream*, 25.
56. Feminist publishing history is chronicled in Nicci Gerrard, *Into the Mainstream*, Patricia Duncker, 'A Note on the Politics of Publishing', in *Sisters and Strangers: An Introduction to Contemporary Feminist Fiction* (Oxford: Blackwell, 1992), Eileen Cadman, Gail Chester and Agnes Pivot, *Rolling Our Own: Women as Printers, Publishers and Distributors* (London: Minority Press Group, 1981), Ursula Owen, 'Feminist Publishing', in Peter Owen, ed., *Publishing: The Future* (London: Peter Owen, 1988), 86–100, Florence Howe, 'Feminist Publishing', in Altbach et al., *International Book Publishing*, 130–8, and Carmen Callil, 'Women, Publishing and Power', in *Writing: A Woman's Business*, 183–92, and most recently and in greatest depth in Murray's *Mixed Media*.
57. Interview with Peter Straus, Publisher of Picador, Macmillan, 19 July 1999.
58. Interview with Kirsty Fowkes, Editor, Hodder & Stoughton Publishers, 13 July 2000.
59. De Bellaigue, *British Book Publishing*, 182–6.

60. 'Push' marketing promotes to the next group in the marketing channel, whereas 'pull' promotion appeals directly to consumers. Dibb et al., *Marketing: Concepts and Strategies*, 472–3.
61. Interview with David Godwin, David Godwin Associates, 11 May 1998.
62. Lucy Ellmann, *Man or Mango?* (London: Review, 1998); Ronan Bennett, *The Catastrophist* (London: Review, 1997).
63. Interview with Alexandra Pringle.
64. Peter Straus, 'Format', in Peter Owen, ed., *Publishing Now* (London: Peter Owen, 1996; revised edn., 1st edn. 1993), 68–74, 73.
65. Peter Straus, 'Format', 69.
66. Peter Straus, 'Format', 69.
67. The floor plans described are derived from the layout of Waterstone's, on Broad Street in Oxford, from Blackwell's, on Broad Street in Oxford, Borders on Magdalen Street in Oxford and The QI Bookshop on Turl Street in Oxford on 6 September 2006.
68. Alan Hollinghurst's books are *The Swimming Pool Library* (London: Chatto & Windus, 1988), *The Folding Star* (London: Chatto & Windus, 1994), *The Spell* (London: Chatto & Windus, 1998) and *The Line of Beauty* (London: Picador, 2004). There wasn't a named gay and lesbian section in any of the four bookshops on the dates visited.
69. The Travel Bookshop is at 13–15 Blenheim Crescent, London W11 2EE.
70. Michel Foucault, *The Order of Things: An Archaeology of the Human Sciences* (London: Routledge, 1994; first published in the UK in 1970; first published in France in 1966).
71. Foucault, *The Order of Things*, xviii.
72. My article 'A Common Ground? Book Prize Culture in Europe' considers the varying role of literary prizes, and the ways in which research into them can be conducted. In *Javnost The Public* 11: 4 (2004), 37–47.
73. Jonathan Taylor, Chairman of Booker plc and The Booker Prize Management Committee, Introduction to *Booker 30: A Celebration of 30 Years of The Booker Prize for Fiction 1969–1998* (Great Britain: Booker plc, 1998), 5.
74. Pico Iyer, in 'The Empire Writes Back', *Time* (8 February 1993), 54–9 sees the Booker Prize at the forefront of the promotion of a new set of post-colonial or 'World Fiction' writers (54). Graham Huggan, in *The Post-Colonial Exotic*, particularly in chapter 4, 'Prizing Otherness: A Short History of the Booker', 105–23, analyses the ironies of the Booker Prize's relation to the colonial past (including Booker's history as a distribution company in Guyana) and post-colonial present.
75. 'Prizes and Awards', in *Writers' & Artists' Yearbook 1998* (London: A&C Black, 1998), 488–515.
76. Todd, *Consuming Fictions*, 128.
77. Todd, *Consuming Fictions*, 128.
78. Rose Tremain, *Music and Silence* (London: Chatto & Windus, 1999); David Cairns, *Berlioz Volume Two: Servitude and Greatness 1832–1869* (London: Allen Lane, 1999); Seamus Heaney, *Beowulf* (London: Faber and Faber, 1999).
79. Kate Atkinson, *Behind the Scenes at the Museum* (London: Doubleday, 1995).
80. Ted Hughes, *Birthday Letters* (London: Faber and Faber, 1998).
81. Interview with Bud McLintock of Karen Earl Ltd., Director of the Whitbread Book Awards, 30 June 2000.

82. Connor, *The English Novel in History*, 22–23. Michael Hayes makes the same argument in his chapter on 'Popular Fiction', in Clive Bloom and Gary Day, eds., *Literature and Culture in Modern Britain. Volume Three: 1956–1999* (Harlow: Longman, 2000), 76–93, 77.

4. Icons and Phenomenons

1. Mitchinson, 'Bestseller Genes', 25.
2. Sutherland, *Reading the Decades*, 7.
3. Bloom, *Bestsellers*, 15.
4. Sebastian Faulks, *Birdsong* (London: Hutchinson, 1993).
5. Nick Hornby, *High Fidelity* (London: Gollancz, 1995).
6. For the construction of this case study, I am indebted to Geoff Mulligan, Publishing Director, Secker & Warburg. Mulligan's article 'Promoting the Captain' in *The Bookseller*, 29 May 1998, 34, provides further information.
7. Paul Wood, 'Death Cheats Two Wartime Lovers', *Independent*, 11 January 1999, 8 (main section).
8. Louis de Bernières, *The War of Don Emmanuel's Nether Parts* (London: Secker & Warburg, 1990); *Señor Vivo and the Coca Lord* (London: Secker & Warburg, 1991); *The Troublesome Offspring of Cardinal Guzman* (London: Secker & Warburg, 1992). Print run information from Interview with Geoff Mulligan.
9. According to Random House's celebratory advert in *The Bookseller*, 12 February 1999, 19.
10. Joanna Pitman, 'Word of Mouth', *The Times*, 15 November 1997, 16 (Metro section).
11. Nicholas Best, 'Drugs and Thugs', *Financial Times*, 6 July 1991, 9 (Weekend section).
12. Louis de Bernières, 'The Brass Bar', *Granta 43: Best of Young British Novelists*, Spring 1993, 23–31. The choice of twenty writers was made by Bill Buford, A. S. Byatt, John Mitchinson and Salman Rushdie.
13. Interview with Geoff Mulligan.
14. Interview with Geoff Mulligan.
15. Interview with Geoff Mulligan.
16. '"Can YOU Recommend a Really Good Book?"', presenter for *Captain Corelli's Mandolin* produced by Secker & Warburg n.d. [1993/4?].
17. '"Can YOU Recommend a Really Good Book?"'
18. '"Can YOU Recommend a Really Good Book?"'
19. Peter Silverton, 'Word of Mouth', *Observer*, 27 July 1997, 4 (Review section).
20. Silverton, 'Word of Mouth', 4. Random House posted a 'Reading Guide' to *Captain Corelli's Mandolin* on their website (www.randomhouse.co.uk/offthepage/guidehtm?command=search&db=/catalog/main.txt&eqisbndata+0749397543, accessed 4 February 1999) – an example of the publisher intersecting with the word-of-mouth phenomenon they instigated. (This theme is explored in more detail in the article 'Marionettes and Puppeteers?: The Relationship between Book Club Readers and Publishers' by Danielle Fuller, DeNel Rehberg Sedo and Claire Squires, forthcoming in a volume of essays on reading groups edited by DeNel Rehberg Sedo, and in Long's *Book Clubs*, in the chapter on 'Reading Groups and the Challenge of Mass Communication and Marketing', 189–218.)
21. The list is printed in Holgate and Wilson-Fletcher, *The Test of Time*, 216–20.

22. Silverton, 'Word of Mouth', 4.
23. Silverton, 'Word of Mouth', 4.
24. Book Marketing Ltd./The Reading Partnership's *Reading the Situation: Book Reading, Buying and Borrowing Habits in Britain* (London: Book Marketing, 2000), 11.
25. Interview with Geoff Mulligan.
26. See, for example, John Cunningham, 'Interview: Louis de Bernières', *Guardian*, 23 August 1997, 3 (G2 section).
27. Sven Birkerts, *The Gutenberg Elegies: The Fate of Reading in an Electronic Age* (London: Faber and Faber, 1996; first published in the US in 1994), 7.
28. See, for example, the discussion that arose around the film deal for the novel in John Harlow, 'Will Tom Cruise Pluck Corelli's Mandolin?', *Sunday Times*, 3 January 1999, 7 (main section). The controversy that developed about Louis de Bernières' negative portrayal of the Greek communist resistance suggests that these are matters of political as well as aesthetic judgement. See, for example, Helena Smith, 'Mandolin Man Changes His Tune as Cameras Roll', *Observer*, 4 June 2000, 3 (main section) and Seumas Milne, 'A Greek Myth', *Guardian*, 29 July 2000, 10–19 (Weekend section).
29. Adams and Barker, 'A New Model for the Study of the Book', 14.
30. Amis's side of the quarrel is documented in his memoir *Experience* (London: Jonathan Cape, 2000).
31. Martin Amis, *Money* (London: Jonathan Cape, 1984); Martin Amis, *London Fields* (London: Jonathan Cape, 1989). See Todd, *Consuming Fictions*, 85, for more on the 1989 Booker arguments.
32. Martin Amis, *Time's Arrow* (London: Jonathan Cape, 1991).
33. Jonathan Wilson, 'The Literary Life: A Very English Story', *The New Yorker*, 6 March 1995, 96–104.
34. Amis, in fact, deserted HarperCollins to return to his previous house, Jonathan Cape, for the publication of his subsequent works including *Night Train* (London: Jonathan Cape, 1997) and *Heavy Water and Other Stories* (London: Jonathan Cape, 1998).
35. Moran, *Star Authors*, 151–3; Delany, *Literature, Money and the Marketplace*, 180–4; Gardiner, '"What is an Author?"'
36. Gardiner, '"What is an Author?"', 67, 72.
37. Daragh O'Reilly, 'Martin Amis on Marketing', in Stephen Brown, ed., *Consuming Books: The Marketing and Consumption of Literature* (London: Routledge, 2006), 73–82, 77.
38. Gerald Howard, 'Slouching Towards Grubnet: The Author in the Age of Publicity', *Review of Contemporary Fiction* 16: 1 (Spring 1996), 44–53, cited in Moran, *Star Authors*, 152.

5. Marketing Stories

1. For the construction of this case study I am indebted to Robin Robertson (Welsh's editor), Deputy Publishing Director of Jonathan Cape.
2. James Naughtie, 'Teenage Passions', *Daily Telegraph*, 18 July 1998, 1 (Arts & Books section).
3. Welsh, *Trainspotting*, 339, 329.
4. Welsh, *Trainspotting*, 344.

5. Welsh, *Trainspotting*, 339–40.
6. Irvine Welsh, 'The First Day of the Edinburgh Festival', in Hamish Whyte and Janice Galloway, eds., *Scream, If You Want to Go Faster (New Writing Scotland 9)* (Aberdeen: Association for Scottish Literary Studies, 1991), 145–55.
7. Irvine Welsh, *Past Tense: Four Stories from a Novel* (South Queensferry: Clocktower Press, n.d. [1992]).
8. Duncan McLean, ed., *Ahead of its Time: A Clocktower Press Anthology* (London: Vintage, 1998), xiv.
9. *Rebel Inc.* 1 (May 1992), as mentioned by Peter Kravitz in his Introduction to his edited *The Picador Book of Contemporary Scottish Fiction* (London: Picador, 1997), xi–xxxvi, xvii.
10. See Kravitz, ed., *The Picador Book of Contemporary Scottish Fiction*, xvii.
11. Widely reported and confirmed to be 'not far off' the actual sum in Interview with Robin Robertson, Deputy Publishing Director of Jonathan Cape, 7 May 1999.
12. Irvine Welsh, *Porno* (London: Jonathan Cape, 2002).
13. See, for example, Alan Taylor's 'Scottish Efflorescence' in *The New Yorker*, 25 December 1995 and 1 January 1996, 97, which is followed by a double-page photograph of eleven Scottish writers by Richard Avedon, 98–9: Alan Warner, Kathleen Jamie, Duncan McLean, Robert Crawford, Janice Galloway, Robin Robertson, Don Paterson, John Burnside, Alasdair Gray, A. L. Kennedy and Welsh himself.
14. 'Generation Ecstasy: Forty Things that Started with an E', *The Face*, October 1995, 120.
15. Interview with Robin Robertson.
16. Sarah Champion, ed., *Disco Biscuits* (London: Sceptre, 1997).
17. See Rasselas, 'Noises Off', *Sunday Times*, 1 June 1997, 6 (Culture section). Books endorsed by Welsh include Matthew Collin and John Godfrey's *Altered State: The Story of Ecstasy Culture and Acid House* (London: Serpent's Tail, 1997): ' "Brilliant" – Irvine Welsh', reads the front cover.
18. McLean, *Ahead of its Time*, xi; Kevin Williamson, ed., *Children of Albion Rovers* (Edinburgh: Rebel Inc., 1997; 2nd edn.; 1st edn. 1996), 230.
19. For these biographical details, see Andy Beckett, 'Raving with an MBA', *Independent on Sunday*, 23 April 1995, 38 (Review section) and John Walsh, 'The Not-So-Shady Past of Irvine Welsh', *Independent*, 15 April 1995, 25 (Weekend section). It is possible that the mischievous Welsh was creating yet another persona for the media, and never was a property dealer. Nevertheless, the point stands: Welsh *was* studying for an MBA when he began to write, a fact that only became widely known some time after publication.
20. Irvine Welsh, *Trainspotting and Headstate* (London: Minerva, 1996), 6–7.
21. Welsh, *Trainspotting*, 14–27.
22. Welsh, *Trainspotting*, 27.
23. For example, see John Walsh, 'The Not-So-Shady Past of Irvine Welsh'; Nicholas Lezard, 'Junk and the Big Trigger', *Independent on Sunday*, 29 August 1993, 28 (Sunday Review section); Nick Hornby, 'Chibs with Everything', *Times Literary Supplement*, 28 April 1995, 23.
24. Alan Freeman, 'Ghosts in Sunny Leith: Irvine Welsh's *Trainspotting*', in Susanne Hagemann, ed., *Studies in Scottish Fiction: 1945 to the Present* (Frankfurt: Peter Lang, 1996), 251–62, 257–8.

25. A report of Welsh's arrest, allegedly drunk, at a football match, is made in 'This is the Age of the Trainspotter', *The Times*, 28 January 1996. Alan Chadwick's 'End of the Line for Gravy Trainspotters?', *Sunday Times*, 8 November 1998, mentions Welsh's links with popstars including Primal Scream and Oasis.
26. Welsh, *Trainspotting*, 78.
27. Melvin Burgess, *Junk* (London: Andersen, 1996).
28. For the construction of this case study I am indebted to Gillon Aitken, Barker's agent, and Clare Alexander, Barker's former publisher at Viking.
29. Nicci Gerrard, 'Hype, hype hurrah!', *Observer*, 6 August 1995, 15 (The Observer Review section).
30. Barker's previous novels are *Union Street* (London: Virago, 1982); *Blow Your House Down* (London: Virago, 1984); *The Century's Daughter* (London: Virago, 1986); *The Man Who Wasn't There* (London: Virago, 1989); *Regeneration* (London: Viking, 1991) and *The Eye in the Door* (London: Viking, 1993).
31. Information about Arundhati Roy from Interview with David Godwin. By 2002, Roy would publish her second substantial volume, but it would be a collection of journalism and essays rather than a work of fiction, *The Algebra of Infinite Justice* (London: Flamingo, 2002). The publication of another novel only occurred in 2007.
32. Interview with Gillon Aitken and Clare Alexander, Gillon Aitken Associates Ltd., 19 July 1999.
33. Peter Parker, 'The War that Never Becomes the Past', *Times Literary Supplement*, 8 September 1995, 5.
34. Peter Kemp, 'What an Unlovely War', *Sunday Times*, 10 September 1995, 13 (Books section).
35. Salman Rushdie, *The Moor's Last Sigh* (London: Jonathan Cape, 1995). See, for example, John Walsh, 'Northern Realism wins over Rushdie Favourite', *Independent*, 8 November 1995, 3 (main section).
36. Mark Lawson, 'Pick of the Year', *Sunday Times*, 19 November 1995, 3 (Books section).
37. Valerie Grove, 'I Know in my Bones that Book Prizes are Just Three Lemons in a Row', *The Times*, 29 September 1995, 17 (main section).
38. Richard Todd claims in *Consuming Fictions*, 76, that, 'It could be argued that the award to Pat Barker for *The Ghost Road* in 1995 (whether consciously or not) took account of the fact that the winning book was the culmination of a highly acclaimed trilogy', but hard evidence to support this theory is unavailable, although it may eventually become so via the Booker Prize Archive at Oxford Brookes University (http://www.brookes.ac.uk/services/library/speccoll/booker.html).
39. Francis Spufford, 'Exploding Old Myths', *Guardian*, 9 November 1995, 2–3 (Section 2).
40. George Walden, 'Why Pat Barker Won the Booker', *The Times*, 8 November 1995, 15 (main section).
41. George Walden, 'Why Pat Barker Won the Booker', 15.
42. Hugh Cecil, *The Flower of Battle: British Fiction Writers of the First World War* (London: Secker & Warburg, 1995).
43. Geoff Dyer, *The Missing of the Somme* (London: Hamish Hamilton, 1994), 18.
44. Dyer, *The Missing of the Somme*, 77.

45. Keith Miller, 'Dying for Happiness', *Times Literary Supplement*, 4 October 1996, 25.
46. DS, 'NB', *Times Literary Supplement*, 17 November 1995, 18.
47. In a letter in response to the *TLS* diarist, Walden argued that he had never in fact forgotten the more subtle manifestations of historical fiction, and that his views 'may have been inadvertently misconstrued'. Nevertheless, the polemic will inevitably be remembered rather than the retraction. See George Walden, 'Fiction, Nostalgia and Escapism', *Times Literary Supplement*, 24 November 1995, 17.
48. 'Sound of Silence', *Guardian*, 13 November 1995, 12 (main section).
49. Jason Cowley, 'Was the Pity All in the Poetry?', *Sunday Times*, 8 November 1998, 2–3, 2.
50. Niall Ferguson, *The Pity of War* (London: Allen Lane, 1998); Lyn MacDonald, *To the Last Man: Spring 1918* (London: Viking, 1998); John Keegan, *First World War* (London: Hutchinson, 1998); Cowley, 'Was the Pity All in the Poetry?', 2.
51. Cowley, 'Was the Pity All in the Poetry?', 2.
52. Discussed in Alan Riding, 'Testifying to the Ravages of Granddad's War', *New York Times*, 6 December, 17 (Section C). Angela Carter is mentioned as the mentor offering advice to Barker.
53. For example, Rachel Cusk, 'The Apple of Our Sisters' Eyes', *Guardian*, 26 October 1995, 5 (G2 section) and Sarah Baxter, 'Why Did the Apple Crumble?', *Observer*, 29 October 1995, 9 (The Review section).
54. Paul Taylor, 'Hero at the Emotional Front', *Independent on Sunday*, 2 June 1991, 32 (The Sunday Review section).
55. Catherine Bennett, 'The House that Carmen Built', *Guardian*, 14 June 1993, 10–11 (G2 section), 11.
56. Interview with Gillon Aitken and Clare Alexander.
57. Pat Barker, *The Man Who Wasn't There* (London, Penguin 1990; paperback edn.).
58. Interview with Gillon Aitken and Clare Alexander.
59. Interview with Gillon Aitken and Clare Alexander.
60. Taylor, 'Hero at the Emotional Front', 32.
61. Justine Picardie, 'The Poet who Came Out of his Shell Shock', *Independent*, 25 June 1991, 19 (main section).
62. Pat Barker, *Another World* (London: Viking, 1998). Michèle Roberts, 'Male Insensitivity, Female Nagging and Children's Selfishness', *Independent on Sunday*, 18 October 1998, 11 (Culture section).
63. Kate Kellaway, 'Billy, Don't be a Hero', *Observer*, 27 August 1995, 16 (The Observer Review section).
64. DS, 'NB', *Times Literary Supplement*, 5 January 1996, 14.
65. Jackie Wullschlager, 'Sanity, Madness and Unholy Innocence', *Financial Times*, 6 July 1991, 9 (Weekend FT section).
66. Barker talks about the influence of her grandparents in John Ezard, 'Warring Fictions', *Guardian*, 11 September 1993, 28 (Outlook section).
67. 195.157.68.238/research/summary2000.html, accessed 15 October 2002.
68. Lawson, 'Pick of the Year', 3.
69. For the construction of this case study I am indebted to David Godwin (Roy's agent) and Philip Gwyn Jones, Editorial Director of Flamingo (Roy's editor).

70. Roy, *The God of Small Things*, v.
71. Scott Hughes, 'CV: David Godwin, Literary Agent', *Independent*, 20 October 1997, 5 (Media + section).
72. Jason Cowley, 'Goddess of Small Things', *The Times*, 18 October 1997, 17 (Metro section).
73. Patrick French, 'The Many Lures of the Orient', *Sunday Times*, 30 June 1996, 13 (Books section).
74. Marianne MacDonald, 'Book Watch', *Independent*, 6 September 1996, 9 (main section).
75. 'Diary', *Sunday Times*, 18 May 1997, 6 (Books section).
76. Boyd Tonkin, 'Preface to 1997', *Independent*, 28 December 1996, 4 (The Long Weekend section). Jackie Wullschlager's 'Hedonism – and Feminism', *Financial Times*, 28 December 1996, xiv (Weekend section) was another preview mentioning Roy's book.
77. Arundhati Roy, 'Things Can Change in a Day', *Granta 57: India*, Spring 1997, 257–88.
78. Harvey Porlock, 'Critical List', *Sunday Times*, 29 June 1997, 2 (Books section).
79. Peter Popham, 'Rushdie Started It. And It Won't Stop', *Independent on Sunday*, 7 February 1999, 4 (Culture section). Later in the same year Tarun J. Tejpal's article 'New Gold-Rush in the East' in the *Guardian*, 14 August 1999, 3 (Saturday Review section), similarly suggests *The God of Small Things*' place in the altering landscape from the point of view of the Indian publisher of the novel.
80. English writes that 'The Booker's chief administrator, Martin [sic] Goff, who should be regarded as a major figure in the history of prizes, was fully and actively complicit in exploiting the association of the Booker with scandal, wagering that the prize stood to reap the greatest symbolic profit precisely from its status as a kind of cultural embarrassment' ('Winning the Culture Game', 115).
81. Damian Whitworth and Erica Wagner, 'Booker Prize Goes to Debut Novelist', *The Times*, 15 October 1997, 1 (main section).
82. Dalya Alberge, 'Literary Recluse Faces Booker Shortlist Limelight', *The Times*, 16 September 1997, 1 (main section).
83. Michael Gorra, 'Living in the Aftermath', *London Review of Books*, 19 June 1997, 22.
84. Peter Kemp, 'Losing the Plot', *Sunday Times*, 21 September 1997, 3 (Books section).
85. Valentine Cunningham, 'Manufacturing a Masterpiece', *Prospect*, December 1998, 56–8.
86. Jan McGirk, 'Indian Literary Star Faces Caste Sex Trial', *Sunday Times*, 29 June 1997, 19 (main section).
87. Peter Popham, 'Under Fire, but India is in my Blood', *Independent on Sunday*, 21 September 1997, 17 (main section).
88. Simon Barnes, 'Passage to the India in All of Us', *The Times*, 18 October 1997, 22 (main section).
89. Blake Morrison, 'The Country Where Worst Things Happen', *Independent on Sunday*, 1 June 1997, 33 (The Sunday Review section).
90. Jackie Wullschlager, 'Prose Full of Promise', *Financial Times*, 3 January 1998, v (Weekend section).

91. Amit Chaudhuri, 'Lure of the Hybrid', *Times Literary Supplement*, 3 September 1999, 5–6, 5.
92. Chaudhuri, 'Lure of the Hybrid', 5.
93. Chaudhuri, 'Lure of the Hybrid', 6.
94. Graham Huggan, *The Postcolonial Exotic*.
95. Salman Rushdie, '"Commonwealth Literature" Does Not Exist', in *Imaginary Homelands: Essays and Criticism 1981–1991* (London: Granta, 1991), 61–70, 66.
96. Cowley, 'Goddess of Small Things', 16.
97. The edition of *The New Yorker* is 23 and 30 June 1997, with the photograph on 118–19. Cowley, 'Goddess of Small Things', 17.
98. Chaudhuri, 'The Lure of the Exotic', 5.
99. Popham, 'Under Fire, but India is in my Blood', 17.
100. Rushdie, 'Imaginary Homelands', in *Imaginary Homelands*, 9–21, 10.
101. Cowley, 'Goddess of Small Things', 17.
102. Jack O'Sullivan, 'Have You Heard the One About the Oriental Fantasy?', *Independent*, 17 September 1997, 23 (main section).
103. O'Sullivan, 'Have You Heard the One About the Oriental Fantasy?', 23.
104. Interview with David Godwin.

6. Crossovers

1. Bret Easton Ellis, *Less Than Zero* (London: Picador, 1986; first published in the US in 1985), *The Rules of Attraction* (London: Picador, 1988; first published in the US in 1987).
2. Charles Bremner, 'Setting a Beast to Catch a Beastie', *The Times*, 19 November 1990, 12 (main section).
3. Jon Heilpern, 'Dressed to Kill and Bound for the Best-seller Lists', *Independent on Sunday*, 25 November 1990, 11 (main section).
4. Patrick Bateman's occasional admissions of his violent deeds are either misheard or disregarded by those to whom he confesses, for example the following conversation in a nightclub:

   > 'Well?'
   > 'I'm into, oh, murders and executions mostly. It depends.' I shrug.
   > 'Do you like it?' she asks, unfazed.
   > 'Um . . . It depends. Why?' I take a bite of sorbet.
   > 'Well, most guys I know who work in mergers and acquisitions don't really like it,' she says. (Ellis, *American Psycho*, 206.)

5. Harvey Porlock, 'On the Critical List', *Sunday Times*, 28 April 1991, 7 (Books section).
6. Porlock, 'On the Critical List', 7. *Dirty Weekend* is a novel by Helen Zahavi (London: Picador, 1991), also subject to that week's 'review of reviews'.
7. www.panmacmillan.com/ppm/imprints/Picador.htm, accessed 27 June 2000.
8. Suzanne Moore, 'Can't Pay, Won't Pay', *Independent*, 26 September 1991, 21.
9. Interview with Peter Straus.

10. Interview with Peter Straus.
11. For the construction of this case study, I am indebted to Peter Straus, Publisher of Picador, and Gillon Aitken (Fielding's agent).
12. www.amazon.co.uk/exec/obidos/tg/stores/detail/-/books/0330332767/customer-reviews/qid=1035649491/sr=1–4/ref=sr_1_3_4/ref=cm_cr_dp_2_1/026–5624646–4387602, accessed 5 March 1999.
13. Interview with Peter Straus.
14. Cherry Norton, 'She's Successful, Attractive But Has Yet to Find the Right Man. Is it Down to Chance or, as New Study Claims, Evolution', *Sunday Times*, 7 June 1998, 17 (main section).
15. Katharine Viner, 'Suddenly, the Thirtysomething Single Woman is a Media Celebrity', *Guardian*, 11 September 1997, 2–3 (G2 section), 2. Fielding's first reference to 'Singletons' is in *Bridget Jones's Diary*, 42.
16. Viner, 'Suddenly, the Thirtysomething Single Woman is a Media Celebrity', 2.
17. Viner, 'Suddenly, the Thirtysomething Single Woman is a Media Celebrity', 2.
18. 'The Diary of Bridget Jones', *Independent*, 28 February 1995, 19 (Section 2).
19. Mentioned in Lydia Slater, 'Poignant, Funny and Truthful', *Daily Telegraph*, 8 November 1997, 15 (main section), Robert Yates, 'Bridget of Madison County', *Observer*, 31 May 1998, 20 (The Review section) and Decca Aitkenhead, 'Bridget Jones: Don't Ya Just Love Her?', *Guardian*, 8 August 1997, 17 (main section).
20. The apparent trivia of these accounts was counterbalanced by a contemporaneous manifestation: that of the journalistic 'sickness' narratives, for example Oscar Moore's *Guardian* PWA column that detailed the progressions of his AIDS, John Diamond's record of his cancer in *The Times*, and Ruth Picardie's occasional pieces about her breast cancer in the *Observer*.
21. Lydia Slater, 'Poignant, Funny and Truthful', 15.
22. Cosmo Landesman, 'Naughty Little Nietzschean, *Sunday Times*, 11 January 1998, 7 (News Review section).
23. Interview with Peter Straus. Helen Fielding, *Cause Celeb* (London: Picador, 1994).
24. Interview with Gillon Aitken. *Bridget Jones's Diary* is subtitled *A Novel*, to indicate its generic status as a novel, but is rarely quoted in full.
25. Interview with Peter Straus.
26. Joanna Pitman, 'Write On, Sisters', *The Times*, 11 October 1997, 16–17 (Metro section), 17.
27. Interview with Peter Straus.
28. Nicola Shulman, 'Some Consolations of the Single State', *Times Literary Supplement*, 1 November 1996, 26.
29. Fielding, *Bridget Jones's Diary*, front flap.
30. Interview with Peter Straus. In 1998, Picador published a 'Special gold-leaf type, commemorative-style, limited, important MILLION COPY CHARDONNAY EDITION', to celebrate the million paperback sales (London: Picador, 1998).
31. Helen Fielding, *Bridget Jones: The Edge of Reason* (London: Picador, 1999).
32. For example, Gill Hornby's 'Weight of the Single State', *The Times*, 19 October 1996, 10 (The Directory section); Kathy O'Shaughnessy's 'Authentic Tales of the Single Life', *Daily Telegraph*, 23 November 1996, 4 (Arts & Books section) and Nicola Shulman, 'Some Consolations of the Single State', 26.

33. Gill Hornby, 'Weight of the Single State', 10; Penny Perrick, 'Sex and the Single Girl', *Sunday Times*, 20 October 1996, 12 (Books section).
34. Shulman, 'Some Consolations of the Single State', 26.
35. Catherine Bennett, 'Old Girls', *Guardian*, 17 January 1998, 23 (main section).
36. In referring to the 'New Feminism', Bennett would seem to be commenting generally on the situation of feminist debate in the late 1990s, but also specifically to Natasha Walter's *The New Feminism* (London: Little, Brown, 1998). In interview, Fielding mentioned her (failed) attempt to write a Mills & Boon novel, see Slater, 'Poignant, Funny and Truthful', 15.
37. Bidisha, 'Banish these Publishing Ghettoes', *Independent*, 16 July 1998, 4 (Thursday Review section).
38. In *The Feminist Bestseller: From Sex and the Single Girl to Sex and the City* (Basingstoke: Palgrave Macmillan, 2005), Imelda Whelehan sets about this task, including a lengthy analysis of Bridget Jones and the chicklit phenomenon.
39. Amanda Loose, 'Holidays Ready Booked', *The Times*, 19 August 1998, 3 (Crème de la Crème section).
40. Mike Gayle, *My Legendary Girlfriend* (London: Hodder & Stoughton, 1998). Jamie Hodder-Williams discussed the label used by Hodder & Stoughton and then taken up by the media. (Interview with Jamie Hodder-Williams.) The *Mirror* used the strapline 'Here comes the male Bridget Jones' in a review of *My Legendary Girlfriend*, 'Now on Sale…Round-Up' on 14 August 1998, 17 (The A List section). The *Guardian* was more cynical in its comments on the 'Bestsellers' on 1 August 1998, discussing 'The much-hyped Mike Gayle – "the male Bridget Jones" (they wish!)', 11 (Saturday section).
41. Emma Forrest, 'Not with a Bang but with a Simper', *Guardian*, 31 August 1998, 9 (G2 section). She refers to Isabel Wolff's *The Trials of Tiffany Trott* (London: HarperCollins, 1998); Jane Green's *Straight Talking* (London: Mandarin, 1997); Kate Morris's *Jemima J – Single Girl's Diary* (London: Penguin, 1998); and Freya North's *Chloe* (London: William Heinemann, 1997).
42. Interview with Peter Straus.
43. Pitman, 'Write On, Sisters', 17.
44. Sutherland, *Bestsellers*, 35–6.
45. Ideas suggested by Joanne Knowles in her paper ' "Hurrah for the Singletons!" 1990s Fictions of the Single Woman', at *Contemporary British Women's Writing 1960–Present Day*, University of Leicester, 1 July 2000.
46. The 'crossover' phenomenon is due to be addressed in greater detail than available here by Rachel Falconer in her forthcoming *Crossover Fiction and Cross-Reading in the UK: Contemporary Writing for Children and Adults* (London: Routledge, 2007).
47. Philip Pullman, 'Writing Children's Fiction: or You Cannot Be Serious', in Barry Turner, ed., *The Writer's Handbook 2000* (London: Macmillan, 1999), 216–18, 217.
48. Julia Eccleshare, 'A Fast Track for Children's Books', *Publishers Weekly Special Report: British Publishing 2004*, 8 March 2004, 16–18, 16.
49. James Meek, 'To 3,000 Little Fans, With Love', *Guardian*, 11 March 2004.
50. Public Lending Right, 'Wilson Topples Cookson', http://www.plr.uk.com/trends/pressrelease/feb2004.htm, 2004, accessed 22 May 2006; Public

Lending Right, 'Jacqueline Wilson: UK's Most Borrowed Author for Third Year Running', http://www.plr.uk.com/trends/pressrelease/feb2006(1).htm, 2006, accessed 22 May 2006.

51. *Children's Writers' and Artists' Yearbook* (London: A&C Black, 2004).
52. Julia Eccleshare, 'A Golden Time for Children's Books', *Publishers Weekly*, 18 February 2002, 20–4, 20.
53. Robert McCrum, 'Why Eng Lit Smites Pop Culture', *Observer*, 30 January 2000.
54. Boyd Tonkin, 'Once Upon a Time in the Marketing Department...', *Independent*, 6 November 2002.
55. Fiachra Gibbons, 'Booker Prize: Snubbed Unknown Sweeps Giants Off Shortlist', *Guardian*, 17 September 2003.
56. David Almond, *The Fire-Eaters* (London: Hodder Children's, 2003).
57. Mark Haddon, *The Talking Horse and the Sad Girl and the Village Under the Sea* (London: Picador, 2005); *A Spot of Bother* (London: Jonathan Cape, 2006).
58. Nicholas Clee, 'The Bookseller', *Guardian*, 28 June 2003.
59. Wendy Parsons and Catriona Nicholson, '"Talking to Philip Pullman": An Interview', *The Lion and the Unicorn* 23:1 (January 1999), 116–34, 126.
60. Melvin Burgess, *Junk; Doing It* (London: Andersen, 2003).
61. My study *Philip Pullman, Master Storyteller: A Guide to the Worlds of* His Dark Materials (London: Continuum, 2006) explores Pullman's writing in more detail.
62. http://www.commonwealthwriters.com/worldreaders/haddon.html, accessed 22 May 2006.
63. http://www.commonwealthwriters.com/worldreaders/haddon.html, accessed 22 May 2006.
64. English, *The Economy of Prestige*, 10.
65. See Alastair Niven, 'A Common Wealth of Talent', *Booker 30. A Celebration of the Booker Prize for Fiction. 1969–1998*, London: Booker plc, 1998, 40–2.
66. See http://www.brookes.ac.uk/services/library/speccoll/booker.html
67. Whitbread Book Awards, http://www.whitbread-bookawards.co.uk/about.cfm?page=62, accessed 18 April 2006.
68. Robert McCrum, 'Pullman Gives His Readers Precisely the Satisfactions They Look For in a Novel', *Observer*, 22 October 2000.
69. http://www.commonwealthwriters.com/worldreaders/haddon.html, accessed 22 May 2006.
70. An argument made by Christine Evain in '"Whatever the trick is, you have it": International Marketing of Canadian-Authored Books in Relation to Commonwealth Literary Prizes', in Guignery and Gallix, eds., *Pre- and Post-Publication Itineraries*.
71. See my 'A Common Ground? Book Prize Culture in Europe' for a framework through which the various uses to which literary prizes are put can be understood.
72. This peritextual marketing item is thus named and discussed with regards to its frequent use in the French literary marketplace by Genette in *Paratexts*, 8, 27–8.
73. Justine Jordan, 'Preview: Fiction: Seconds Out', *Guardian*, 27 December 2003. The publisher conveniently changed the preview to read 'this year' rather than 'next year'.

74. David Mitchell, *Ghostwritten* (London: Sceptre, 1999); *number9dream* (London: Sceptre, 2001).
75. Lawrence Norfolk and Tibor Fischer, eds., *New Writing 8* (London: Vintage, 1999).
76. All of these writers are quoted in the *Cloud Atlas* hardback cover copy. David Mitchell, 'The January Man', *Granta 81: Best of Young British Novelists* (2003), 135–48. Earlier editions were *Granta 43: Best of Young British Novelists 2* (1993) and *Granta 7: Best of Young British Novelists* (1983).
77. Mitchell wrote about the influence of Calvino's novel on *Cloud Atlas* in a newspaper article, 'Rereadings: Enter the Maze', *Guardian*, 22 May 2004.
78. Mark Sanderson, 'The Literary Life', *Sunday Telegraph*, 7 March 2004.
79. Eileen Battersby, 'Now, For my Next Trick…', *Irish Times*, 6 March 2004; Theo Tait, 'From Victorian Travelogue to Airport Thriller', *Daily Telegraph*, 28 February 2004.
80. Neel Mukherjee, 'Dances with Genres', *The Times*, 21 February 2004.
81. Matt Thorne, 'Welcome to a World Where Fabricants Live on Soap', *Independent on Sunday*, 29 February 2004.
82. Jan Dalley's 'Rich Mix Make Man Booker Prize Final Six', *Financial Times*, 22 September 2004 reports Mitchell's publisher's comments on the positive effect of the longlisting and shortlisting of *Cloud Atlas*. Sales figures courtesy of Nielsen Bookscan.
83. Alan Hollinghurst, *The Line of Beauty* (London: Picador, 2004). One of the judges, Rowan Pelling, described the difficult decision in her article 'Only After We Went to the Loo Did the Winner Emerge', *Independent on Sunday*, 24 October 2004.
84. Hartley, *Reading Groups*; Long, *Book Clubs*.
85. Suki Dhanda, 'Our Top 50 Players', 4.
86. As announced in Louise Jury and Boyd Tonkin, 'Does Richard and Judy's Book Club Guarantee Success for These Ten Titles?', *Independent*, 10 December 2004. Carlos Ruiz Zafon, *The Shadow of the Wind* (London: Weidenfeld & Nicolson, 2004); Audrey Niffenegger, *The Time Traveler's Wife* (London: Jonathan Cape, 2004); Andrew Taylor, *The American Boy* (London: Flamingo, 2003); Justin Cartwright, *The Promise of Happiness* (London: Bloomsbury, 2004); Karen Joy Fowler, *The Jane Austen Book Club* (London: Viking, 2004); William Brodrick, *The Sixth Lamentation* (London: Time Warner, 2003); Jodi Picoult, *My Sister's Keeper* (London: Hodder & Stoughton, 2005); Paula Byrne, *Perdita: The Life of Mary Robinson* (London: HarperCollins, 2004); and Chris Heath, *Feel* (London: Ebury Press, 2004).
87. Quoted in Louise Jury, '£50,000 Buys Me Time, Says Booker Winner Hollinghurst as He Takes a Break from Writing', *Independent*, 21 October 2004. Yann Martel, *Life of Pi* (Edinburgh: Canargate, 2002).
88. Giles Hattersley, 'She's Choosing Your Books', *Sunday Times*, 13 August 2006.
89. Leo Hickman and Grundy Northedge, 'The G2 Graphic: The Publishing Industry', *Guardian*, 10 October 2005. The actual sales figures are slightly complicated because the cheaper paperback edition of the book was only published very shortly before it was featured on Richard & Judy. Sales figures from Nielsen Bookscan.
90. 'Literary Lion with a Line to Richard and Judy', *Sunday Times*, 24 April 2005.

Conclusion: Writing Beyond Marketing

1. Sage, 'Living on Writing', 267.
2. Zadie Smith, 'The Waiter's Wife', in *Granta 67: Women and Children First*, Autumn 1999, 127–42; 'Stuart', in *The New Yorker*, 27 December 1999 and 3 January 2000, 60–7.
3. Benedicte Page, 'Chewing up the Past', *The Bookseller*, 15 October 1999, 38.
4. *Book Sales Yearbook 2002. Book 2: The Year in Detail: Subjects, Books, Authors* (London: Bookseller Publications, 2002), reported *White Teeth* as the second bestselling paperback fiction title by volume in 2001, 44.
5. Roger Tagholm, 'Something to Get Your Teeth Into', *Publishing News*, 12 November 1999, 18.
6. *The Bookseller*, 10 September, 1999, front cover.
7. *The Bookseller*, 10 September, 1999, inside front cover. The biography reads, 'Zadie Smith is in her early twenties and lives in North-West London. *White Teeth* is her first novel.'
8. See Janine di Giovanni, 'Poached, Lunched and Published', *The Times*, 8 December 1997, 16; David Rennie, 'Finals Chapter', *Daily Telegraph*, 11 December 1997, 27; and Cole Moreton, 'Some Kind of Success', *Independent on Sunday*, 4 January 1998, 26 (The Sunday Review section).
9. Alex Renton, 'Next Big Hype', *Evening Standard*, 4 January 2000, 25.
10. Sam Wallace, 'Cutting Her Teeth with a Book Deal', *Daily Telegraph*, 15 January 2000, 18 (main section); Simon Hattenstone, 'White Knuckle Ride', *Guardian*, 11 December 2000, 6–7 (G2 section), 7.
11. Zadie Smith, *The Autograph Man* (London: Hamish Hamilton, 2002).
12. Robert McCrum, 'If 1900 was Oysters and Champagne, 2000 is a Pint of Lager and a Packet of Crisps', *Observer*, 24 December 2000, 19 (Review section). He refers to Hanif Kureishi, *The Buddha of Suburbia* (London: Faber and Faber), 1990.
13. Zadie Smith, 'Mrs Begum's Son and the Private Tutor', in Martha Kelly, ed., *The May Anthology of Oxford and Cambridge Short Stories 1997*, selected and introduced by Jill Paton Walsh (Oxford and Cambridge: Varsity Publications Ltd and Cherwell (Oxford Student Publications Ltd), 1997), 89–113.
14. Salman Rushdie, *The Satanic Verses* (London: Viking, 1988).
15. Despite affirming that Rushdie and Kureishi were 'heroes of mine' in 1998 (in Moreton, 'Some Kind of Success', 26), by the time of publication in 2000 Smith was saying that ' "I think some writers, not just me, feel that you're being compared to Rushdie or Kureishi just because there are Asian characters in your book, and if that's the case, it's a waste of time and a pain in the ass because there are thousands of books with white people in them and they're not all the same" '. See Christina Patterson, 'Zadie Smith – A Willesden Ring of Confidence', *Independent*, 22 January 2000, 9 (Weekend Review section).
16. Fiachra Gibbons, 'The Route to Literary Success: Be Young, Gifted and Very Good Looking', *Guardian*, 28 March 2001, 3 (main section).
17. Sarah Sands, 'Zadie, the Woman Who Reinvented the Novelist', *Daily Telegraph*, 24 March 2000, 28 (main section).
18. Smith, *White Teeth*, 115.
19. Smith, *White Teeth*, 118.

20. Smith, *White Teeth*, 398.
21. Monica Ali, *Brick Lane* (London: Doubleday, 2003); Andrea Levy, *Small Island* (London: Review, 2004).
22. Smith, *White Teeth*, 443.
23. Smith, *White Teeth*, 3, 441.
24. Smith, *White Teeth*, 397.
25. Smith, *White Teeth*, 462.
26. Smith, *White Teeth*, 462.

Bibliography

Adams, Thomas R., and Barker, Nicolas, 'A New Model for the Study of the Book', in Nicolas Barker, ed., *A Potencie of Life: Books in Society. The Clark Lectures 1986–1987. The British Library Studies in the History of the Book* (London: The British Library, 1993), 5–43.

Adorno, Theodor, *The Culture Industry: Selected Essays on Mass Culture*, edited with an Introduction by J. M. Bernstein (London: Routledge, 1991).

Aitkenhead, Decca, 'Bridget Jones: Don't Ya Just Love Her?', *Guardian*, 8 August 1997, 17 (main section).

Alberge, Dalya, 'Literary Recluse Faces Booker Shortlist Limelight', *The Times*, 16 September 1997, 1 (main section).

ALCS, 'What are Words Worth?', http://www.alcs.co.uk/multimedia/pdf2/word2.pdf, accessed 25 March 2007.

Ali, Monica, *Brick Lane* (London: Doubleday, 2003).

Almond, David, *The Fire-Eaters* (London: Hodder Children's, 2003).

Altbach, Philip G., 'Literary Colonialism: Books in the Third World', in Bill Ashcroft, Gareth Griffiths and Helen Tiffin, eds., *The Post-Colonial Studies Reader* (London: Routledge, 1995), 485–90.

Amis, Martin, *Money* (London: Jonathan Cape, 1984).

——*London Fields* (London: Jonathan Cape, 1989).

——*Time's Arrow* (London: Jonathan Cape, 1991).

——*The Information* (London: Flamingo, 1995).

——*Night Train* (London: Jonathan Cape, 1997).

——*Heavy Water and Other Stories* (London: Jonathan Cape, 1998).

——*Experience* (London: Jonathan Cape, 2000).

Anderson, Chris, *The Long Tail: How Endless Choice is Creating Unlimited Demand* (London: Random House, 2006).

Ash, Timothy Garton, *History of the Present: Essays, Sketches and Despatches from Europe in the 1990s* (London: Penguin, 2000 updated edn.; 1st edn. 1999).

Athill, Diana, *Stet* (London: Granta, 2000).

Atkinson, Kate, *Behind the Scenes at the Museum* (London: Doubleday, 1995).

Atwood, Margaret, *The Blind Assassin* (London: Bloomsbury, 2000).

Bagdikian, Ben, *The Media Monopoly* (Boston: Beacon Press, 1983).

Barker, Nicolas, 'Intentionality and Reception Theory', in Nicolas Barker, ed., *A Potencie of Life: Books in Society. The Clark Lectures 1986–1987. The British Library Studies in the History of the Book* (London: The British Library, 1993), 195–210.

Barker, Pat, *Union Street* (London: Virago, 1982).

——*Blow Your House Down* (London: Virago, 1984).

——*The Century's Daughter* (London: Virago, 1986).

——*The Man Who Wasn't There* (London: Virago, 1989).

——*Regeneration* (London: Viking, 1991).

——*The Eye in the Door* (London: Viking, 1993).

——*The Ghost Road* (London: Viking, 1995).

——*Another World* (London: Viking, 1998).
Barker, R. E., and Davies, G. R., *Books Are Different: An Account of the Defence of the Net Book Agreement Before the Restrictive Practices Court in 1962* (London: Macmillan, 1966).
Barker, Richard, 'A Tale of Two Cities', *Bookseller*, 30 April 1999, 30–2.
Barnes, Simon, 'Passage to the India in All of Us', *The Times*, 18 October 1997, 22 (main section).
Batt, Anne, 'A Book is Not a Tin of Beans...', *Daily Express*, 8 May 1967.
Battersby, Eileen, 'Now, For my Next Trick...', *Irish Times*, 6 March 2004.
Baverstock, Alison, *Are Books Different?: Marketing in the Book Trade* (London: Kogan Page, 1993).
——*How to Market Books* (London: Kogan Page, 2000; 3rd edn.).
Baxter, Sarah, 'Why Did the Apple Crumble?', *Observer*, 29 October 1995, 9 (The Review section).
Beckett, Andy, 'Raving with an MBA', *Independent on Sunday*, 23 April 1995, 38 (Review section).
Bedford, Martyn, *The Houdini Girl* (London: Viking, 1999; paperback edn. Penguin, 2000).
Belfer, Lauren, *City of Light* (London: Sceptre, 1999).
Bellaigue, Eric de, *British Book Publishing as a Business Since the 1960s: Selected Essays* (London: The British Library, 2004).
Bennett, Catherine, 'The House that Carmen Built', *Guardian*, 14 June 1993, 10–11 (G2 section).
——'Old Girls', *Guardian*, 17 January 1998, 23 (main section).
Bennett, Peter D, ed., *Dictionary of Marketing Terms* (Chicago: American Marketing Association, 1988).
Bennett, Ronan, *The Catastrophist* (London: Review, 1997).
Bernières, Louis de, *The War of Don Emmanuel's Nether Parts* (London: Secker & Warburg, 1990).
——*Señor Vivo and the Coca Lord* (London: Secker & Warburg, 1991).
——*The Troublesome Offspring of Cardinal Guzman* (London: Secker & Warburg, 1992).
——'The Brass Bar', *Granta 43: Best of Young British Novelists*, Spring 1993, 23–31.
——*Captain Corelli's Mandolin* (London: Secker & Warburg, 1994).
Best, Nicholas, 'Drugs and Thugs', *Financial Times*, 6 July 1991, 9 (Weekend section).
'Bestsellers', *Guardian*, 1 August 1998, 11 (Saturday section).
Bidisha, 'Banish these Publishing Ghettoes', *Independent*, 16 July 1998, 4 (Thursday Review section).
Birkerts, Sven, *The Gutenberg Elegies: The Fate of Reading in an Electronic Age* (London: Faber and Faber, 1996; first published in the US in 1994).
Blake, Carole, *From Pitch to Publication: Everything You Need to Get Your Novel Published* (London: Macmillan, 1999).
Bloom, Clive, *Bestsellers: Popular Fiction Since 1900* (Basingstoke: Palgrave Macmillan, 2002).
Bloom, Harold, *The Western Canon: The Books and School of the Ages* (New York: Harcourt Brace, 1994).
Bone, Alison, 'Output Surges 11%', *The Bookseller*, 9 September 2005, 7.
Book Marketing Limited, *Book Facts 2001: An Annual Compendium* (London: Book Marketing Ltd., 2001).

——*Books and the Consumer: Summary Report on the Findings of the 2004 Survey* (London: BML, 2005).

——*Expanding the Book Market: A Study of Reading and Buying Habits in GB* (London: BML, 2005).

Book Marketing Limited/The Reading Partnership, *Reading the Situation: Book Reading, Buying and Borrowing Habits in Britain* (London: Book Marketing, 2000).

Book Publishing in Britain (London: Bookseller Publications, 1999).

Book Retailing – UK (London: Mintel International Group Limited, 2000), accessed via http://reports.mintel.com, 25 July 2003.

Book Sales Yearbook 2002. Book 2: The Year in Detail: Subjects, Books, Authors (London: Bookseller Publications, 2002).

Bookseller, *Who Owns Whom: Book Publishing and Retailing 1980–1989* (London: J. Whitaker & Sons, 1990).

——12 February 1999, 19.

——'Winning Prizes: The Sales Effect', *The Bookseller*, 9 July 1999, 19.

——10 September 1999.

——'John Murray: Gentlemen Overcome by Arrivistes?', *The Bookseller*, 17 May 2002, 26.

Bourdieu, Pierre, 'The Field of Cultural Production, or: The Economic World Reversed', in *The Field of Cultural Production: Essays on Art and Literature*, translated by Randal Johnston (Cambridge: Polity Press, 1993), 29–73. Originally published in *Poetics* 12/4–5 (1983), 311–56.

Bremner, Charles, 'Setting a Beast to Catch a Beastie', *The Times*, 19 November 1990, 12 (main section).

Brodrick, William, *The Sixth Lamentation* (London: Time Warner, 2003).

Brown, Dan, *The Da Vinci Code* (London: Bantam, 2003).

Brown, Iain D., and Fletcher, Jo, eds., *Superstores – Super News?: The Report of Fiona Stewart, 1998 Tony Godwin Award Recipient* (London: The Tony Godwin Memorial Trust, 1999).

Brown, Stephen, ed., *Consuming Books: The Marketing and Consumption of Literature* (London: Routledge, 2006).

Brown, Stephen, *Wizard! Harry Potter's Brand Magic* (London: Cyan Books, 2005).

Brown, Stephen, Doherty, Anne Marie and Clarke, Bill, *Romancing the Market* (London: Routledge, 1998).

Burgess, Melvin, *Junk* (London: Andersen, 1996).

——*Doing It* (London: Andersen, 2003).

Bury, Liz, and Kean, Danuta, 'Browser to Buyer, Amazon Style', *The Bookseller*, 7 January 2005, 26–7.

Byatt, A. S., *Possession* (London: Chatto & Windus, 1990).

——'Fathers', in *On Histories and Stories: Selected Essays* (London: Chatto & Windus, 2000), 9–35.

Byrne, Paula, *Perdita: The Life of Mary Robinson* (London: HarperCollins, 2004).

Cadman, Eileen, Chester, Gail and Pivot, Agnes, *Rolling Our Own: Women as Printers, Publishers and Distributors* (London: Minority Press Group, 1981).

Cairns, David, *Berlioz Volume Two: Servitude and Greatness 1832–1869* (London: Allen Lane, 1999).

Callil, Carmen, 'Women, Publishing and Power', in *Business: Women, Writing and the Marketplace* (Manchester: Manchester University Press, 1998), 183–92.

Callil, Carmen, and Tóibín, Colm, *The Modern Library: The Two Hundred Best Novels in English Since 1950* (London: Picador, 1999).

'"Can YOU Recommend a Really Good Book?"', presenter for *Captain Corelli's Mandolin* produced by Secker & Warburg n.d. [1993/4?].
Carey, John, *The Intellectuals and the Masses* (London: Faber and Faber, 1992).
Carr, Caleb, *The Alienist* (London: Little, Brown, 1994).
Cartwright, Justin, *The Promise of Happiness* (London: Bloomsbury, 2004).
Cavallo, Guglielmo, and Chartier, Roger, 'Introduction', in Guglielmo Cavallo and Roger Chartier, *A History of Reading in the West*, translated by Lydia G. Cochrane (Cambridge: Polity Press, 1999; first published in Italy in 1995), 1–36.
Cecil, Hugh, *The Flower of Battle: British Fiction Writers of the First World War* (London: Secker & Warburg, 1995).
Chadwick, Alan, 'End of the Line for Gravy Trainspotters?', *Sunday Times*, 8 November 1998.
Champion, Sarah, ed., *Disco Biscuits* (London: Sceptre, 1997).
Chandler, Charles, 'No Experience Necessary (Or, How I Learned to Stop Worrying and Love Marketing)', in Stephen Brown, ed., *Consuming Books: The Marketing and Consumption of Literature* (London: Routledge, 2006), 167–74.
Chaudhuri, Amit, 'Lure of the Hybrid', *Times Literary Supplement*, 3 September 1999, 5–6.
Children's Writers' and Artists' Yearbook (London: A&C Black, 2004).
Clark, Giles, *Inside Book Publishing* (London: Routledge, 2001; 3rd edn.).
Clee, Nicholas, 'The Bookseller', *Guardian*, 28 June 2003.
Collin, Matthew, and Godfrey, John, *Altered State: The Story of Ecstasy Culture and Acid House* (London: Serpent's Tail, 1997).
Competition Commission, http://www.competition-commission.org.uk/inquiries/ref2005/hmv/, accessed 29 September 2006.
Connolly, Cyril, ed., 'Questionnaire: The Cost of Letters', *Horizon* 14: 81 (1946), 140–75.
Connor, Steven, *The English Novel in History 1950–1995* (London: Routledge, 1996).
Coser, Lewis A., Kadushin, Charles and Powell, Walter W., *Books: The Culture and Commerce of Publishing* (New York: Basic Books, 1982).
Cowley, Jason, 'Goddess of Small Things', *The Times*, 18 October 1997, 17 (Metro section).
——'Was the Pity All in the Poetry?', *Sunday Times*, 8 November 1998, 2–3.
Craig, Amanda, *A Vicious Circle* (London: Fourth Estate, 1997; paperback edn., first published in 1996).
Croce, Benedetto, 'Criticism of the Theory of Artistic and Literary Kinds', in David Duff, ed., *Modern Genre Theory*, translated by Douglas Ainslie (Harlow: Longman, 2000; first published in Italy in 1902), 25–8.
Cunningham, John, 'Interview: Louis de Bernières', *Guardian*, 23 August 1997, 3 (G2 section).
Cunningham, Valentine, 'Manufacturing a Masterpiece', *Prospect*, December 1998, 56–8.
Cusk, Rachel, 'The Apple of Our Sisters' Eyes', *Guardian*, 26 October 1995, 5 (G2 section).
Dalley, Jan, 'Rich Mix Make Man Booker Prize Final Six', *Financial Times*, 22 September 2004.
Dalrymple, William, *From the Holy Mountain: A Journey in the Shadow of Byzantium* (London: Flamingo, 1998; paperback edn., first published in 1997).

Darnton, Robert, 'What is the History of Books?', in *The Kiss of Lamourette: Reflections in Cultural History* (London: Faber and Faber, 1990), 107–35. First published in *Daedalus* (Summer 1982), 65–83.

——'First Steps Towards a History of Reading', in *The Kiss of Lamourette: Reflections in Cultural History* (London: Faber and Faber, 1990), 154–87. First published in the *Australian Journal of French Studies* 23 (1986), 5–30.

Delany, Paul, *Literature, Money and the Market: From Trollope to Amis* (Basingstoke: Palgrave Macmillan, 2002).

'Detective Fiction', in Margaret Drabble, ed., *The Oxford Companion to English Literature* (Oxford: Oxford University Press, 2000; 6th edn.).

Dhanda, Suki, 'Our Top 50 Players in the World of Books', *Observer*, 5 March 2006, 4–7.

'Diary', *Sunday Times*, 18 May 1997, 6 (Books section).

Dibb, Sally, Simkin, Lyndon, Pride, William M. and Ferrell, O. C., *Marketing: Concepts and Strategies* (Boston: Houghton Mifflin, 2001; 4th edn.).

DS, 'NB', *Times Literary Supplement*, 17 November 1995, 18.

——'NB', *Times Literary Supplement*, 5 January 1996, 14.

Duff, David, 'Key Concepts', in David Duff, ed., *Modern Genre Theory* (Harlow: Longman, 2000), x–xvi.

Duncker, Patricia, 'A Note on the Politics of Publishing', in *Sisters and Strangers: An Introduction to Contemporary Feminist Fiction* (Oxford: Blackwell, 1992).

Dyer, Geoff, *The Missing of the Somme* (London: Hamish Hamilton, 1994).

Eccleshare, Julia, 'A Golden Time for Children's Books', *Publishers Weekly*, 18 February 2002, 20–4.

——'A Fast Track for Children's Books', *Publishers Weekly Special Report: British Publishing 2004*, 8 March 2004, 16–18.

Eliot, Simon, 'Continuity and Change in British Publishing, 1770–2000', *Publishing Research Quarterly*, 19: 2 (Summer 2003), 37–50.

Ellis, Bret Easton, *Less Than Zero* (London: Picador, 1986; first published in the US in 1985).

——*The Rules of Attraction* (London: Picador, 1988; first published in the US in 1987).

——*American Psycho* (London: Picador, 1991).

Ellmann, Lucy, *Man or Mango?* (London: Review, 1998).

English, James F., 'Winning the Culture Game: Prizes, Awards, and the Rules of Art', *New Literary History* 33: 1, (2002) 109–35.

——*The Economy of Prestige: Prizes, Awards, and the Circulation of Cultural Value* (Cambridge, Mass.: Harvard University Press, 2005).

English, James F., ed., *A Concise Companion to Contemporary British Fiction* (Oxford: Blackwell Publishing, 2006).

English, James F. and Frow, John, 'Literary Authorship and Celebrity Culture', in James F. English, ed., *A Concise Companion to Contemporary British Fiction* (Oxford: Blackwell Publishing, 2006), 39–57.

Epstein, Jason, *Book Business: Publishing Past Present and Future* (New York: W. W. Norton, 2001).

Evain, Christine, '"Whatever the trick is, you have it": International Marketing of Canadian-Authored Books in Relation to Commonwealth Literary Prizes', in Vanessa Guignery and François Gallix, eds., *Pre- and Post-Publication Itineraries of the Contemporary Novel in English* (Paris: Éditions Publibook Université, 2007).

Ezard, John, 'Warring Fictions', *Guardian*, 11 September 1993, 28 (Outlook section).
Faber, Geoffrey, *A Publisher Speaking* (London: Faber and Faber, 1934).
Farrell, Winslow, *How Hits Happen: Forecasting Unpredictability in a Chaotic Marketplace* (London: Orion Business, 1998).
Faulks, Sebastian, *Birdsong* (London: Hutchinson, 1993).
Feather, John, *A History of British Publishing* (London: Routledge, 2006; 2nd edn.).
Feeny, Catherine, '"I Haven't Actually Read Your Book, Catherine..."', *Independent*, 10 March 2000, 6 (World Book Day 2000 supplement).
Ferguson, Niall, *The Pity of War* (London: Allen Lane, 1998).
Fetterley, Judith, *The Resisting Reader: A Feminist Approach to American Fiction* (Bloomington: Indiana University Press, 1978).
Fielding, Helen, *Cause Celeb* (London: Picador, 1994).
——'The Diary of Bridget Jones', *Independent*, 28 February 1995, 19 (Section 2).
——*Bridget Jones's Diary* (London: Picador, 1996).
——*Bridget Jones: The Edge of Reason* (London: Picador, 1999).
Fill, Chris, *Marketing Communications: Contexts, Contents and Strategies* (London: Prentice Hall, 1999; 2nd edn.).
Fish, Stanley, *Self-Consuming Artifacts: The Experience of Seventeenth-Century Literature* (Berkeley: University of California Press, 1972).
——*Is There a Text in This Class? The Authority of Interpretive Communities* (Cambridge, Mass.: Harvard University Press, 1980).
Forrest, Emma, 'Not with a Bang but with a Simper', *Guardian*, 31 August 1998, 9 (G2 section).
Forsyth, Patrick, and Birn, Robin, *Marketing in Publishing* (London: Routledge, 1997).
Foucault, Michel, 'What is an Author?', in Josué V. Harari, *Textual Strategies: Perspectives in Post-Structuralist Criticism* (London: Methuen & Co, 1980; English translation first published in the US in 1979), 141–60.
——*The Order of Things: An Archaeology of the Human Sciences* (London: Routledge, 1994; first published in the UK in 1970; first published in France in 1966).
Fowler, Karen Joy, *The Jane Austen Book Club* (London: Viking, 2004).
Freeman, Alan, 'Ghosts in Sunny Leith: Irvine Welsh's *Trainspotting*', in Susanne Hagemann, ed., *Studies in Scottish Fiction: 1945 to the Present* (Frankfurt: Peter Lang, 1996), 251–62.
French, Patrick, 'The Many Lures of the Orient', *Sunday Times*, 30 June 1996, 13 (Books section).
Gardiner, Juliet, 'Recuperating the Author: Consuming Fictions of the 1990s', *The Papers of the Bibliographical Society of America* 94: 2 (2000), 255–74.
——'"What is an Author?" Contemporary Publishing Discourse and the Author Figure', *Publishing Research Quarterly* 16: 1 (Spring 2000), 63–76.
Gaskell, Philip, *A New Introduction to Bibliography* (Oxford: Clarendon Press, 1972).
Gasson, Christopher, *Who Owns Whom in British Book Publishing* (London: Bookseller Publications, 1998).
——*Who Owns Whom in British Book Publishing* (London: Bookseller Publications, 2002).
Gayle, Mike, *My Legendary Girlfriend* (London: Hodder & Stoughton, 1998).
'Generation Ecstasy: Forty Things that Started with an E', *The Face*, October 1995, 120.

Genette, Gérard, *Fiction and Diction*, translated by Catherine Porter (Ithaca: Cornell University Press, 1993; originally published in France in 1991).

——*Paratexts: Thresholds of Interpretation*, translated by Jane E. Lewin (Cambridge: Cambridge University Press, 1997; first published in France in 1987).

Gerrard, Nicci, *Into the Mainstream* (London: Pandora, 1989).

——'Hype, hype hurrah!', *Observer*, 6 August 1995, 15 (The Observer Review section).

Gibbons, Fiachra, 'The Route to Literary Success: Be Young, Gifted and Very Good Looking', *Guardian*, 28 March 2001, 3 (main section).

——'Booker Prize: Snubbed Unknown Sweeps Giants Off Shortlist', *Guardian*, 17 September 2003.

Giovanni, Janine di, 'Poached, Lunched and Published', *The Times*, 8 December 1997, 16.

Gordon, Giles, 'Proper Publishing Goes Bung', *Bookseller*, 25 January 2002, 27–8.

Gorra, Michael, 'Living in the Aftermath', *London Review of Books*, 19 June 1997, 22.

Granta 7: Best of Young British Novelists (1983).

Granta 43: Best of Young British Novelists 2 (1993).

Green, Jane, *Straight Talking* (London: Mandarin, 1997).

Grove, Valerie, 'I Know in my Bones that Book Prizes are Just Three Lemons in a Row', *The Times*, 29 September 1995, 17 (main section).

Guterson, David, *Snow Falling on Cedars* (London: Bloomsbury, 1995).

Hackley, Chris, 'I Write Marketing Textbooks but I'm Really a Swill Guy', in Stephen Brown, ed., *Consuming Books: The Marketing and Consumption of Literature* (London: Routledge, 2006).

Haddon, Mark, *The Curious Incident of the Dog in the Night-Time* (London/Oxford: Jonathan Cape/David Fickling, 2003).

——*The Talking Horse and the Sad Girl and the Village Under the Sea* (London: Picador, 2005).

——*A Spot of Bother* (London: Jonathan Cape, 2006).

Hamilton, Alex, 'Top Hundred Chart of 1996 Fastsellers', in *Writers' & Artists' Yearbook 1998* (London: A&C Black, 1998), 261–8.

——'Fastsellers 2000: The Hot Paperbacks', *Guardian*, 6 January 2001, 10 (Saturday Review section).

Hare, Steve, ed., *Penguin Portrait: Allen Lane and the Penguin Editors 1935–1970* (London: Penguin, 1995).

Harlow, John, 'Will Tom Cruise Pluck Corelli's Mandolin?', *Sunday Times*, 3 January 1999, 7 (main section).

Harris, Joanne, *Chocolat* (London: Black Swan, 2000; first published in 1999).

Hartley, Jenny, *Reading Groups* (Oxford: Oxford University Press, 2001).

——*The Reading Groups Book 2002–2003 Edition* (Oxford: Oxford University Press, 2002).

Hattenstone, Simon, 'White Knuckle Ride', *Guardian*, 11 December 2000, 6–7 (G2 section).

Hattersley, Giles, 'She's Choosing Your Books', *Sunday Times*, 13 August 2006.

Hayes, Michael, 'Popular Fiction', in Clive Bloom and Gary Day, eds., *Literature and Culture in Modern Britain. Volume Three: 1956–1999* (Harlow: Longman, 2000), 76-93.

Heaney, Seamus, *Beowulf* (London: Faber and Faber, 1999).

Heath, Chris, *Feel* (London: Ebury Press, 2004).
Heilpern, Jon, 'Dressed to Kill and Bound for the Best-seller Lists', *Independent on Sunday*, 25 November 1990, 11 (main section).
Hickman, Leo, and Northedge, Grundy, 'The G2 Graphic: The Publishing Industry', *Guardian*, 10 October 2005.
Høeg, Peter, *Miss Smilla's Feeling for Snow*, translated by F. David (London: Harvill, 1993; first published in Denmark in 1992).
Hoggart, Richard, *The Uses of Literacy* (London: Chatto & Windus, 1957).
Holbrook, Morris B., 'On the Commercial Exaltation of Artistic Mediocrity: Books, Bread, Postmodern Statistics, Surprising Success Stories, and the Doomed Magnificence of Way Too Many Big Words', in Stephen Brown, ed., *Consuming Books: The Marketing and Consumption of Literature* (London: Routledge, 2006), 96–113.
Holgate, Andrew, and Wilson-Fletcher, Honor, eds., *The Cost of Letters: A Survey of Literary Living Standards* (Brentford: Waterstone's Booksellers Ltd, 1998).
——*The Test of Time: What Makes a Classic a Classic?* (Brentford: Waterstone's, 1999).
Hollinghurst, Alan, *The Swimming Pool Library* (London: Chatto & Windus, 1988).
——*The Folding Star* (London: Chatto & Windus, 1994).
——*The Spell* (London: Chatto & Windus, 1998).
——*The Line of Beauty* (London: Picador, 2004).
Hornby, Gill, 'Weight of the Single State', *The Times*, 19 October 1996, 10 (The Directory section).
Hornby, Nick, 'Chibs with Everything', *Times Literary Supplement*, 28 April 1995, 23.
——*High Fidelity* (London: Gollancz, 1995).
Howard, Gerald, 'Slouching Towards Grubnet: The Author in the Age of Publicity', *Review of Contemporary Fiction* 16: 1 (Spring 1996), 44–53.
Howe, Florence, 'Feminist Publishing', in Philip G. Altbach and Edith S. Hoshimo, eds., *International Book Publishing: An Encyclopaedia* (London: Fitzroy Dearborn, 1995), 130–8.
http://www.commonwealthwriters.com/worldreaders/haddon.html, accessed 22 May 2006.
Huggan, Graham, *The Postcolonial Exotic: Marketing the Margins* (London: Routledge, 2001).
Hughes, Scott, 'CV: David Godwin, Literary Agent', *Independent*, 20 October 1997, 5 (Media + section).
Hughes, Ted, *Birthday Letters* (London: Faber and Faber, 1998).
Interview with Alexandra Pringle, Editor-in-Chief, Bloomsbury, 13 July 2000.
Interview with Andrew Miller, 30 June 2000.
Interview with Bud McLintock of Karen Earl Ltd., Director of the Whitbread Book Awards, 30 June 2000.
Interview with David Godwin, David Godwin Associates, 11 May 1998.
Interview with Eric Anderson (Chair of the Judges of the 1999 Whitbread Awards), Lincoln College, Oxford, 9 March 2000.
Interview with Erica Wagner, Literary Editor of *The Times*, 1 February 2000.
Interview with Geoff Mulligan, Publishing Director of Secker & Warburg, 15 April 1999.
Interview with Gillon Aitken and Clare Alexander, Gillon Aitken Associates Ltd., 19 July 1999.

Interview with Jamie Hodder-Williams, Sales and Marketing Director, Hodder & Stoughton General Division, Hodder Headline, 13 July 2000.
Interview with John Carey, Merton College, Oxford, 12 February 2001.
Interview with Kirsty Fowkes, Editor, Hodder & Stoughton Publishers, 13 July 2000.
Interview with Mark Le Fanu, General Secretary of The Society of Authors, 20 July 1999.
Interview with Martyn Goff, Administrator of the Booker Prize, 21 March 2000.
Interview with Pat Kavanagh, Literary Agent at PFD, 25 July 2000.
Interview with Peter Straus, Publisher of Picador, Macmillan, 19 July 1999.
Interview with Philip Gwyn Jones, Editorial Director of Flamingo, HarperCollins, 11 May 1999.
Interview with Robert McCrum, Literary Editor of the *Observer*, 1 February 2000.
Interview with Robin Robertson, Deputy Publishing Director of Jonathan Cape, 7 May 1999.
Iser, Wolfgang, *The Implied Reader: Patterns of Communication in Prose Fiction from Bunyan to Beckett* (Baltimore: Johns Hopkins University Press, 1974).
Iyer, Pico, 'The Empire Writes Back', *Time* (8 February 1993), 54–9.
James, Elizabeth, ed., *Macmillan: A Publishing Tradition* (Basingstoke: Palgrave Macmillan, 2002).
Johnston, Paul, *Body Politic* (London: Hodder & Stoughton, 1997).
Jones, Derek, ed., *Censorship: A World Encyclopedia Volume 3: L–R* (London: Fitzroy Dearborn Publishers, 2001).
Jordan, Justine, 'Preview: Fiction: Seconds Out', *Guardian*, 27 December 2003.
Jury, Louise, '£50,000 Buys Me Time, Says Booker Winner Hollinghurst as He Takes a Break from Writing', *Independent*, 21 October 2004.
Jury, Louise and Tonkin, Boyd, 'Does Richard and Judy's Book Club Guarantee Success for These Ten Titles?', *Independent*, 10 December 2004.
Kean, Danuta, *Book Retailing in Britain* (London: Bookseller Publications, 2001).
——'Bungs – Are They Fair Trade?', *Bookseller*, 15 February 2002, 26–9.
Kean, Danuta, ed., *In Full Colour: Cultural Diversity in Publishing Today* (London: Bookseller Publications, 2004).
Keegan, John, *First World War* (London: Hutchinson, 1998).
Kellaway, Kate, 'Billy, Don't be a Hero', *Observer*, 27 August 1995, 16 (The Observer Review section).
Kemp, Peter, 'What an Unlovely War', *Sunday Times*, 10 September 1995, 13 (Books section).
——'Losing the Plot', *Sunday Times*, 21 September 1997, 3 (Books section).
Kneale, Matthew, 'Re-animating the Past', *Waterstone's Books Quarterly*, Issue 2, 2001, 22–5.
Knowles, Joanne, '"Hurrah for the Singletons!" 1990s Fictions of the Single Woman', at *Contemporary British Women's Writing 1960–Present Day*, University of Leicester, 1 July 2000.
Kotei, S. I. A., 'The Book Today in Africa', in Bill Ashcroft, Gareth Griffiths and Helen Tiffin, eds., *The Post-Colonial Studies Reader* (London: Routledge, 1995), 480–4.
Kotler, Philip, *Marketing Management: Analysis, Planning, Implementation and Control* (Englewood Cliffs, NJ: Prentice Hall, 1996; 9th edn.).
KPMG, *The UK Book Industry: Unlocking the Supply Chain's Hidden Prize*, February 1998.

——*Tackling Returns*, August 1999.

Kravitz, Peter, ed., *The Picador Book of Contemporary Scottish Fiction* (London: Picador, 1997).

Kreitzman, Leon, 'Shop Around the Clock', *Bookseller*, 26 March 1999, 36.

Kureishi, Hanif, *The Buddha of Suburbia* (London: Faber and Faber), 1990.

Landesman, Cosmo, 'Naughty Little Nietzschean, *Sunday Times*, 11 January 1998, 7 (News Review section).

Lane, Michael, *Books and Publishers: Commerce Against Culture in Postwar Britain* (Lexington, Mass.: Lexington Books, 1980).

Lawson, Mark, 'Pick of the Year', *Sunday Times*, 19 November 1995, 3 (Books section).

Leavis, F. R., *Mass Civilisation and Minority Culture* (Cambridge: Minority Press, 1930).

Leavis, Q. D., *Fiction and the Reading Public* (London: Peregrine, 1979; first published in 1932).

Legat, Michael, *An Author's Guide to Literary Agents* (London: Robert Hale, 1995).

——*An Author's Guide to Publishing* (London: Robert Hale, 1998; 3rd edn.), 82.

Levy, Andrea, *Small Island* (London: Review, 2004).

Lewis, Jeremy, *Kindred Spirits: Adrift in Literary London* (London: HarperCollins, 1995).

——*Penguin Special: The Life and Times of Allen Lane* (London: Viking, 2005).

Lezard, Nicholas, 'Junk and the Big Trigger', *Independent on Sunday*, 29 August, 1993, 28 (The Sunday Review section).

'Literary Lion with a Line to Richard and Judy', *Sunday Times*, 24 April 2005.

Litt, Toby, *Adventures in Capitalism* (London: Secker & Warburg, 1996).

——*Beatniks* (London: Secker & Warburg, 1997).

——*Corpsing* (London: Hamish Hamilton, 2000; paperback edn. Penguin, 2000).

Lockerbie, Catherine, 'Return of Reading's Red Letter Day', *The Scotsman*, 10 April 1999, 10.

Long, Elizabeth, *Book Clubs: Women and the Uses of Reading in Everyday Life* (Chicago: University of Chicago Press, 2003).

Look, Hugh, 'Stars for all the Write Reasons', *The Bookseller*, 10 July 1998, 27.

Loose, Amanda, 'Holidays Ready Booked', *The Times*, 19 August 1998, 3 (Crème de la Crème section).

MacDonald, Lyn, *To the Last Man: Spring 1918* (London: Viking, 1998).

MacDonald, Marianne, 'Book Watch', *Independent*, 6 September 1996, 9 (main section).

Martel, Yann, *Life of Pi* (Edinburgh: Canongate, 2002).

Maschler, Tom, *Publisher* (London: Picador, 2005).

Matthews, Nicole, and Moody, Nickianne, eds., *Judging a Book by its Cover: Fans, Publishers, Designers and the Marketing of Books* (London: Ashgate, forthcoming).

McAleer, Joseph, *Passion's Fortune: The Story of Mills & Boon* (Oxford: Oxford University Press, 1999).

McCrum, Robert, 'Why Eng Lit Smites Pop Culture', *Observer*, 30 January 2000.

——'Pullman Gives His Readers Precisely the Satisfactions They Look For in a Novel', *Observer*, 22 October 2000.

——'If 1900 was Oysters and Champagne, 2000 is a Pint of Lager and a Packet of Crisps', *Observer*, 24 December 2000, 19 (Review section).

McDonald, Peter, *British Literary Culture and Publishing Practice 1880–1914* (Cambridge: Cambridge University Press, 1997).

McGirk, Jan, 'Indian Literary Star Faces Caste Sex Trial', *Sunday Times*, 29 June 1997, 19 (main section).

McGowan, Ian, 'The United Kingdom', in Philip G. Altbach and Edith S. Hoshimo, eds., *International Book Publishing: An Encyclopaedia* (London: Fitzroy Dearborn, 1995), 565–74.

McKenzie, D. F., 'Trading Places? England 1689–France 1789)', in Haydn T. Mason, ed., *The Darnton Debate* (Oxford: Voltaire Foundation, 1998), 1–24.

McLean, Duncan, ed., *Ahead of its Time: A Clocktower Press Anthology* (London: Vintage, 1998).

McPhee, Hilary, *Other People's Words* (Sydney: Picador Australia, 2001).

Meek, James, 'To 3,000 Little Fans, With Love', *Guardian*, 11 March 2004.

Miller, Andrew, *Ingenious Pain* (London: Sceptre, 1997).

——*Casanova* (London: Sceptre, 1998).

——*Oxygen* (London: Sceptre, 2001).

Miller, Karl, *Authors* (Oxford: Oxford University Press, 1989).

Miller, Keith, 'Dying for Happiness', *Times Literary Supplement*, 4 October 1996, 25.

Miller, Laura J., 'The Best-Seller List as Marketing Tool and Historical Fiction', *Book History* 3 (2000), 286–304.

——*Reluctant Capitalists: Bookselling and the Culture of Consumption* (Chicago: University of Chicago Press, 2006).

Milne, Seumas, 'A Greek Myth', *Guardian*, 29 July 2000, 10–19 (Weekend section).

Milner, Andrew, *Literature, Culture and Society* (London: UCL Press, 1996).

Mitchell, David, *Ghostwritten* (London: Sceptre, 1999).

——*number9dream* (London: Sceptre, 2001).

——'The January Man', *Granta 81: Best of Young British Novelists* (2003), 135–48.

——*Cloud Atlas* (London: Sceptre, 2004).

——'Rereadings: Enter the Maze', *Guardian*, 22 May 2004.

Mitchinson, John, 'Bestseller Genes', *The Bookseller*, 2 April 1999, 24–6.

Moore, Suzanne, 'Can't Pay, Won't Pay', *Independent*, 26 September 1991, 21.

Moran, Joe, *Star Authors: Literary Celebrity in America* (London: Pluto Press, 2000).

Moreton, Cole, 'Some Kind of Success', *Independent on Sunday*, 4 January 1998, 26 (The Sunday Review section).

Morris, Kate, *Jemima J – Single Girl's Diary* (London: Penguin, 1998).

Morrison, Blake, 'The Country Where Worst Things Happen', *Independent on Sunday*, 1 June 1997, 33 (The Sunday Review section).

Mukherjee, Neel, 'Dances with Genres', *The Times*, 21 February 2004.

Mulligan, Geoff, 'Promoting the Captain', *The Bookseller*, 29 May 1998, 34.

Murray, Simone, 'From Literature to Content: Media Multinationals, Publishing Practice and the Digitisation of the Book', at *SHARP 2002*, Institute of English Studies, School of Advanced Study, University of London, July 2002.

——*Mixed Media: Feminist Presses and Publishing Politics* (London: Pluto Press, 2004).

——'Publishing Studies: Critically Mapping Research in Search of a Discipline', at *SHARP 2006*, The Hague/Leiden, July 2006.

Naughtie, James, 'Teenage Passions', *Daily Telegraph*, 18 July 1998, 1 (Arts & Books section).

Niffenegger, Audrey, *The Time Traveler's Wife* (London: Jonathan Cape, 2004).

Niven, Alastair, 'A Common Wealth of Talent', *Booker 30. A Celebration of the Booker Prize for Fiction. 1969–1998*, London: Booker plc, 1998, 40–2.

Norfolk, Lawrence, and Fischer, Tibor, eds., *New Writing 8* (London: Vintage, 1999).

Norrie, Ian, *Mumby's Publishing and Bookselling in the Twentieth Century* (London: Bell and Hyman, 1982; 6th edn.).

North, Freya, *Chloe* (London: William Heinemann, 1997).

Norton, Cherry, 'She's Successful, Attractive But Has Yet to Find the Right Man. Is it Down to Chance or, as New Study Claims, Evolution', *Sunday Times*, 7 June 1998, 17 (main section).

'Now on Sale…Round-Up', *Mirror*, 14 August 1998, 17 (The A List section).

O'Reilly, Daragh, 'Martin Amis on Marketing', in Stephen Brown, ed., *Consuming Books: The Marketing and Consumption of Literature* (London: Routledge, 2006), 73–82.

O'Shaughnessy, Kathy, 'Authentic Tales of the Single Life', *Daily Telegraph*, 23 November 1996, 4 (Arts & Books section).

O'Sullivan, Jack, 'Have You Heard the One About the Oriental Fantasy?', *Independent*, 17 September 1997, 23 (main section).

Ong, Walter, 'The Writer's Audience is Always a Fiction', *PMLA* (*Publication of the Modern Language Association of America*) 90 (1975), 9–21.

Opacki, Ireneusz, 'Royal Genres', in David Duff, ed., *Modern Genre Theory* (Harlow: Longman, 2000), 118–26. First published in 1963, translated by David Malcolm.

Owen, Lynette, *Selling Rights* (Abingdon: Routledge, 2006; 5th edn.).

Owen, Ursula, 'Feminist Publishing', in Peter Owen, ed., *Publishing: The Future* (London: Peter Owen, 1988), 86–100.

Page, Benedicte, 'Chewing up the Past', *The Bookseller*, 15 October 1999, 38.

Parker, Peter, 'The War that Never Becomes the Past', *Times Literary Supplement*, 8 September 1995, 5.

Parsons, Wendy, and Nicholson, Catriona, '"Talking to Philip Pullman": An Interview', *The Lion and the Unicorn* 23: 1 (January 1999), 116–34.

Patten, Chris, *East and West: The Last Governor General of Hong Kong on Power, Freedom and the Future* (London: Macmillan, 1998).

Patterson, Christina, 'Zadie Smith – A Willesden Ring of Confidence', *Independent*, 22 January 2000, 9 (Weekend Review section).

Pelling, Rowan, 'Only After We Went to the Loo Did the Winner Emerge', *Independent on Sunday*, 24 October 2004.

Perrick, Penny, 'Sex and the Single Girl', *Sunday Times*, 20 October 1996, 12 (Books section).

Phillips, Angus, 'How Books are Positioned in the Market', in Nicole Matthews and Nickianne Moody, eds., *Judging a Book by its Cover: Fans, Publishers, Designers and the Marketing of Books* (London: Ashgate, forthcoming).

Picardie, Justine, 'The Poet who Came Out of his Shell Shock', *Independent*, 25 June 1991, 19 (main section).

Picoult, Jodi, *My Sister's Keeper* (London: Hodder & Stoughton, 2005).

Pitman, Joanna, 'Write On, Sisters', *The Times*, 11 October 1997, 16–17 (Metro section).

——'Word of Mouth', *The Times*, 15 November 1997, 16 (Metro section).

Pool, Kate, 'Love, Not Money: The Survey of Authors' Earnings', *The Author* 111: 2 (2000), 58–66.

Popham, Peter, 'Under Fire, but India is in my Blood', *Independent on Sunday*, 21 September 1997, 17 (main section).

——'Rushdie Started It. And It Won't Stop', *Independent on Sunday*, 7 February 1999, 4 (Culture section).

Porlock, Harvey, 'On the Critical List', *Sunday Times*, 28 April 1991, 7 (Books section).

——'Critical List', *Sunday Times*, 29 June 1997, 2 (Books section).

Powers, Alan, 'Jeff Fisher', in *Front Cover: Great Book Jackets and Cover Design* (London: Mitchell Beazley, 2001), 128–9.

'Prizes and Awards', in *Writers' & Artists' Yearbook 1998* (London: A&C Black, 1998), 488–515.

Public Lending Right, 'Wilson Topples Cookson', http://www.plr.uk.com/trends/pressrelease/feb2004.htm, 2004, accessed 22 May 2006.

——'Jacqueline Wilson: UK's Most Borrowed Author for Third Year Running', http://www.plr.uk.com/trends/pressrelease/feb2006 (1).htm, 2006, accessed 22 May 2006.

Pullman, Philip, *Northern Lights* (London: Scholastic, 1995).

——*The Subtle Knife* (London: Scholastic, 1997).

——'Writing Children's Fiction: or You Cannot Be Serious', in Barry Turner, ed., *The Writer's Handbook 2000* (London: Macmillan, 1999), 216–18.

——*The Amber Spyglass* (London: Scholastic, 2000).

Radway, Janice, *Reading the Romance: Women, Patriarchy, and Popular Literature* (Chapel Hill: University of North Carolina Press, 1984).

——*A Feeling for Books: The Book-of-the-Month Club, Literary Taste, and Middle-Class Desire* (Chapel Hill: University of North Carolina Press, 1997).

Rasselas, 'Noises Off', *Sunday Times*, 1 June 1997, 6 (Culture section).

Rebel Inc. 1 (May 1992).

Rees, Emlyn, *The Book of Dead Authors* (London: Headline Review, 1997; paperback edn. Headline Review, 1998).

Rennie, David, 'Finals Chapter', *Daily Telegraph*, 11 December 1997, 27.

Renton, Alex, 'Next Big Hype', *Evening Standard*, 4 January 2000, 25.

Rickett, Joel, 'Publishing by Numbers?', *Bookseller*, 1 September 2000, 20–2.

——'Year-in-View of the Publishing Industry', in *Writers' and Artists' Yearbook 2006* (London: A&C Black, 2005; 99th edn.), 270–3.

Riding, Alan, 'Testifying to the Ravages of Granddad's War', *New York Times*, 6 December, 17 (Section C).

Roberts, Michèle, 'Male Insensitivity, Female Nagging and Children's Selfishness', *Independent on Sunday*, 18 October 1998, 11 (Culture section).

Rolph, C. H., ed., *The Trial of Lady Chatterley* (Harmondsworth: Penguin, 1961).

Rose, Jonathan, 'The History of Books: Revised and Enlarged', in Haydn T. Mason, ed., *The Darnton Debate: Books and Revolution in the Eighteenth Century. Studies on Voltaire and the Eighteenth Century* 359 (Oxford: Voltaire Foundation, 1998), 83–104.

——*The Intellectual Life of the British Working Classes* (New Haven: Yale University Press, 2001).

Rowling, J. K., *Harry Potter and the Philosopher's Stone* (London: Bloomsbury, 1997).

——*Harry Potter and the Chamber of Secrets* (London: Bloomsbury, 1998).

——*Harry Potter and the Prisoner of Azkaban* (London: Bloomsbury, 1999).

——*Harry Potter and the Goblet of Fire* (London: Bloomsbury, 2000).

——*Harry Potter and the Order of the Phoenix* (London: Bloomsbury, 2003).

——*Harry Potter and the Half-Blood Prince* (London: Bloomsbury, 2005).

——*Harry Potter and the Deathly Hallows* (London: Bloomsbury, 2007).
Roy, Arundhati, *The God of Small Things* (London: Flamingo 1997).
——'Things Can Change in a Day', *Granta 57: India*, Spring 1997, 257–88.
——*The Algebra of Infinite Justice* (London: Flamingo, 2002).
Royle, Jo, Cooper, Louise and Stockdale, Rosemary, 'The Use of Branding by Trade Publishers: An Investigation into Marketing the Book as a Brand Name Product', *Publishing Research Quarterly* 15: 4 (Winter 1999/2000), 3–13.
Rubin, Joan Shelley, *The Making of Middle/Brow Culture* (Chapel Hill: University of North Carolina Press, 1982).
Rushdie, Salman, *Midnight's Children* (London: Jonathan Cape, 1981).
——*The Satanic Verses* (London: Viking, 1988).
——' "Commonwealth Literature" Does Not Exist', in *Imaginary Homelands: Essays and Criticism 1981–1991* (London: Granta, 1991), 61–70.
——*The Moor's Last Sigh* (London: Jonathan Cape, 1995).
Sage, Lorna, 'Living on Writing', in Jeremy Treglown and Bridget Bennett, eds., *Grub Street and the Ivory Tower: Literary Journalism and Literary Scholarship from Fielding to the Internet* (Oxford: Clarendon Press, 1998), 262–76.
Sanderson, Mark, 'The Literary Life', *Sunday Telegraph*, 7 March 2004.
Sands, Sarah, 'Zadie, the Woman Who Reinvented the Novelist', *Daily Telegraph*, 24 March 2000, 28 (main section).
Schiffrin, André, *The Business of Books: How International Conglomerates Took Over Publishing and Changed the Way We Read* (London: Verso, 2000).
Scott, Linda M., 'The Bridge from Text to Mind: Adapting Reader-Response Theory to Consumer Research', *Journal of Consumer Research* 21 (December 1994), 461–80.
Seabrook, John, *Nobrow: The Culture of Marketing the Marketing of Culture* (London: Methuen, 2000).
Shankar, Avi, 'Book-Reading Groups: A "Male Outsider" Perspective', in Stephen Brown, ed., *Consuming Books: The Marketing and Consumption of Literature* (London: Routledge, 2006), 114–25.
Shulman, Nicola, 'Some Consolations of the Single State', *Times Literary Supplement*, 1 November 1996, 26.
Silverton, Peter, 'Word of Mouth', *Observer*, 27 July 1997, 4 (Review section).
Simmonds, Posy, *Literary Life* (London: Jonathan Cape, 2003).
Simons, Judy, and Fullbrook, Kate, eds., *Writing: A Woman's Business: Women, Writing and the Marketplace* (Manchester: Manchester University Press, 1998).
Slater, Lydia, 'Poignant, Funny and Truthful', *Daily Telegraph*, 8 November 1997, 15 (main section).
Smith, Helena, 'Mandolin Man Changes His Tune as Cameras Roll', *Observer*, 4 June 2000, 3 (main section).
Smith, P. R., *Marketing Communications: An Integrated Approach* (London: Kogan Page, 1998; 2nd edn.).
Smith, Zadie, 'Mrs Begum's Son and the Private Tutor', in Martha Kelly, ed., *The May Anthology of Oxford and Cambridge Short Stories 1997*, selected and introduced by Jill Paton Walsh (Oxford and Cambridge: Varsity Publications Ltd and Cherwell (Oxford Student Publications Ltd.), 1997), 89–113.
——'Stuart', in *The New Yorker*, 27 December 1999 and 3 January 2000, 60–7.
——'The Waiter's Wife', in *Granta 67: Women and Children First*, Autumn 1999, 127–42.

——*White Teeth* (London: Hamish Hamilton, 2000).

——*The Autograph Man* (London: Hamish Hamilton, 2002).

Sobel, Dava, *Longitude: The True Story of a Lone Genius Who Solved the Greatest Scientific Problem of His Time* (London: Fourth Estate, 1996).

'Sound of Silence', *Guardian*, 13 November 1995, 12 (main section).

Spufford, Francis, 'Exploding Old Myths', *Guardian*, 9 November 1995, 2–3 (Section 2).

Squires, Claire, 'Toby Litt', in Michael Molino, ed., *Dictionary of Literary Biography 267: Twenty-First-Century British and Irish Novelists* (Detroit: The Gale Group, 2002), 164–71.

——*Zadie Smith's* White Teeth *: A Reader's Guide* (London: Continuum, 2002).

——'A Common Ground? Book Prize Culture in Europe', *Javnost The Public* 11:4 (2004): 37–47.

——'Novelistic Production and the Publishing Industry in Britain and Ireland', in Brian W Shaffer, ed., *A Companion to the British and Irish Novel 1945–2000* (Oxford: Blackwell Publishing, 2005) 177–93.

——*Philip Pullman, Master Storyteller: A Guide to the Worlds of* His Dark Materials (London: Continuum, 2006).

——'Literary Prizes, Literary Categories and Children's Literature in the 1990s-2000s', in Vanessa Guignery and François Gallix, eds., *Pre- and Post-Publication Itineraries of the Contemporary Novel in English* (Paris: Éditions Publibook Université, 2007).

——'Judging on a Cover: Book Marketing and the Booker Prize', in Nicole Matthews and Nickianne Moody, eds., *Judging a Book by its Cover: Fans, Publishers, Designers and the Marketing of Books* (London: Ashgate, forthcoming).

Stevenson, Randall, *The Last of England? The Oxford English Literary History. Volume 12 1960–2000* (Oxford: Oxford University Press, 2004).

Stockmann, Doris, 'Free or Fixed Prices on Books – Patterns of Book Pricing in Europe', *Javnost The Public* 11: 4 (2004), 49–64.

Straus, Peter, 'Format', in Peter Owen, ed., *Publishing Now* (London: Peter Owen, 1996; revised edn., 1st edn. 1993), 68–74.

Suleiman, Susan, and Crosman, Inge, *The Reader in the Text: Essays on Audience and Interpretation* (Princeton: Princeton University Press, 1980).

Sutherland, John, *Fiction and the Fiction Industry* (London: Athlone Press, 1978).

——*Bestsellers: Popular Fiction of the 1970s* (London: Routledge & Kegan Paul, 1981).

——*Reading the Decades: Fifty Years of the Nation's Bestselling Books* (London: BBC, 2002).

Sylge, Caroline, 'Reviews – Who Needs Them?', *The Bookseller*, 27 February 1998, 26–9.

Tagholm, Roger, 'Something to Get Your Teeth Into', *Publishing News*, 12 November 1999, 18.

Tait, Theo, 'From Victorian Travelogue to Airport Thriller', *Daily Telegraph*, 28 February 2004.

Taylor, Alan, 'Scottish Efflorescence', in *The New Yorker*, 25 December 1995 and 1 January 1996, 97.

Taylor, Andrew, *The American Boy* (London: Flamingo, 2003).

Taylor, D. J., *A Vain Conceit: British Fiction in the 1980s* (London: Bloomsbury, 1989).

Taylor, Jonathan, 'Introduction', in *Booker 30: A Celebration of 30 Years of The Booker Prize for Fiction 1969-1998* (Great Britain: Booker plc, 1998).

Taylor, Paul, 'Hero at the Emotional Front', *Independent on Sunday*, 2 June 1991, 32 (The Sunday Review section).

Tejpal, Tarun J, 'New Gold-Rush in the East', *Guardian*, 14 August 1999, 3 (Saturday Review section).

'This is the Age of the Trainspotter', *The Times*, 28 January 1996.

Thompson, John B., *Books in the Digital Age: The Transformation of Academic and Higher Education Publishing in Britain and the United States* (Cambridge: Polity, 2005).

Thomson, Rupert, *The Book of Revelation* (London: Bloomsbury, 1999; paperback edn. Bloomsbury, 2000).

Thorne, Matt, 'Welcome to a World Where Fabricants Live on Soap', *Independent on Sunday*, 29 February 2004.

Todd, Richard, *Consuming Fictions: The Booker Prize and Fiction in Britain Today* (London: Bloomsbury, 1996).

——'Literary Fiction and the Book Trade', in James F. English, ed., *A Concise Companion to Contemporary British Fiction* (Oxford: Blackwell Publishing, 2006), 19–38.

Todorov, Tzvetan, *Genres in Discourse*, translated by Catherine Porter (Cambridge: Cambridge University Press, 1990; first published in France in 1978).

Tomalin, Claire, *Several Strangers: Writing from Three Decades* (London: Viking, 1999).

Tonkin, Boyd, 'Preface to 1997', *Independent*, 28 December 1996, 4 (The Long Weekend section).

——'Historical', in Jane Rogers, ed., *Good Fiction Guide* (Oxford: Oxford University Press, 2001), 62–4

——'Lord Byron's Publisher Bids Farewell to Independence', *Independent*, 11 May 2002, 9.

——'Once Upon a Time in the Marketing Department…', *Independent*, 6 November 2002.

Tremain, Rose, *Music and Silence* (London: Chatto & Windus, 1999).

Viner, Katharine, 'Suddenly, the Thirtysomething Single Woman is a Media Celebrity', *Guardian*, 11 September 1997, 2–3 (G2 section).

Walden, George, 'Why Pat Barker Won the Booker', *The Times*, 8 November 1995, 15 (main section).

——'Fiction, Nostalgia and Escapism', *Times Literary Supplement*, 24 November 1995, 17.

Wallace, Sam, 'Cutting Her Teeth with a Book Deal', *Daily Telegraph*, 15 January 2000, 18 (main section).

Walsh, John, 'The Not-So-Shady Past of Irvine Welsh', *Independent*, 15 April 1995, 25 (Weekend section).

——'Northern Realism wins over Rushdie Favourite', *Independent*, 8 November 1995, 3 (main section).

Walter, Natasha, *The New Feminism* (London: Little, Brown, 1998).

Warburg, Fredric, *An Occupation for Gentlemen* (London: Hutchinson, 1959).

Welsh, Irvine, 'The First Day of the Edinburgh Festival', in Hamish Whyte and Janice Galloway, eds., *Scream, If You Want to Go Faster (New Writing Scotland 9)* (Aberdeen: Association for Scottish Literary Studies, 1991), 145–55.

——*Past Tense: Four Stories from a Novel* (South Queensferry: Clocktower Press, n.d. [1992]).
——*Trainspotting* (London: Secker & Warburg, 1993).
——*Trainspotting and Headstate* (London: Minerva, 1996).
——*Porno* (London: Jonathan Cape, 2002).
Wernick, Andrew, 'Authorship and the Supplement of Promotion', in Maurice Biriotti and Nicola Miller, eds., *What is an Author?* (Manchester: Manchester University Press, 1993), 85–103.
Whelehan, Imelda, *The Feminist Bestseller: From Sex and the Single Girl to Sex and the City* (Basingstoke: Palgrave Macmillan, 2005).
Whitbread Book Awards, http://www.whitbread-bookawards.co.uk/about.cfm?page=62, accessed 18 April 2006.
Whiteside, Thomas, *The Blockbuster Complex: Conglomerates, Show Business, and Book Publishing* (Middletown: Wesleyan University Press, 1981).
Whitworth, Damian, and Wagner, Erica, 'Booker Prize Goes to Debut Novelist', *The Times*, 15 October 1997, 1 (main section).
Williamson, Kevin, ed., *Children of Albion Rovers* (Edinburgh: Rebel Inc., 1997; 2nd edn.; 1st edn. 1996).
Willison, Ian R., 'Massmediatisation: Export of the American Model?', in Jacques Michon and Jean-Yves Mollier, eds., *Les Mutations de Livre et de l'Edition Dans le Monde du XVIIIe Siècle à l'An 2000: Actes du Colloque International Sherbrooke 2000* (Saint-Nicolas: Les Presses de l'Université Laval, 2001).
Wilson, Jonathan, 'The Literary Life: A Very English Story', *The New Yorker*, 6 March 1995, 96–104.
Wirtén, Eva Hemmungs, *Global Infatuation: Explorations in Global Publishing and Texts* (Uppsala: Avdelningen för litteratursociologi vid Litteraturventenskapliga Institutionen i Uppsala, 1998).
——*No Trespassing: Authorship, Intellectual Property Rights, and the Boundaries of Globalization* (Toronto: University of Toronto Press, 2004).
Wolff, Isabel, *The Trials of Tiffany Trott* (London: HarperCollins, 1998).
Wood, Paul, 'Death Cheats Two Wartime Lovers', *Independent*, 11 January 1999, 8 (main section).
Wullschlager, Jackie, 'Sanity, Madness and Unholy Innocence', *Financial Times*, 6 July 1991, 9 (Weekend FT section).
——'Hedonism – and Feminism', *Financial Times*, 28 December 1996, xiv (Weekend section).
——'Prose Full of Promise', *Financial Times*, 3 January 1998, v (Weekend section).
Yates, Robert, 'Bridget of Madison County', *Observer*, 31 May 1998, 20 (The Review section).
Zafon, Carlos Ruiz, *The Shadow of the Wind* (London: Weidenfeld & Nicolson, 2004).
Zahavi, Helen,*Dirty Weekend* (London: Picador, 1991).

Index